Russia's Food Policies and Globalization

RURAL ECONOMIES IN TRANSITION

Series Editors

Zvi Lerman
The Hebrew University of Jerusalem
Csaba Csaki
The World Bank and the Budapest Economics University
Johan Swinnen
Katholieke Universiteit Leuven

Much of the world's rural population lives in transition countries that are attempting to transform their economies from the centrally planned socialist system to a market-oriented system. The Rural Economies in Transition series evaluates the deep impact these transformations are having in Central and Eastern Europe, the former Soviet Union, and Asia. Based on original empirical work by international teams at the cutting edge of research, each volume presents the results of one complete empirical study devoted to a single country or region. The editors have designed the series to provide agricultural, development, and political economists, as well as scholars in other disciplines, with authoritative and up-to-date factual information about rural transition. The editors welcome manuscript submissions from scholars engaged in original empirical research in the field.

Private Agriculture in Armenia, by Zvi Lerman and Astghik Mirzakhanian
Romanian Agriculture and Transition toward the EU, edited by
    Sophia Davidova and Kenneth J. Thomson
Transition, Institutions, and the Rural Sector, edited by Max Spoor
*Greening Industrialization in Asian Transitional Economies: China and
    Vietnam,* edited by Arthur Mol and J. van Buuren
*Agriculture in Transition: Land Policies and Evolving Farm Structures in Post-
    Soviet Countries,* by Zvi Lerman, Csaba Csaki, and Gershon Feder
*Building Market Institutions in Post-Communist Agriculture: Land, Credit, and
    Assistance,* edited by David A. J. Macey, William Pyle, and Stephen K.
    Wegren
*Cooperation in the Romanian Countryside: An Insight into Post-Soviet Agricul-
    ture,* by Rachel, Sabates-Wheeler
Russia's Food Policies and Globalization, by Stephen K. Wegren

Russia's Food Policies and Globalization

Stephen K. Wegren

LEXINGTON BOOKS

Lanham • Boulder • New York • Toronto • Oxford

LEXINGTON BOOKS

Published in the United States of America
by Lexington Books
An imprint of The Rowman & Littlefield Publishing Group, Inc.
4501 Forbes Boulevard, Suite 200, Lanham, Maryland 20706

PO Box 317
Oxford
OX2 9RU, UK

British Library Cataloguing in Publication Information Available

Library of Congress Cataloging-in-Publication Data

Wegren, Stephen K., 1956-
  Russia's food policies and globalization / Stephen K. Wegren.
     p. cm. — (Rural economies in transition)
  Includes index.
  ISBN 0-7391-0687-2 (cloth : alk. paper)
  1. Food industry and trade—Government policy—Russia (Federation) 2. Food industry
and trade—Government policy—Soviet Union. I. Title. II. Series.
HD9015.R92W44 2005
338.1'947—dc22   2004019395

Printed in the United States of America

♾™ The paper used in this publication meets the minimum requirements of American
National Standard for Information Sciences—Permanence of Paper for Printed Library
Materials, ANSI/NISO Z39.48–1992.

For my mother

Contents

Tables

Introduction

Peruse the shelves of a university library and you will find numerous books on food policy—there are books about food policy in developing states or different types of economic systems in general, about food policy in broad regions such as Africa, East Asia, or Latin America, or about food policy in specific countries, such as Mexico, the Philippines, or even the United States. One might also run across individual chapters in edited books and collections on food policy in the USSR and other Communist nations. Oddly, there is no literature on food policy in post-communist states. This relative neglect is curious because food policy is one of the most vitally important aspects of economic reform, affecting the entire basket of market reforms. The neglect is also curious because changes in food policy have significant ramifications for how former communist states integrate into the world economy, how globalization affects their societies, and how receptive post-communist nations are to the dual processes of integration and globalization.

The core of the book focuses on three main questions. The first question is: "What is the nature of Russia's domestic food policies?" The intent is to analyze policies, patterns, and actors, comparing how they differ from the Soviet period, and how they reflect the functioning of a market economy.

The second question is: "What is the nature of Russia's external (foreign) food policies?" The focus is on policies such as import quotas, tariffs, and other protective measures, as well as export policies. The intent is not only to compare policies and patterns from the Soviet era, but also to show the effects of trade policies on prospects for global economic integration.

The third question is: "What is the effect of Russia's food policies (domestic and international) on global integration?" In other words, what influence do food policies have on efforts to integrate into the global economy? The focus is on the tension between protecting domestic producers—political constituents—and opening the economy to meet international standards for inclusion in the World Trade Organization and perhaps later, the European Union.

Based on these broad questions, the investigation of Russia's food policies is placed between two scholarly literatures. The first literature, on post-communist agrarian reform, continues to expand, focusing mostly on farm restructuring, land privatization, the development of private farming, and issues related to assistance and credit.[1] Recently a literature has emerged on Russian agrarian reform that increasingly focuses on the nature and degree of change that has occurred since the breakup of the Soviet Union.[2] While the literature on post-communist and Russian agrarian reform continues to grow, it is lacking in that there has been scant attention to some of the most basic issues: how do food policies affect these societies' ability to feed themselves, what are the nature of food trade policies (both domestic and external), what happens to food after it is produced, how is food traded, and how do Russia's trade polices affect efforts to integrate into the global economy?[3]

The relative neglect of Russian food policy among area experts is odd because the privatization of land and farming enterprises in the early 1990s was expected to lead to specific economic benefits, for example, increased food production, increased efficiency, lower consumer subsidies by the state, *as well as* better quality and higher selection for consumers. By focusing on the privatization of land and enterprises, only one part of the reform equation is being considered. Without a consideration of Russia's food policies, we are unable to understand how food supplies are managed and how food markets operate in contemporary Russia. If the existing literature is any guide, it is as our attention should be directed only to food production and not to distribution processes or trade policies which comprise food policy.

The second scholarly literature concerns globalization and economic integration. The interesting question is what is the relationship between food policy and globalization. Within the globalization literature, some key catch words are integration, interdependence, state sovereignty, free trade, global markets, and global communications. While it is commonly acknowledged that Russia desires to become more economically integrated globally, there has been little analysis of the relationship between different aspects of food policies and Russia's ongoing international integration, although some attention has been given to this question for Eastern European nations.[4] Food policies affect Russia's international political and economic relations by influencing food import and export policies, trade regulations and tariffs, and import quotas. These considerations in turn are instrumental to Russia's integration into the world economy. Thus, this book makes a fourfold contribution to the existing literature.

(1) Analytically and conceptually, the book "brings the state back in" by focusing on state interventions and state policies that shape and influence food policies. For that reason, the unit of analysis is the state for most of the chapters, though not all. The rationale is that the state defines the nature of domestic and foreign food policies, and different actors within the food system react and adjust to those policy parameters.

(2) Substantively, this book begins to fill the void in the food policy literature by analyzing Russia. To my knowledge, no book-length study exists that analyzes Russia's food trade policies. As Russia expands its international ties and becomes more tied into the world economy, this topic and the issues relevant to it will become increasingly important.

(3) In terms of scope, this book makes a contribution by examining both domestic and foreign food policies. Chapter 1 focuses on food production trends and food consumption, but the remaining five chapters are devoted to food trade policies and patterns of food trade.

(4) Finally, the book makes a contribution by comparing the nature of Russia's food policies across time. For purposes of comparison, some attention is devoted to the Soviet period, but the bulk of the book examines food policy in the post-Soviet period, from 1992 to the end of 2003.

The Argument in Brief

The broad arguments of the book are severalfold. First, to pose the question whether food policies in post-Soviet Russia facilitate or hinder global integration suggests that sufficient change has occurred to warrant writing a book about the subject. Thus, the first argument in the chapters to follow is that since Russia embarked upon agrarian reform in the early 1990s, there has been significant institutional, policy, and behavioral change in Russia's rural economy.[5] As subsequent chapters document, some of the most important changes have been in the arena of food policy. The core elements in post-Communist Russian food policy have changed in a number of ways from the food policy that was pursued in the Soviet Union. Procurement and marketing policies have been liberalized, reducing the importance of compulsory deliveries at fixed prices. Food producers have more marketing choices, and state procurements capture a much smaller percentage of food products than previously. Retail food prices have been decontrolled, exposing the Russian consumer to the market value of the goods purchased. Control over exports has also been liberalized. Producers and processors are able to establish direct links with trading partners abroad. In theory at least, farms are able to engage in export operations once their obligation to their respective food funds has been met and after paying the required export duties. All of these changes are important and represent significant movement toward a more competitive, market-oriented economy.

The second broad argument is that just because significant change has occurred is not to say that original expectations of what reform would do have been met; it is not to deny that problems continue to exist in Russia's rural transition; and it is not to suggest that further progress is not needed. Specifically, the second broad argument maintains that while Russia's domestic procurement system and wholesale trade system have been deregulated and liberalized, at the same time, significant protectionist measures have been adopted at the regional level that affect domestic wholesale trade.

The third broad argument is that significant protectionist impulses and policies have arisen at the regional and federal levels that affect foreign food trade. As such, there are countermarket tendencies at work in Russian reform. The danger for reform is that the present import policy may retard the transformation of the agroindustrial complex and the food-producing sector in Russia because it protects farms from the competition they need to stimulate reform in their operations. Without competition from imports, the main impetus to change comes in response to state purchase prices, which are subject to political pressures.

In recent years a coalition of interests has come together to support restrictive food import policies. That coalition includes the government, urban and industrial interests, large farms and private farmers, and commodity-specific interest groups, all of whom have given either implicit or tacit support to the government's import policies. The genesis of this coalition originated from a need to protect the financial status of the agrarian sector.

The final broad argument is that significant obstacles exist that hinder Russia's global integration. On a number of dimensions it is not at all clear that Russia is able to compete successfully in a free trade regime. In fact, it may be argued that at this stage of development, Russia has become more interdependent with the rest of the world, but due to the nature of food policies and the way that market reforms are developing within Russia, actual integration remains elusive.

What Is Food Policy?

It is necessary to say a few words about what food policy is before proceeding to an examination of domestic and external food policies in Russia. At the outset it is important to note three key facts: (1) "food policy" is really an umbrella term for food policies; (2) food policies have domestic and foreign dimensions; and (3) food policy is about policy *choices*. Specifically, with regard to the latter point, food policy is about choices made by governments. Thus, there is nothing deterministic about what food policy should be, or will be, in a given country. Instead, food policy is comprised of choices made by policymakers. As decision makers, they are of course subject to various influences, but in general they are free actors whose decisions reflect values about how food producers, food traders, and food consumers are to be treated. Food policies vary from nation to nation, although they may be categorized analytically, and food policies vary as well according to the type of political and economic system, the level of development, the condition of domestic agriculture, and a host of other variables.

At the broadest level, choices concerning food policies encompass the entire cycle of food, from "farm to table," including: food production, food processing, domestic food trade, and foreign food trade (both imports and exports). Each specific aspect of food policy entails decisions about how different actors in the food system are to be treated, how trade is to be regulated, and what are the opportunity structures that exist for actors within the system. For example, in the realm of food production, policy choices have to be made concerning subsidy policies, pricing policies of inputs needed by producers, policies regarding the cost of transporting food to processing and retail points, rural credit policy, and financial support for rural infrastructure. As concerns postproduction processes, that is, domestic food trade, food policy choices concern the degree of regulation of the wholesale market, the system of wholesale prices and the government's role in that system, whether to regulate patterns of food trade, and if so, how, the degree of state intervention in wholesale markets and state influence over wholesale prices, and how to support the creation of new wholesale actors in the domestic trade system. In the realm of foreign food trade, the range of policy choices include how open or closed the economy should be to imports, whether to impose tariffs or quotas on imports, and if so, at what level, and whether to impose export tariffs or to offer export subsidies, and if so, at what level.

The effects of choices about food policy are also important. Choices about food policies affect how different segments of the population are treated. From a political standpoint, food policy has enormous implications as trade policy influences the nature of bilateral and multilateral international relations. In addition, there are domestic considerations, as food policy affects how domestic regional food markets operate, whether they are open or closed, and therefore fundamentally affect not only food producers and processors as political constituents, but also consumers as constituents. Furthermore, from a social standpoint, food policy has implications for food consumption, demographic, and health trends. Domestic distribution processes and trade policies are equally important to actual food production because ill-conceived or poorly implemented domestic trade policies can turn abundance into hunger, with potential political consequences thereafter. On the other hand, well-conceived and well-implemented food policies can prevent food shortages from causing widespread social unrest, hunger, or even starvation.

Analytic Considerations of Food Policy

Food policy encompasses efforts by the state to influence the decision-making environment and behaviors of food producers, food marketing agents, and food trade policies. To analyze the entire spectrum of policy decisions that comprise food policy as a whole is an enormous undertaking and would include, in essence, the entire agricultural system and its various components. Therefore, the focus in this book is more limited. While some attention is paid to production and consumption trends in chapter 1, the primary focus is on the role of the state and the degree to which it intervenes in the nation's food system. Stated differently, the analysis of Russia's food policies focuses on domestic food policies and patterns of trade, as well as on international food policies and patterns of trade. Thus, the focus herein is more on food trade than on food production. Subsequent chapters will examine the degree of state regulation of domestic and international food trade, patterns of food trade, and content of food trade.

Having said that, it is necessary to be explicit about the effects and impact of food policy on different aspects of a nation's agricultural system.

(1) Food policy affects food production. Food producers respond to input and purchase prices, to subsidy levels, to production incentives and disincentives, to the terms of trade, and to marketing opportunities. A food policy that is too restrictive for producers will curtail motivations to increase production, or will lead them to withhold sales to the state.

(2) Food policy affects distribution and the functioning of the wholesale system. Marketing agents depend upon freedom and latitude to operate; the role of marketing agents and the degree of regulation over food trade can either alleviate or exacerbate food shortages.

(3) Food policy affects international-domestic trade linkages. A food policy that is too open runs the danger of undermining domestic farms by exposing them to foreign competition. In Russia, food and trade policy define the environment in which reorganized state and collective farms operate, as well as influencing the prospects for success of newly created private peasant farms.

(4) Food policy affects consumption. Consumers respond to the retail price for food, and retail prices are influenced by government policies. Food prices paid by the population reflect the strategies governments use to benefit or protect certain segments of the population. Retail food prices have political ramifications, and disputes over the correct price policy to pursue, or how to influence prices, often are contentious political issues in developing nations.[6]

(5) Food policy and domestic politics have reciprocal effects on each other. Food policy reflects values about how to maintain political stability. Differences

in food policies are often at the root of how political elites perceive political stability, and reflect the relationship between the government and the governed. Different types of political systems, and different states, pursue different policies and strategies in providing food for their populations. Significant differences in food policy are observed between communist and non-communist states, between heavily state-interventionist and regulated and those which are market oriented and laissez faire.

(6) Food policy affects international trade linkages and integration. Whether food trade will be unregulated or subject to high quotas and tariffs, or whether domestic producers must worry about foreign imports and restricted exports, are important considerations that will influence the health of the agrarian sector and thus the outcome of Russian agricultural reform. The foreign trade aspect of food policy also affects the nation's balance of payments accounts.

Structure of the Book

As indicated above, the book is set within the broad framework of rural change in Russia. A main argument of the book is that substantial change has occurred within the arena of food policy, and these changes reflect broader processes of transition in the agricultural system as a whole. The goal in presenting an original analysis of domestic and international food policies in Russia is to contribute broadly to the:

(1) understanding of the nature of domestic food policies in Russia;

(2) understanding of the degree to which Russia's domestic food policies operate according to market economics;

(3) understanding of the extent to which domestic producers are successful in lobbying the government to protect their interests;

(4) illuminating of the pressures and obstacles to "free trade" in Russia; and

(5) understanding of the difficulties that transitional states face in their international food policies during the era of globalization.

The book is organized in the following manner:

Chapter 1 reviews trends in food production and consumption during 1980-2002 by way of context for subsequent chapters. The chapter examines food production and consumption trends during the Soviet and post-Soviet periods. The chapter shows that significant differences exist between Soviet and Russian food production trends in: (a) the relationship between food production and population growth; (b) volumes of food production; (c) food supplies to the population; and (d) sectoral performance.

Chapter 2 examines domestic and external food policies and food trade patterns during the latter Soviet period by way of providing a basis for comparison to the post-Soviet period. In particular, in domestic food policy this chapter demonstrates that: (a) the Soviet procurement system deprived producers (large farms) of the freedom to search out the highest bidder for food. At the same time, the procurement system provided farms secure outlets for the sale of their produce; (b) the procurement system locked farms into certain production modalities; (c) the procurement price system did not reward the efficient and sent the wrong signals to producers; (d) over time, state channels of trade accounted for a greater percentage of domestic food trade, until perestroika began dismantling the command economy; and (e) the retail price system was political in nature and was intended to protect urban consumers from the true cost of food. As such, retail prices sent the wrong signals to consumers and producers, with the consequence of long lines and chronic shortages. The chapter also surveys the Soviet foreign trade system, changes in Soviet foreign trade policies and strategies under Gorbachev, and patterns of foreign food trade in the latter Soviet period.

Chapter 3 focuses on policy changes in the post-Soviet period that affect the domestic food system. The chapter demonstrates that Russian food policy is considerably different from its Soviet predecessor. In particular, this chapter argues that the nature and degree of state (federal) intervention in food trade has changed in fairly radical ways. Policy changes in the procurement price system and in the procurement system are examined, as well as retail price policy, all of which show that significant change has taken place in the way the agricultural sector is managed. Finally, the chapter surveys different rural and commodity interest groups that exert an influence on the creation and implementation of food policies.

Chapter 4 analyzes patterns of domestic food trade during the post-Soviet period, showing that patterns of food trade have changed in significant ways in comparison to the Soviet period. State channels of trade are much less dominant, while private channels have emerged as common outlets for wholesale food trade. Barter has also become more important compared to the Soviet period. Large farms continue to be the primary supplier of food to the wholesale food system. Special attention is given to the role of food processors in domestic food trade, and the development of commodity exchanges. Household food production tends, on the other hand, to be consumed. Survey data are analyzed in order to understand some of the factors that contribute to food sales by large farms and by households. Finally, the chapter shows that federal withdrawal from regulation over domestic food trade has been partially offset by increased regional interventions, mainly for local political reasons.

Chapter 5 analyzes external (international) food policies and trade patterns during the post-Soviet period. After surveying the post-Soviet foreign trade system, state regulation, and foreign trade, the bulk of the chapter is devoted to an analysis of foreign food policies in post-Soviet Russia. Significant change in the nature of the food trade system, as well as in patterns of trade and content of food trade, are shown. Because imports and exports are no longer centrally managed, patterns of external food trade have changed so that most food trade is conducted with non-CIS nations, and high value animal husbandry products have replaced grain as Russia's primary import.

The concluding chapter, chapter 6, ties the preceding chapters together by addressing the question of how Russia's domestic and external food policies affect its efforts at international integration. The chapter argues that with regard to its food policies, and perhaps more broadly, Russia has become more interdependent but has not fully integrated. A large part of the reason Russia remains unintegrated is its protectionist trade policies. A brief discussion of globalization is presented. Thereafter, the chapter investigates reasons why Russia has become more protectionist under President Vladimir Putin, starting with a section that examines structural factors to trade protectionism that affect food trade, that is, factors that are common transnationally. A subsequent section then examines factors that are unique to Russia, including the rise of concerns over Russia's "food security." A third section examines general policy issues surrounding Russia's accession to the World Trade Organization, in addition to specific concerns about the effects of accession on Russian agriculture. A final section analyzes different domestic factors in agriculture that affect the ability of Russia to compete during global integration. The conclusion summarizes Russia's prospects for global integration.

This book reflects the interest I have had in the political and economic dimensions of food policies for several years. The completion of this project was facilitated by research support from the National Council for Eurasian and East European Research, and by the John G. Tower Center for Political Studies at Southern Methodist University. I am grateful for that support. In addition, during the several years of collecting information and thinking about this topic, there have been many individuals who helped me cultivate this interest. Particular thanks are extended (in alphabetical order) to Vladimir Belen'kiy, Sergei Khokhlov, Sergei Kiselev, Olga Kniazeva, Andrei Morozov, Allan Mustard, Valeri Patsiorkovski, Iosif Rogov, Natalia Shagaida, Vasilii Uzun, and Arkadii Zlochevskii. I thank each of these individuals for their willingness to help me obtain the information I needed to complete this project. I would also like to thank Zvi Lerman, who as editor of the Lexington series "Rural Economies in Transition" initially supported the project and encouraged me to pursue it. Zvi also read and commented on the text. As usual, any mistakes or errors remain my responsibility. Serena Krombach supported the project at Lexington books, and I am grateful to her. Finally, I express my appreciation to Christine Carberry, who expertly prepared the index.

Notes

1. See, for example, Zvi Lerman, Csaba Csaki, and Gershon Feder, *Land Policies and Evolving Farm Structures in Transition Countries*, Policy Research Working Paper 2794 (Washington, DC: The World Bank, 2002); and David A. J. Macey, William Pyle, and Stephen K. Wegren, eds., *Building Market Institutions in Post-Communist Agriculture: Land, Credit, and Assistance* (Lanham, MD: Lexington Books, 2004).
2. Stephen K. Wegren, *Agriculture and the State in Soviet and Post-Soviet Russia* (Pittsburgh: University of Pittsburgh Press, 1998); and see David J. O'Brien and Stephen K. Wegren, eds., *Rural Reform in Post-Soviet Russia* (Washington and Baltimore: Woodrow Wilson Center Press and Johns Hopkins University Press, 2002).
3. For Russia, exceptions include: The World Bank, *Food and Agricultural Policy Reforms in the Former USSR: An Agenda for the Transition* (Washington, DC: The World Bank, 1992); Stephen K. Wegren, "From Farm to Table: The Food System in Post-Communist Russia," *Communist Economies and Economic Transformation*, 8, no. 2

(1996): 149-83; Grigory Ioffe and Tatyana Nefedova, "Russian Agriculture and Food Processing: Vertical Cooperation and Spatial Dynamics," *Europe-Asia Studies*, 53, no. 3 (2001): 389-418.

4. Jason G. Hartell and Johan F. M. Swinnen, eds., *Agriculture and East-West European Integration* (Aldershot, UK: Ashgate, 2000).

5. See in particular: David J. O'Brien, Valeri V. Patsiorkovski, and Larry D. Dershem, *Household Capital and the Agrarian Problem in Russia* (Aldershot, UK: Ashgate, 2000); A. V. Petrikov, ed., *Agrarnaia Reforma v Rossii: kontseptsii, opyt, perspektivy* (Moscow: Russian Institute of Agrarian Problems and Information, 2000); A. V. Petrikov, ed., *Rynochnaia transformatsiia sel'skogo khoziaistva: desiatiletnii opyt i perspektivy* (Moscow: Russian Institute of Agrarian Problems and Information, 2000); O'Brien and Wegren, eds., *Rural Reform in Post-Soviet Russia*, pt. 1; and V. V. Patsiorkovskii, *Sel'skaia Rossiia, 1991-2001 gg.* (Moscow: Finansy i statistika, 2003).

6. See Paul Streeten, *What Price Food? Agricultural Price Policies in Developing Countries* (Ithaca: Cornell University Press, 1987).

Chapter One

Food Production and Consumption, 1980-2002

This book begins with a survey of food production and food consumption during the latter part of the Soviet period and the first ten years of the post-Soviet period, or roughly 1980 through 2002. The intent is threefold: (1) to provide a review and comparison of production and consumption trends during the latter Soviet period and into the post-Soviet period; (2) to indicate who the main producers were or are; and (3) to provide a context for the examination of Russian food policies and patterns of food trade in subsequent chapters.

The chapter demonstrates that considerable change has occurred in terms of dominant food producers, food production levels, and per capita consumption levels from the Soviet to the post-Soviet period. The chapter shows that significant differences exist between Soviet and Russian food production trends in: (1) the relationship between food production and population growth; (2) volumes of food production; (3) food supplies to the population; and (4) sectoral performance. Generally speaking, the analysis shows that in the transition from Soviet to post-Soviet agriculture, the collective sector as a food producer has become relatively less important, and the private sector as a food producer has become relatively more important.

The chapter focuses on production and consumption, while only briefly reviewing the factors that influence production trends; an extensive discussion would take us far from the original intent.[1] The chapter is organized into three main sections. The first section analyzes food production trends, main producers, and food consumption during the latter Soviet period. The second section examines the same aspects in the post-Soviet period, during 1992-2002. The post-Soviet period has witnessed new research opportunities, and thus a third section uses survey data on rural households to provide an analysis of who produces food in rural Russia according to income category.

The Soviet Period

During the Soviet period there were two primary food producers: large farming enterprises called state farms (*sovkhozy*) and collective farms (*kolkhozy*), and rural households most of which were located within the structure of a large farm and used a household land plot (*lichnoe podsobnoe khoziaistvo*) which were referred to as "personal auxiliary plots," or more simply, "private plots." Private plots were very small, an average of .20 hectares per collective farm family, although plot sizes varied by size of the family, region of the USSR, and profession.[2] Virtually all food was produced from these two sources of production, with state and collective farms the dominant producer. However, it should be noted, at least in passing, that households also had access to other forms of land for personal or family use. These land plots, within a collective setting, were called "collective gardens" and also were very small. Sometimes industrial enterprises would allocate land to its workers for their personal use, with a part of the production being paid to the enterprise as implied rent. Finally, households often used the land surrounding their country dachas for growing food. Food produced on household plots was both consumed and sold, although the vast majority was consumed. Surveys in the 1980s showed that about 90 percent of household production was consumed, although the actual percentage varied by product, region, family size, and level of income.[3] Food production trends for both types of producers are reviewed below.

Trends in Food Production, 1980-1991

Soviet agriculture suffered from a number of problems. Weather, drought, and natural disasters are a constant concern in Russian agriculture, as in other nations. It is often argued that most of Russia's agricultural land is of poor quality. Although the Soviet Union was a large country, much of its agricultural land was located in northern regions or regions where agricultural production was not advantageous. For this reason, in 1990 of the 640.7 million hectares of land that were considered agricultural land, only 213.8 million hectares (or about one-third) were considered arable land.[4]

Beyond weather and nature in general, during the Soviet period food production was insulated from influences of supply and demand. Instead, production was largely a function of economic decisions made for political reasons. Food production was also affected by general economic conditions, including, but not limited to, the level of farm mechanization, access to quality seed, fertilizer, and spare parts, the presence and condition of harvesting equipment, the availability of storage facilities, the level of development of food distribution networks, and other factors related to rural infrastructure.[5] During the Brezhnev period in particular (1964-1982), considerable financial resources were poured into agriculture to modernize and mechanize production processes, to irrigate lands, and to use more mineral fertilizers. But in general, food production during the Soviet period was a function of planning and not driven by consumer demand.

Soviet agriculture was also hampered by several policy and structural constraints. A short list of policy obstacles and structural impediments that confronted state and collective farms includes the following, all of which were well documented in the Soviet press over the years:

(1) Farms did not control input prices or availability of supplies;

(2) Farms did not control the quality or quantity of inputs;

(3) Farms did not control the quality of cadres or specialists assigned to the farm;

(4) Farms did not control procurement prices they received;

(5) Farm managers and directors could not fire slackers or drunks;

(6) Farms suffered from shortages of inputs, various types of transport, including refrigerated units, as well as shortages of storage and spare parts;

(7) Farms suffered from inadequate rural infrastructure, and most capital investments were directed toward "productive" purposes (food production);

(8) Farms suffered from an inability to retain skilled workers, due in part to the wage policies set by the state and the low level of rural amenities which reflected state investment priorities.

In addition to the list above, state and collective farms suffered from poor coordination by planners, duplication of authority, and problems from interministerial competition. In the early 1980s the agroindustrial complex was managed by no fewer than eleven different ministries.[6] The point is that given the range of economic factors over which farms had no control (not to mention a politically motivated retail price system), and given bureaucratic infighting and lack of coordination among regulatory agencies, it is hardly surprising that collective farms did not produce "efficiently." The real question is how they managed to improve food production during much of the 1960s and 1970s, and into the 1980s.

Regarding the price system, it is important to note that documented inefficiencies in Soviet-era production also resulted from the political choices Soviet leaders made about domestic food policy. The purpose of domestic food policy was to protect urban consumers from the true cost of food, which imposed unequal terms of trade on the rural sector. This pro-urban political goal of food policy was sometimes overlooked by Western analysts, as state subsidy policies and procurement price policies improved the economic environment for state and collective farms, starting with Khrushchev in 1953 and continuing under Brezhnev after 1965.[7] Despite seemingly "pro-rural" policy changes under Khrushchev and Brezhnev, the real aim was to moderate the intensity of Stalin-era urban bias so that the rapidly growing urban population could be fed. As such, the real beneficiaries of agricultural policy change were urban dwellers. A perfect example to illustrate the point is agricultural subsidies.[8]

During 1965-1980, agricultural subsidies increased severalfold, rising from 2 billion rubles in 1965 to 37 billion rubles in 1980, continuing to rise thereafter to nearly 100 billion rubles by 1987. Such a precipitous increase would appear to have benefited state and collective farms. However, of the 98.8 billion rubles the USSR spent on agricultural subsidies in 1987, 54 billion, or 55 percent, were retail price subsidies for consumers, and only 5.8 billion rubles were input subsidies intended for producers.[9] In 1991, retail price subsidies for consumers reached 80 percent of the total subsidy level allocated to agriculture.[10] Therefore, the essence of Soviet food policy (broadly defined) was decidedly *not* pro-rural, as described by former USSR President and General Secretary Mikhail Gorbachev, who also served as party secretary for agriculture during 1978-1985:

> The traditional concept of the peasant as a second class citizen had a
> further negative effect. . . .The countryside, with 100 million people,
> received only 10 percent of electric power. . . .A gas network was in-
> troduced in urban areas but farmers were deprived of it, and there
> were no plans to make gas available to them. . . .Rural areas were

> badly off for roads, schools, medical services, public services, news-
> paper and magazine supplies, cinemas and cultural entertainment. . .
> .Statements claiming that agriculture was 'unprofitable' were found
> to be wrong. All data pointed to the fact that much more was si-
> phoned off from agriculture than invested in it. And, of course, the
> nation's economic development had been achieved at the expense of
> the countryside.[11]

As a result of these and other problems, variations in food production, particularly for cereal crops, were symptomatic of the Soviet food system. Particularly in the last three five-year plans, the plan targets for food production were not realized.

Generally speaking, however, basic food production was not the key problem that plagued Soviet agriculture (though with some exceptions for specific commodities in the latter Soviet period). Despite deficiencies in the Soviet agricultural system, food production increased for most of the post-Stalin period, excepting a period during the late 1970s and early 1980s due to a string of bad harvests and drought. Even during the period of its worst performance, the early 1980s, followed by collapse of the economic system at the end of the decade, the gross value of agricultural production in the Russian Republic increased. During 1981-1985 the gross value of Russian agricultural production averaged 92.4 billion rubles annually, which increased to 103 billion rubles during 1986-1990 (measured in 1983 prices).[12] Some of the increase in value is accounted for by higher procurement prices during 1986-1989, which actually outstripped increases in retail prices. However, gross volumes of output increased over time as well. During 1960-1990, average Russian grain production increased during every five-year plan period except the Eleventh five-year plan (1981-1985), and the same was true for grain yields as well.[13] The average production level of high-preference items such as beef and pork increased during every five-year plan period from 1956 to 1990 in the USSR. Output of other animal products increased as well during every five-year plan in the post-Stalin period, including poultry, milk, wool, and eggs.[14] Thus, it is important to note that well-known consequences of the Soviet food system felt by consumers—long lines, chronic shortages, poor quality, and selection—flowed not so much from production as from politically motivated retail price strategies and an inadequate food distribution system.[15]

Nonetheless, for the most part, the USSR did feed itself. The fact that the USSR increased agricultural output was a rather remarkable feat, given the fact that: (a) the wholesale price structure provided few incentives for farms to maximize production and rewarded the least efficient farms with higher procurement prices; (b) the wholesale price structure provided few incentives to curb waste or use inputs efficiently; (c) the wholesale price structure provided incentives to engage in such "irrational" actions as using bread for livestock feed; (d) the wholesale price structure often favored industrial inputs and discriminated against agricultural products; (e) the retail price structure encouraged excess consumer consumption, leading to long lines and chronic shortages; and

(f) food trade in general was used for political purposes and not for comparative advantage.

In terms of production of specific food commodities, *sovkhozy* and *kolkhozy* on the one hand, and private plots on the other hand, played somewhat different roles. As would be expected, state and collective farms were the primary producers of food in the USSR. During the last year of the Soviet Union, state and collective farms accounted for 69 percent of the total ruble value of agricultural output, including 66 percent of plant products and 72 percent of animal products.[16] State and collective farms were the dominant producers of grains and cereals, technical crops used by industry, and feed crops, accounting for nearly all production. Households were important producers of meat, milk, potatoes, vegetables, and eggs. Food production levels and trends for the Russian Republic are presented in table 1.1.

Table 1.1. Average Food Production in Russian Republic, 1976-1991

	1976-1980 average	1981-1985 average	1986-1990 average	1991 only	% Produced by State/ Collective Farms, 1991
Grains, clean weight (million tons)	106	92	104.3	89.1	94
Sugar Beets (mt)	25.4	25.1	33.2	24.3	99
Sunflower Seed (mt)	2.5	2.3	3.1	2.9	96.5
Flax (thous.tons)	157	152	124	102	98
Potatoes (mt)	40.9	38.4	35.9	34.3	25
Vegetables (mt)	10.4	12.1	11.2	10.4	46
Meat, carcass weight (mt)	7.3	8	9.6	9.3	70
Milk (mt)	48.2	48.7	54.2	52	74
Eggs (billions)	36.7	43.1	47.9	47.1	78
Wool (thous. tons)	222	221	225	204	72

Source: *Rossiiskaia Federatsii v 1992 godu: statisticheskii ezhegodnik* (Moscow: Goskomstat, 1993), 412-13, 420, 473.

The data in the last column, which shows the percentage of output produced by state and collective farms, actually understate the importance of the collective sector in Soviet agriculture, for two reasons. First, 1991 was not an especially good year for Soviet agriculture, and production levels were below recent averages of the 1986-1990 period. Second, in the latter 1980s, production from households began to reverse its long-term decline relative to public production.

As food production on large farms increased significantly during the 1950s and 1960s—part of a deliberate plan—the hope, and intent, of Soviet leaders was to supplant "private" food with production from the public collective sphere. Indeed, over time, private production declined in importance and in its contribution to the national food supply.[17] But the goal to eliminate private production altogether proved to be unattainable, and Soviet leaders not only acknowledged the continued importance of private production, but at various times adopted policies to benefit plot operators.[18] At the 1978 July plenum, Soviet leader Brezhnev admitted that these small individually operated plots of land were an "important source" of food for the nation.[19] By the early 1980s, due to poor production performance on large farms, Soviet leaders loosened most restrictions on private plots.[20] Gorbachev further liberalized conditions and encouraged cooperation between large farms and individual plot operators. As a result, during the latter 1980s, production from private plots and other nonstate production, which had experienced a long-term decline since the 1940s, began to revive in terms of volumes of production and as a component of rural household income. In 1991, the last year of Soviet rule, private production accounted for nearly one-third of household income for a collective farm family, an increase of 30 percent over 1985.[21] Moreover, in that same year, the ruble value of production from private sources accounted for 31 percent of national food production, whereas during 1981-1985 it averaged 25 to 26 percent. This is an impressive statistic given the fact that output from large farms increased as well during the 1986-1990 period. The growth in output from private production lasted until the middle of the 1990s, but private producers remained the majority producer throughout the decade of the 1990s and into the twenty-first century as will be seen below.

Food Consumption Trends, 1980-1991

During the Soviet period food consumption data tend to be aggregated, and specific data by region, social class, and urban/rural division are difficult to find. Aggregate data show that from 1960 through 1990, the total population in the Russian Republic increased by 24.3 percent.[22] During that same time span in the Russian Republic (1960 through 1990), grain production increased by 36 percent, meat production by 102 percent, and milk production by 50 percent.

Thus, over a three-decade timeframe, food output increased faster than total population growth, resulting in an impressive increase in per capita consumption. By the mid-1980s, average caloric intake in the USSR was about 3,400 calories a day, equaling or exceeding the level of several OECD nations. (It should be noted that caloric intake was not calculated on actual consumption, but rather on food production divided by the population, and therefore actual caloric intake was likely to have been considerably lower.)[23] Per capita consumption trends in the Russian Republic for major food groups are indicated in table 1.2.

The consumption patterns displayed in the table are not unique to Russia or the Soviet system. Instead, an increase in fats and proteins from animal husbandry products, attendant with a decrease in cereals and starches, is a natural process called Bennett's law. Bennett's law states that the proportion of calories derived from starchy foods falls as income rises.[24] Thus, similar to the pattern found cross-nationally, changing mixes of food consumption in Soviet Russia reflected higher household income and increased standards of living.

Table 1.2. Per Capita Food Consumption in Russian Republic, 1971-1991 (in kilograms unless otherwise noted)

	1971-1975 average	1980 only	1981-1985 average	1986-1990 average	1991 only
Cereals	136	126	122	118	120
Meat and Meat Products	56	59	64	70	69
Fish and Fish Products	19.8	22.5	22.3	21.9	15.8
Milk and Milk Products	324	328	330	377	347
Eggs (#)	228	279	293	310	288
Sugar	42.7	46.7	46.6	48.2	37.8
Vegetable Oil	7.6	9.1	9.7	10.2	7.8
Potatoes	132	118	113	109	112
Vegetables and Melons	81	94	97	94	86
Fruits and Berries	NA	30	42	42	35

NA=data not available.
Source: *Narodnoe khoziaistvo RSFSR*, various years and pages.

The achievements in production and increased consumption should be qualified by noting that especially during the late 1980s, even increased food production did not compensate for deteriorating domestic food supplies. By the late 1980s, the state supply network of retail stores was not able to satisfy consumer demand. Shelves were empty, lines were long, and selection was poor. In the winter of 1990-1991, food rationing was introduced in many Russian cities for the first time since World War II.[25] Therefore, more and more demand was satisfied through purchases at urban collective farm markets where prices were much higher than prices in the state retail network. Another important source was food stores attached to factories and other workplaces where employees could purchase food at state prices.

The Post-Soviet Period

Trends in post-communist Russia stand in sharp contrast to the latter Soviet period on a number of dimensions. First, during most of the 1990s, gross food production declined significantly, measured either in ruble value or in physical volume. In the Russian Republic, as was seen above, during most of the post-Stalin period food production was *increasing* faster than total population growth. During the post-Soviet period through 2002, food production *decreased* faster than the decline in the Russian population. Second, per capita food consumption levels decreased, and the dietary structure of Russians changed as well. Post-Soviet trends and differences with the Soviet period are examined in detail in the sections below.

Food Production Trends, 1992-2002

In the post-Soviet period, there are three main food producers: (1) large agricultural enterprises, which are successors to former state and collective farms; (2) peasant households, or *krest'ianskie khoziaistva*; and (3) private farms. During the immediate post-Soviet period, several significant changes occurred in food production trends in comparison to the Soviet period.

The first change was a significant decrease in the amount of food that was produced. During 1992 through 2002, the total Russian population declined about 2.5 percent, while the gross value of agricultural production decreased 35-40 percent. The decline in food production was due to a variety of different factors—lower consumer demand as a result of sharply higher retail prices, reduction in livestock herds, curtailment of the amount of land cultivated, reduced use of mineral fertilizers and pesticides, substitution of manual for mechanized labor as spare parts became expensive and farms were unable to replace older machinery due to cost considerations, and sharply higher production costs including fuels, electricity, seeds, and transport. As a result, national food production declined steadily during 1992-1998, reaching its nadir in that year, before rebounding during 1999-2002. Nonetheless, even after stabilization was achieved and gross food production began to increase after 1998, output levels were considerably lower than in 1992. For example, from all types of farms in 2002, production of food grains was 74 percent the level of 1992, the production of feed grains was 64 percent, meat production was 55 percent, milk production was 71 percent, and egg production was 84 percent. The main food commodities that had production levels nearly equal to or greater than 1992 were potatoes and vegetables—95 percent and 122 percent of 1992 levels—respectively.[26]

A second change was the decline of large agricultural enterprises in their share of overall agricultural output. For example, in 1991 large farming enterprises produced 69 percent of total agricultural output, while households produced 31 percent (expressed as the nominal ruble value of output). But during the 1990s most of the food production decline was experienced by large agricultural enterprises. Using an index of physical volume of output (1990=100), the nadir was reached in 1998 when domestic agricultural production by large agricultural enterprises declined to 36 percent of 1990 levels.[27] After 1998, agricultural production began to rebound, and in 2002 large enterprises accounted for 42.2 percent of production, and households produced 53.8 percent, while private farmers contributed about 4 percent of total agricultural output.[28] (As during the Soviet period, it should be noted that households do not produce all types of produce, but concentrate mostly on potatoes, vegetables, meat, milk, and eggs.)

A third change was a reversal in the decline of output by households. The increase in household production helped to compensate for some of the production declines experienced by large farms.[29] The increase in household output was due in part to an expansion of land used by households, suggesting that households took advantage of reform opportunities. Household uses of land include private plots, collective gardens, dacha plots, and individual gardens. To illustrate, during 1990-2002, the amount of land used by households for food production on private plots increased from 3.2 million hectares (ha) in 1990 to 6.9 million ha in 2002.[30] The average size of a private plot more than doubled, from .20 ha in 1990 to .43 ha in 2002. Moreover, in 2002, approximately 35 million families operated some form of household agriculture, whether it be private plots, collective and individual fruit gardens, or collective and individual vegetable gardens.[31]

The increased contribution by households actually began under Gorbachev, but the trend accelerated in the early post-Soviet period. Within the overall trend of higher household production, the greatest increases in physical volumes of output from households occurred during 1992-1995, and thereafter declined through 1999 before stabilizing and increasing somewhat during 2000-2002.[32] During 1995-1998, increases in the relative contribution of agricultural output from households were due more to declines in output among large agricultural enterprises than increases in physical output by the household sector.[33] Nonetheless, the combination of increased household production and decreased production on large farms led to household production reaching its maximum contribution level in 1998, at which time households produced nearly 59 percent of the nation's food (in ruble value).[34] In 2002, households produced 93 percent of the nation's potatoes, 82 percent of its vegetables, 89 percent of its berries, 90 percent of its honey, and more than half of its cattle, poultry, pork, and milk. For several of these products, the contribution to the nation's food supply, expressed as a percentage, was double the 1990 level.[35]

While household output alone is not sufficient to provide the nation with a full range of food products, household production is important in that it provides an important source of food for rural dwellers—a segment of the population that in general saw its standard of living decline during the 1990s. For example, in 1997, household food production accounted for 46 percent of the value of food consumed by rural families, but less than 9 percent for urban families.[36] Production from rural households, therefore, clearly was the strategy of first choice to cushion rural families from the full effects of market reform.

A fourth contrast with the Soviet period is food production from the private farming sector. The contribution to the nation's food supply from private farms during the 1990s was disappointing, averaging 2 to 3 percent of total agricultural production for most of the decade. Private farmers never became the significant producer hoped for by reformers. Under Putin, however, several new trends emerged that augur well for the private farming sector. First, food production from private farmers increased, from 2.5 percent of national production in 1999 to 4 percent at the end of 2002, although output differed significantly from product to product.[37] This increase occurred in an environment of increased food production by large farming enterprises, and thus the improvement was real, not just relative.

In addition, from 1999 to the beginning of 2003, significant increases in land holdings by private farmers occurred. The amount of agricultural land used by private farmers increased from 13.4 million hectares in 1999 to 16.7 million hectares at the beginning of 2003, an increase of over 24 percent. During this time, the amount of arable land used by private farmers increased more than 26 percent, to 13 million hectares. There was also significant consolidation among farms. While the number of private farms during 1999-2003 increased by less than 3,000 (261,100 to 264,000), the average size of a farm increased 22 percent, from 55 hectares to 67 hectares, of which 49 hectares were arable.[38]

Private farmers also emerged as significant producers of certain plant products, specifically grains and sunflower seed. In 2002, for example, private farmers produced over 12 percent of the nation's grain and 20 percent of its sunflower seeds. During 1999-2003 the production of grains by private farmers nearly tripled.[39] Moreover, as the federal government intervened in the grain market to support domestic wholesale prices after the 2001 and 2002 harvests, private farmers benefited from price supports.

A final contrast with the Soviet period concerns sectoral performance. During the latter Soviet period, animal husbandry and meat production increased slowly but steadily, while the nation imported large quantities of grain. In the post-Soviet period, the animal husbandry sector has been especially hard hit. The reasons for the decline are varied: competition from imports, declining consumer demand due to higher retail prices, declining herd sizes due to increased production costs, and deliberate farm restructuring of production mix. The result was that, among all types of food producers, the number of dairy cows and beef cattle declined from 54.7 million in 1992 to 26.5 million by the end of 2002—a decline of more than 50 percent.[40] In addition, the number of pigs decreased from 35.4 million head in 1992 to a low of 15.7 million head at the end of 2001, a decline of 56 percent.[41] In 2002, a slight increase in the number of pigs occurred, improving to 16.0 million pigs.[42] To put those declines in perspective, during the first seven years of Stalin's collectivization (1928-1934), the number of meat cattle decreased by 40 percent and the number of pigs by 33 percent. As a result of declines in contemporary livestock holdings, cattle herds in 2002 were smaller than herds in 1949.[43]

In addition to declining livestock herds, the production of animal husbandry products trended downward during much of the 1990s. The low point in domestic meat production was in 1999, when 4.3 million tons (carcass weight) were produced, representing a 45 percent decrease in comparison with 1992. Domestic milk production reached its nadir in 1999 and 2000, decreasing by 32 percent in comparison to 1992. Egg production fell to its low point in 1997, dropping by about 25 percent in comparison with 1992.[44] These production data are from all categories of farms. Production declines on large agricultural enterprises were even greater.

The crop sector also experienced declines in output. It is well known that in 1998 Russia had its worst grain harvest in 40 years, totaling only 47.8 million tons, down from over 88 million tons in 1997, due largely to a devastating drought. In February 1999, Minister of Agriculture Viktor Semenov stated that grain reserves had dropped to only one million tons, and during 2000 there were reports of a grain deficits at the national and regional levels. Even though grain harvests rebounded somewhat to 54.7 million tons in 1999 and 65 million tons in 2000, the overall trend was one of drastic decline. Dividing the post-communist era into three three-year periods and one two-year period (1992-94, 1995-97, 1998-2000, and 2001-2002) there was a significant decline in average annual grain production. During 1992-94 the mean output was 95.77 million tons, 73.77 during 1995-97, and only 56 million tons during 1998-2000. There-after, two good harvests in 2001 and 2002 led to a two-year average of 85.9 million tons. Russian food production trends for a variety of products are illus-trated in table 1.3.

Table 1.3. Average Annual Russian Agricultural Production, 1992-2002 (all categories of farms)

	1992-1994	1995-1997	1998-2000	2001-2002
Grains (mil. tons)	95.7	73.7	56	85.9
Sugar Beets (mil. tons)	21.6	16.3	13.3	15.1
Sunflower Seeds (mil. tons)	2.7	3.2	3.7	3.2
Potatoes (mil. tons)	36.5	38.5	32.1	33.9
Vegetables (mil. tons)	9.8	11	11.7	13.1
Meat and Poultry (mil. tons, dead weight)	7.5	5.3	4.4	4.5
Milk (mil. tons)	45.2	36.3	32.2	33.2
Eggs (billion)	40.1	32.6	33.2	35.7

Grain totals after cleaning and drying.
Sources: *Rossiiskii statisticheskii ezhegodnik 1999* (Moscow: Goskom-stat, 1999), 363-71; "Sel'skoe khoziaistvo Rossii v 1999 godu (eko-nomicheskii obzor)," *APK: ekonomika, upravlenie*, no. 4 (April 2000): 26-31; *Sel'skoe khoziaistvo v Rossii* (Moscow: Goskomstat, 2000), various pages; *Agropromyshlennyi kompleks Rossii* (Moscow: Gokom-stat, 2001), 61-81; and *Rossiia v tsifrakh* (Moscow: Goskomstat, 2003), 210, 213.

One of the reasons for the decline in grain output during the 1990s was the decrease in the area of land used for agricultural production, a decrease of about 7 percent. Within that 7 percent drop, land used by private farmers and private plot operators increased while the amount of land used by large agricultural enterprises declined.[45] Importantly, cultivated land used for grain growing declined from 62 million ha in 1992 to a low of 46.5 million ha in 1999.[46] After 1999, there was a slight increase in land used for grains, but even so, in 2002 the amount of cultivated land was still only 76 percent of its 1992 level. Other reasons contributing to the decline in grain production were lower rates of fertilizer application, the virtual cessation of land improvement, drastically fewer numbers of agricultural machines and equipment, as well as spare parts and fuels for them.

As a consequence of these factors, the output of most plant products declined rather significantly during the 1990s before improving in the first years of the twenty-first century. Within the overall downward trend in crop production, there are two exceptions to note. First, the output of industrial crops, such as sunflower seeds, declined marginally, due in part to relatively high export levels. Furthermore, output of vegetables and potatoes either did not decline or did not decline significantly due to changed consumption habits by the population and the popularity of these products grown on household plots.

Food Consumption Trends, 1992-2001

Following price liberalization, which took effect on January 2, 1992, inflation surged throughout the entire economy—reaching 2,600 percent in 1992 and over 900 percent in 1993. Although food commodities for children and certain other items remained price protected, in general food prices shot up as part of the general inflationary process (for more detail see chapter 3). In response to dramatic retail price increases, several trends in food consumption were evident that stand in contrast to the preceding years of the Soviet period.

(1) Compared with food consumption levels during the Soviet period, Russians ate less in the 1990s, measured in per capita consumption and caloric intake. The per capita daily caloric intake declined from a norm of 3,550 to 2,100.[47] Opponents to reform argued that as many as one-third of Russians became undernourished. Hunger, primarily among the old who live on insufficient pensions, became a persistent problem. In April 1999, the World Bank predicted that up to 30 million people in Russia would live in "extreme poverty" in the year 2000.[48] Declines in food production combined with higher prices meant that Russians were consuming, on average, less than they had in 1980. These trends are indicated in table 1.4.

After Putin became president in 2000, real incomes and standards of living began to improve, and this improvement was reflected in somewhat higher consumption levels for certain products. In particular, meat and milk consumption increased the most, which as high-cost/high-preference goods reflected the fact that Russians had more money to spend.[49]

(2) Along with the decline in mean food consumption, the structure of the average Russian diet changed. Russians ate less meat and dairy products and more relatively cheap goods such as bread and potatoes.[50] The former head of the Committee on Agrarian Policy in the Federation Council maintained in 1995 that Russians consumed 75 percent of the protein and 50 percent of the vitamins that minimum health levels dictated.[51] The former chairman of the Duma's

Committee on Labor and Social Welfare claimed that "Today there are entire categories of Russians who are living at the level of the 'blokadeniks' in Leningrad and cannot avail themselves of even 500 grams of bread per day."[52]

Table 1.4. Per Capita Consumption of Food Products, 1980-2002 (includes urban and rural households, in kilograms per year unless otherwise noted)

	1980	1985	1990	1992	1998	1999	2001	2002
Cereals	112	105	97	104	120	111	115	113
Potatoes	117	108	94	107	111	94	93	90
Vegetables	92	91	85	78	83	81	83	83
Fruits and Berries	35	41	37	29	27	22	33	35
Meat and Meat Products	70	70	70	58	58	47	53	58
Eggs (number)	286	265	231	243	198	199	202	209
Milk and Milk Products	390	378	378	294	245	194	214	227
Fish and Fish Products	17	17	15	12	15	13	14	15

Sources: *Prodovol'stvennyi rynok Rossii* (Moscow: Goskomstat, 1999), 56; *Sotsial'noe polozhenie i uroven' zhizni naseleniia Rossii* (Moscow: Goskomstat, 2000), 144; *Prodovol'stvennyi rynok Rossii* (Moscow: Goskomstat, 2003), 176; and *Potreblenie produktov pitaniia v domashnikh khoziaistvakh v 2001-2002 gg.* (Moscow: Goskomstat, 2003), 48.

(3) Higher retail food prices also meant that a greater portion of the family budget was spent purchasing food. According to household survey data from Goskomstat, expenditures on food increased from about one-third of the family budget for urban households in 1991 to 49-50 percent during the third and fourth quarters of 1999, before declining to 39 percent by the fourth quarter of 2000. Rural households spent less on food overall, but food purchases constituted a higher percentage of family income: 56-59 percent during the third and fourth quarters of 1999, before declining to 52 percent by the fourth quarter of 2000.[53] The slight decline in family expenditures on food conforms to Engel's law and is explained by rising real incomes in 2000.[54]

(4) The effect of higher retail prices on low-income families, those with a single parent and two or more children, was even greater. Higher food prices often meant malnutrition and hunger for low-income families. Survey data of Russian households show that families with two or more children had significantly lower per capita consumption of every type of food product than families with zero or one child. The more children in the family, the lower the per capita consumption.[55]

(5) Regional differences in food consumption became evident. Whereas during the Soviet period food consumption patterns were relatively equalized as a result of planned distribution according to leadership priorities, more inequality is evident during the 1990s. While it is true that in the wake of the 1998 financial crisis, regional and city governments intervened to protect consumers by imposing limits on retail food prices, it is also true that northern areas have lost their Soviet-era protection, and now on average have lower per capita consumption means for many products than southern areas.[56] Of course, food consumption data suggest consumption of high-preference items is very sensitive to income levels, with higher income associated with increased consumption of meat and less of carbohydrates.[57] This pattern is perfectly normal and shows that food consumption patterns in Russia conform to patterns predicted by Bennett's law.[58]

(6) Urban-rural differences became evident. Rural dwellers, according to a Goskomstat survey, receive more than one-third of the household's food from their private plot.[59] According to official data, rural dwellers consume more than urban dwellers, and the gap increased since 1991. In 1998, rural dwellers' per capita consumption surpassed urban consumption for bread and bread products, potatoes, vegetables, milk and milk products, and sugar. In sum, rural dwellers consumed on average 3,216 calories a day in 1998, while urban dwellers consumed only 2,612, and rural dwellers had more protein and fat in their diet.[60]

(7) Finally, despite the fact that consumption declined for most food products and for most Russians, somewhat paradoxically food supplies improved during the 1990s. In the Soviet period, food production increased but supplies deteriorated. In the Russian period, although domestic food production declined for much of the 1990s, food supplies are much better. This occurrence is explained by the fact that retail prices began to act as a rationing mechanism, unlike during the Soviet period; by the growing importance of production and sales from the household sector; and by the introduction of an open trade policy which witnessed increased food imports into the country during 1992-1998. Thus, despite declining food production during much of the 1990s, most Russians have had better access to food than previously, food lines have disappeared, and there is improved selection.

Households and Income in Russia: Who Produces?

The sections above reviewed food production and consumption trends at the national level. As was shown above, among the most important changes in food production trends during the post-Soviet period is the fact that households have become a very significant food producer, at least for some products. New research opportunities permit a more detailed examination of household food production and consumption. This section uses survey data to investigate food production and consumption by social class. Per capita income level is used as the independent variable, and food production is the dependent variable. The survey of rural households was conducted in five Russian regions during 2001. Those five regions include: Belgorod oblast, Volgograd oblast, Krasnodar krai,

Novgorod oblast, and the Chuvash Republic. The pretest of the questions was conducted in June 2001 in Riazan oblast, followed by the full survey during July-October 2001. Within each region, four villages were selected, and within each village, 40 households were surveyed, for a total sample of 800 households (160 households in each region). In selecting villages to be surveyed, a primary objective was to gather data from "real" rural Russians, owing to the well-known effects of modernization and urbanization which influence attitudes and behaviors. Previously, when surveying "rural" Russia, it has often been the case that "rural" villages are selected due to their close proximity to an urban center, for the sake of convenience. The consequence of this selection method is that respondents' views do not capture the real attitudes of rural Russia. The selection method used to gather these data focused on remote villages that are located several hours (by bus) from an urban center. Moreover, a cross-section of different types of villages was used: small, middle-sized, economically weak, and economically strong.

For each of the selected villages a stratified sample was composed from the household list of permanent residents which is kept by the village administration for all households within its jurisdiction. This list is updated annually and contains demographic and social characteristics of the households on the list. Households on this list include persons working on large farms, private farmers, persons working in food processing or food trade business, and persons engaged in private household agricultural production and/or processing. One person from each household was interviewed.

Among respondents, the mean household size was three persons, with some, but not significant, regional variation. A large percentage of households consisted of a husband, wife, and third person. The third person was most often an elderly grandparent who tends to stay at home and work the household plot. In all, the survey consisted of more than 100 questions per respondent. The distribution of respondents by income level is indicated in table 1.5.

The table indicates that 193 individuals, or almost a quarter of the sample, have monetary incomes less than one-half of the government-defined subsistence level, and therefore are considered "very poor." Another 345 individuals, or 43 percent of the sample, have incomes from 50 to 90 percent of the subsistence level and are termed "poor." Comprising the "middle class" are 190 individuals (about 24 percent of the sample) who have incomes ranging from 90 percent to 150 percent of the subsistence level. Thirty-nine individuals, or just over 5 percent of the sample, are termed "rich" and have incomes from 150 to 199 percent of the subsistence level. Finally, 33 individuals (4 percent of the sample) have incomes 200 percent or more of the subsistence level and are termed "very rich." A couple of caveats: (1) Income designations assigned by the author are somewhat arbitrary, but do capture, I believe, a close resemblance to reality. (2) Rural monetary incomes are significantly lower than urban incomes—on average less than one-half the urban level. Therefore, the designations in the table are based on rural standards that are not applicable to urban populations. A "rich" urbanite, for example, would be someone with an income much greater than 150 to 199 percent of the subsistence level.

Table 1.5. Distribution of Monetary Income Per Capita for 800 Rural Households

Per Capita Rubles Per Month*	Frequency	Percent of Sample	Percentage of Subsistence Level	Income Designation
0-787	193	24%	0-49.9%	Very Poor
788-1180	232	29.0%	50-74.9%	Poor
1181-1416	113	14.1%	75-89.9%	Poor
1417-1573	56	7.0%	90-99.9%	Middle
1574-1731	36	4.5 %	100-109.9%	Middle
1732-1967	57	7.1%	110-124.9%	Middle
1968-2361	41	5.1%	125-149.9%	Middle
2362-2754	26	3.3%	150-174.9%	Rich
2755-2991	7	.9%	175-189.9%	Rich
2992-3148	6	.8%	190-199.9%	Rich
3149+	33	4.1%	200%+	Very Rich
Total	800	100	NA	NA

NA=not applicable.
*During 2001 the dollar-ruble exchange rate averaged about $1=R29.
Source: Survey data, 2001.

Household Food Producers

For the analysis to follow, access to land and inputs is assumed, although obviously ease of access and level of access vary by region, size of household, and economic status. Aside from access to land and production inputs, there are two sets of factors that influence an increase in households' food production: structural reasons and behavioral reasons. Structural reasons include variables that are either inherent to household members or variables that are not changed easily during the reform period. Examples of structural factors would include, for instance, age, education, and family size. In other words, structural factors are relatively constant and either unchanging (such as education), or change in predictable ways (age).

The second set of factors concern behavioral and adaptive responses to opportunities provided by reform. For example, adaptive responses might include increasing household land plot size, obtaining credit, or engaging in private business. Dividing the sample into income categories, it becomes clear that there are structural differences. For example, the very poorest respondents tend to have the largest household size (3.8 members), have a lower mean age (44.2), and have lower educational levels (10.4) in comparison to the two highest income levels.[61]

Despite certain structural differences among income groups, behavioral responses to reform are more significant. Reflective of behavioral responses are levels of food production. The argument to be developed below is twofold: (1) behavioral-response differences are detectable across income groups; and (2) differences in food production are better understood by behavioral responses than by structural differences. In short, persons in higher income categories responded differently during the reform period. The focus here is on food production, although other research has shown that higher income groups sold more from their household production; participated in private business, thereby reducing dependence on salaries from their primary job for the welfare of the household; and were more likely to acquire additional land during the 1990s.[62]

If this argument is correct, it has importance for the future. Rural economic actors operated in a hostile macroeconomic environment during much of the 1990s which affected the path of rural capitalism.[63] At the village and neighborhood level, rural actors are acutely aware of their relative standing vis-à-vis other members of the community and income strata within the community. If there is compelling evidence that certain groups "won" because of their behavioral responses to reform stimuli, this sends a strong signal to other actors about appropriate strategies to adopt, or what to avoid.[64]

One of the ways in which income groups differed during reform was in food production. Food production alone is not a sufficient measure of adaptation to reform opportunities, and increased food production may be largely a survival strategy. The question of adaptation versus survival requires a broader analysis that would take us far afield from the focus herein, although the author has attempted to disentangle the relevant issues in other research.[65] Nonetheless, per capita food production by category of income do differ significantly, and these trends are shown in table 1.6.

Table 1.6. Per Capita Mean Food Production by Income Category

Per Capita Rubles Per Month	Meat (kg)	Milk (liters)	Eggs (#)	Potatoes (kg)	Vegetables (kg)	Fruit (kg)	Hay (kg)
0-787	67.4	924.4	358.7	281.9	140.8	58.8	800.4
788-1180	89.5	1,245.1	571.3	394.0	221.3	92.5	1,078.0
1181-1416	114.0	1,398.5	573.9	398.1	266.6	107.2	1,240.7
1417-1573	133.3	1,763.4	787.6	457.0	313.6	103.3	1,331.0
1574-1731	124.3	1,688.6	948.4	552.1	400.3	113.5	1,522.2
1732-1967	147.7	1,892.6	741.4	438.1	361.1	95.0	1,874.1
1968-2361	168.6	2,088.3	1,073.6	567.6	340.4	113.9	2,341.9
2362-2754	116.9	2,909.5	1,013.6	506.0	274.8	139.6	3,196.9
2755-2991	109.3	3,600.0	1,854.1	314.2	292.8	126.4	3,650.0
2992-3148	309.3	3,753.3	696.6	477.7	193.3	96.3	3,120.0
3149+	600.6	3,702.3	936.4	741.7	342.5	1,233.4	5,554.5

Production data are annual.
Source: Survey data, 2001.

The data for mean volumes of food production show that the two highest income categories produced significantly more food than the lowest income categories. Furthermore, it is important to note the difference between high-preference and expensive food commodities (primarily meat), and lower-preference and lower-cost foods (such as vegetables and potatoes). It is clear that individuals in lower income categories not only produced less in general—despite more household members—but in particular produced less of high-preference and high-cost food commodities. For example, the highest income individuals produced almost 10 times more meat than the lowest-income individuals, but only about 2.6 times as many potatoes and 2.4 times as many vegetables.

Higher food production by high-income individuals was a result not only of working hard, but also a result of accumulating productive capacity. When reform began, it is reasonable to assume that most rural households were roughly similar in the size of their household plot, and in the number of cows, pigs, etc. In 2001, however, when the survey was conducted, there was evidence of emerging stratification: the highest-income individuals had a mean of 5.82 cows and calves and 5.12 pigs, while the lowest-income individuals had a mean of .99 cows and calves and 1.02 pigs. Further, while household land plots were essentially of equal size, .25 ha for the lowest-income group and .26 for the highest, there were significant differences in the size of rental plots. The lowest-income group had a mean rental plot size of .10 ha while the highest-income group had a mean of 2.1 ha. This is important because the size of household land plots correlate positively with household food production but negatively with food sales, while rental plots correlate positively with food sales. Thus, land plots appear to have different functions. Therefore, differences in food production are attributable to behavioral responses both at present (working hard to produce) and in the past (a pattern of accumulating production capacity). Extrapolating from these survey results, it is clear that among rural household producers, high-income individuals are the most productive and are contributing the most to the national food supply.

The second aspect to note is the relationship between income levels and food consumption. National survey statistics demonstrate an inverse relationship between family size, income, and food consumption: the larger the family, the poorer it is and the less it consumes.[66] To add detail to the picture, the survey data from 800 households show that poorer individuals obtain more of their total income from consumption. For example, the lowest-income group (0-787 rubles per month) obtains 47 percent of total income from consumption; the next-lowest-income group (788-1180 rubles per month) obtains 36 percent of total income from consumption. In contrast, the highest-income group (3149+ rubles per month) obtains only 11 percent of income from consumption, and the next-highest group (2992-3148 rubles per month) obtains only 14 percent from consumption. These statistics reflect higher food production and food sales by upper-income individuals. But beyond that, the data show that those in extreme poverty literally consume their capital and thus are caught in a vicious cycle whereby they must consume to survive but doing so precludes movement out of poverty. In addition, higher percentages of income from consumption affect dietary structure—one consumes what one produces—and the fact that these individuals are so poor makes it unlikely that a lot of food is purchased from outside sources. This reality in turn affects the health of the individual. The policy implication is that as the countryside becomes increasingly stratified, as a result of upper-income individuals and households utilizing the opportunities presented by reform, poor households will fall further behind both in terms of income and in terms of food consumption. The upshot is that the post-Soviet countryside is becoming decidedly less egalitarian than its Soviet predecessor.

Conclusion

The purpose of this chapter has been to place food production and consumption trends within the larger question of rural transformation from the Soviet to the post-Soviet period. The chapter demonstrated that considerable change occurred in terms of which food producers are dominant, food production levels, and per capita consumption levels from the Soviet to the post-Soviet period.

During most of the post-Stalin period, food production and food consumption levels increased, although the latter leveled off by the early 1980s and did not change significantly until consumption levels began to decline during the reform period. State and collective farms in particular increased their levels of food production and reduced the importance of production from households' private plots to the national food supply. Although private plots were relatively large contributors to the nation's total food supply (compared to the amount of land they used), the volume of trade turnover through collective farm markets was small compared to state channels of trade. Overall, a long-term decline was evident in the volume of produce sold on the urban collective farm market, dating from the 1960s to the late 1980s,[67] reflected in the decrease in the number of such markets. By 1988, collective farm market trade accounted for just 2.5 percent of food sales (calculated in 1988 prices), and the number of collective farm markets throughout the USSR had declined from 7,522 in 1970 to 6,098 in 1988.[68] In addition, the percentage of income derived from private plot sales also decreased, from nearly one-half of a collective farmer's income in 1940 to less than one-quarter by 1986.[69]

During the post-Soviet period, notable changes occurred in production trends. Data were presented that showed that food production declined more rapidly than the population decreased. Most significant was the decline in output from large agricultural enterprises; as a result, the relative contribution of output from households increased. In the post-Soviet period, as the importance of production from large farms has decreased, the private sector, in particular household production, has become the dominant sector, measured in ruble value of food output. Private farms did not contribute a lot to the national food supply during the 1990s, but by the beginning of the Putin period there were indicators that the private farming had stabilized and would become more important in the years ahead.

Furthermore, survey data show that the more affluent households produce the most and make the largest contribution to the food supply, despite having fewer members per household. In terms of sectoral production, animal husbandry products and plant products declined, but plant products rebounded faster while livestock herds decreased and stayed low into the new century.

In terms of food consumption trends, during the post-Soviet period per capita caloric intake and per capita consumption declined. Moreover, consumers in Russia changed their diet, consuming less protein and more starches and carbohydrates. Differences in urban-rural consumption patterns became more significant. As a result of higher food prices at retail outlets, families spent more of their household income on food. Finally, as retail prices began to act like a rationing mechanism and as trade policy opened up, food supplies in Russia improved and the long lines that were characteristic of the Soviet period disappeared. These trends, therefore, define the context for an investigation of Russia's food policies, both domestic and external. The following chapter examines domestic food policies and patterns of trade in the Soviet period to provide a context, before turning in subsequent chapters to food and trade policies during the post-Soviet period.

Notes

1. In addition, this topic has been extensively discussed by Western economists. See, for example, D. Gale Johnson and Karen McConnell Brooks, *Prospects for Soviet Agriculture in the 1980s* (Bloomington: Indiana University Press, 1982), 37-57.
2. *Lichnoe podsobnoe khoziaistvo naseleniia v 1988 godu* (Moscow: Goskomstat SSSR, 1989), 9-12.
3. *Lichnoe podsobnoe khoziaistvo naseleniia v 1988 godu*, 9-12.
4. *Rossiiskii statisticheskii ezhegodnik* (Moscow: Goskomstat, 1996), 547.
5. See Anton F. Malish, "The Food Program: A New Policy or More Rhetoric?" in Joint Economic Committee, *Soviet Economy in the 1980s: Problems and Prospects*, Part 2, Joint Committee Print, 97th Congress, 2nd Session (Washington, DC: Government Printing Office, 1982), 47-49.
6. A partial list of ministries that were part of the food production, food processing, and the distribution process includes the following: Ministry of Agriculture, Ministry of Trade, Ministry of Cereal and Grain Production, Ministry of Fruit and Vegetable Farming, Ministry of Machine-building for Animal Husbandry and Feed Production, Ministry of Tractors and Farm Machinery, Ministry of Land Reclamation and Water Resources, Ministry of Meat and Dairy Industry, Ministry of Food Industry, Ministry of Rural Construction, and Ministry of Fertilizer Production. To this list at least three state committees may be added: the State Planning Committee, the Material and Technical Supply Committee, and the Committee for the Supply of Production Equipment to Agriculture. The list of obstacles and coordinating ministries is taken from Stephen K. Wegren, *Agriculture and the State in Soviet and Post-Soviet Russia* (Pittsburgh: Pittsburgh University Press, 1998), 61-62.
7. See I. V. Rusinov, "Agrarnaia politika KPSS v 50-e—pervoi polovine 60-x godov: opyt i uroki," *Voprosy istorii KPSS*, no. 9 (September 1988): 35-49; V. F. Mel'nikov, ed., *Ekonomika sotsialisticheskogo sel'skogo khoziaistva v sovremennykh usloviiakh* (Moscow: Ekonomika, 1971); and A. M. Emel'ianov and S. I. Polovenko, eds., *Ekonomika sel'skogo khoziaistva na sovremennom etape* (Moscow: Moscow State University, 1980).
8. For an excellent analysis of Soviet subsidy policy in agriculture see Vladimir G. Treml, "Subsidies in Soviet Agriculture: Record and Prospects," in Joint Economic Committee, *Soviet Economy in the 1980s: Problems and Prospects*, 171-85.
9. V. Semenov, "Khozrashchet i samofinasirovanie," *APK: ekonomika, upravlenie*, no. 3 (March 1989): 12.

10. World Bank, *Food and Agricultural Policy Reforms in the Former USSR: An Agenda for the Transition* (Washington, DC: The World Bank, 1993), 218.

11. Mikhail Gorbachev, *Memoirs* (New York: Doubleday, 1996), 118-20.

12. World Bank, *Food and Agricultural Policy Reforms in the Former USSR*, 225.

13. Jaclyn Y. Shend, *Agricultural Statistics of the Former USSR Republics and the Baltic States*, Statistical Bulletin No. 863 (Washington, DC: USDA, Economic Research Service, 1993), 99-100.

14. Shend, *Agricultural Statistics of the Former USSR Republics*, 92-95, 184.

15. Of course, to say that Soviet food production increased over time is not to say that the system was efficient. For an analysis on the efficiency of Soviet agriculture see Johnson and Brooks, *Prospects for Soviet Agriculture in the 1980s*, 120-65.

16. *Rossiiskaia Federatsiia v 1992 godu: statisticheskii ezhegodnik* (Moscow: Goskomstat, 1993), 409.

17. See Stephen K. Wegren, "Private Agriculture in the Soviet Union Under Gorbachev," *Soviet Union*, 16, nos. 2-3 (1989): 105-44.

18. For a review of state policy toward private plots, see Z. I. Kalugina, *Lichnoe podsobnoe khoziaistvo v SSSR* (Novosibirsk: Nauka, 1991), 62-68. The classic book on private agriculture which extends the analysis to the first half of the Brezhnev period is by Karl-Eugen Wadekin, *The Private Sector in Soviet Agriculture* (Berkeley: University of California Press, 1973). Over time, however, private plot policy was not consistent. The most notable periods during which Soviet leaders adopted policies to assist private production were 1953-1957, 1965-1966, 1977-1981, and 1987-1988.

19. Emel'ianov and Polovenko, eds., *Ekonomika sel'skogo khoziaistva na sovremennom etape*, 36.

20. See Ann Lane, "USSR: Private Agriculture on Center Stage," in Joint Economic Committee, *Soviet Economy in the 1980s: Problems and Prospects*, 23-40.

21. *Rossiiskaia Federatsiia v 1992 godu*, 163.

22. Within that overall growth, the urban population increased 71 percent while the rural population decreased 30 percent. *Demograficheskii ezhegodnik* (Moscow: Goskomstat, 2000), 19-21.

23. World Bank, *Food and Agricultural Policy Reforms in the Former USSR*, 36-37.

24. C. Peter Timmer, Walter P. Falcon and Scott R. Pearson, *Food Policy Analysis* (Baltimore and London: The World Bank and Johns Hopkins University Press, 1983), 56.

25. See William Moskoff, *Hard Times: Impoverishment and Protest in the Perestroika Years, The Soviet Union 1985-1991* (Armonk, NY: M. E. Sharpe, 1993), 27-54.

26. *Rossiia v tsifrakh* (Moscow: Goskomstat, 2003), 209, 213.

27. *Rossiia v tsifrakh* (Moscow: Goskomstat, 1999), 204.

28. *Rossiia v tsifrakh* 2003, 201.

29. It should be noted that during the early 1990s, the large percentage increases by households occurred mostly as a result of significant declines in food production among large farms.

30. *Sel'skokhoziaistvennaia deiatel'nost' khoziaistv naseleniia v Rossi* (Moscow: Goskomstat, 2003), 12.

31. *Sel'skokhoziaistvennaia deiatel'nost' khoziaistv naseleniia v Rossii* (2003), 12.

32. *Sel'skokhoziaistvennaia deiatel'nost' khoziaistv naseleniia v Rossii* (Moscow: Goskomstat, 1999), 34; *Sel'skokhoziaistvennaia deiatel'nost' khoziaistv naseleniia v Rossii* (2003), 24, 30; and *Rossiia v tsifrakh 2003*, 204

33. See "Razvitie individual'nogo sektora sel'skogo khoziaistva Rossii (ekonomicheskii obzor)," *APK: ekonomika, upravlenie*, no. 3 (March 1999): 57-66; and Z. N. Shuklina,

"Zaniatost' i dokhodnost' v lichnykh podsobnykh khoziaistvakh naseleniia," *Ekonomika sel'skokhoziaistvennykh i pererabatyvaiushchikh predpriiatii*, no. 6 (June 1999): 54-56.
34. *Rossiia v tsifrakh 2003*, 201.
35. *Sel'skokhoziaistvennaia deiatel'nost' khoziaistv naseleniia v Rossii* (2003), 15.
36. *Sel'skokhoziaistvennaia deiatel'nost' khoziaistv naseleniia v Rossii* (1999), 157.
37. *Rossiia v tsifrakh 2003*, 201.
38. See akkor.agris.ru (11 November 2003).
39. See akkor.agris.ru (11 November 2003).
40. *Rossiiskii statisticheskii ezhegodnik 1999*, 370; and "Sel'skoe khoziaistvo Rossii v 2002g," *APK, ekonomika, upravlenie*, no. 3 (March 2003): 26.
41. *Narodnoe khoziaistvo RSFSR v 1992: statisticheskii ezhegodnik* (Moscow: Goskomstat, 1992), 470; I. Terent'ev, "Sostoianie i perspektivy APK," *Ekonomist*, no. 4 (April 2000): 86; and *Rossiia v tsifrakh 2003*, 213.
42. *Sel'skoe khoziaistvo v Rossii* (Moscow: Goskomstat, 2002), 67.
43. *Sel'skoe khoziaistvo v Rossii* (Moscow: Goskomstat, 2000), 67.
44. *Rossiiskii statisticheskii ezhegodnik 1999*, 371-74; and Rossiia v tsifrakh 2003, 213.
45. *Rossiiskii statisticheskii ezhegodnik 1999*, 349.
46. A. Seleznev, "Nekotorye problemy upravleniia APK i puti ikh resheniia," *Ekonomist*, no. 6 (June 2000): 76.
47. S. Piliev, "Ob obespechenii prodovol'stvennoi dostatochnosti naseleniia Rossii," *Ekonomist*, no. 7 (July 1998): 24.
48. *Financial Times*, 19 April 1999, 18.
49. Real incomes for the entire population rose 13 percent in 2000, 10 percent in 2001, and 11 percent in 2002. *Sotsial'noe polozhenie i uroven' zhizni naseleniia Rossii* (Moscow: Goskomstat, 2003), 108.
50. *Potreblenie produktov pitaniia v domashnikh khoziaistvakh v 1997-1999 gg. (po itogam vyborochnogo obsledovaniia biudzhetov domashnikh khoziaistv)* (Moscow: Goskomstat, 2001), 11.
51. V. Zvolinskii, "Prodovol'stvennoe obespechenie—faktor sotsial'no-politicheskoi stabilizatsii obshchestva," *Ekonomist*, no. 9 (September 1995): 91..
52. *Sel'skaia zhizn'*, 15 March 1994, 1.
53. *Statisticheskii biulleten'*, no. 1 (January 2000):19; *Dokhody, raskhody, i potreblenie domashnikh khoziaistv v III-IV kvartalakh 2000 goda (po itogam vyborochnogo obsledovaniia biudzhetov domashnikh khoziaistv)* (Moscow: Goskomstat, 2001), 77.
54. Engels' law states that the proportion of a family's budget devoted to food declines as the family's income increases. Timmer, Falcon, and Pearson, *Food Policy Analysis*, 56.
55. *Potreblenie produktov pitaniia v domanshnikh khoziaistvakh v 1997-1999 gg.,*12-14.
56. *Potreblenie produktov pitaniia v domanshnikh khoziaistvakh v 1997-1999 gg.,*77-82.
57. *Potreblenie produktov pitaniia v domanshnikh khoziaistvakh v 1997-1999 gg.,* 83-88.
58. Bennett's law states that as family income rises, households will consume less starchy products. Timmer, Falcon, and Pearson, *Food Policy Analysis*, 56.
59. *Potreblenie produktov pitaniia v domanshnikh khoziaistvakh v 1997-1999 gg.,*10.
60. *Prodovol'stvennyi rynok Rossii* (Moscow: Goskomstat, 1999), 56.
61. The income category 2,992-3,148 rubles a month has a mean family size of 3.1 members, a mean age of 52.1 years, and an education level of 11.3 for the husband and 12.0 for the wife. The income category 3,149+ rubles a month has a mean family size of 3.0 members, a mean age of 48.4 years, and an education level of 11.3 for the husband and 11.1 for the wife.
62. See Stephen K. Wegren, David J. O'Brien, and Valeri Patsiorkovski, "Winners and Losers in Russian Agrarian Reform," *The Journal of Peasant Studies*, 30, no. 1 (October

2002): 1-29; and Stephen K. Wegren, "Why Rural Russians Participate in the Land Market," *Post-Communist Economies*, 27, no. 4 (December 2003): 483-501.

63. See Stephen K. Wegren, "Russian Agrarian Reform and Rural Capitalism Reconsidered," *The Journal of Peasant Studies*, 26, no. 1 (October 1998): 82-111.

64. Of course, not all actors have equal opportunities or resources, and each faces different constraints.

65. Stephen K. Wegren, "Rural Adaptation in Russia: Who Responds and How Do We Measure It?" *Journal of Agrarian Change*, 4, no. 4 (October 2004): 553-78.

66. See *Potreblenie produktov pitaniia v domashnikh khoziaistvakh v 2001-2002gg.* (Moscow: Goskomstat, 2003), 47-48.

67. Wegren, "Private Agriculture in the Soviet Union under Gorbachev," 128-33.

68. Wegren, "Private Agriculture in the Soviet Union under Gorbachev," 131.

69. *Narodnoe khoziaistvo SSSR za 70 let* (Moscow: Finansy i statistika, 1987), 445.

Chapter Two

Food Policies and Food Trade in the Soviet Period

This chapter surveys the Soviet period, focusing on domestic and external (international) food policies and patterns of trade. For domestic food policies, the focus is on procurement policy and the operation of the procurement system, the procurement price system, as well as patterns and channels of domestic food trade. There is also a section that focuses on food consumers and examines retail price policy as part of the domestic food system. For international food policy, the chapter provides a brief overview of the Soviet system of international trade, starting with a review of the broad characteristics, followed by three subsections: (1) the Soviet foreign trade system; (2) changes in Soviet foreign trade policies and strategies under Gorbachev; and (3) food trade in the latter Soviet period.

The purpose of this chapter is to provide a foundation for the examination of post-Soviet domestic food policies and food trade in subsequent chapters. By providing a basis to which Russian food policy and trade may be compared, my intent is to show that Russian food policy and patterns of trade are considerably different from their Soviet predecessor.

Large Farm Producers: The Food Procurement System

The Soviet procurement system did not regulate food output by households or individual producers who grew food on their private plots, dacha plots, or collective gardens. Of course, households and individuals were allowed to sell produce to the state, largely through so-called consumer cooperatives, but they were not required to do so. Thus, state regulation of quantitative plans for output, the type of food produced, or postproduction use of food pertains to large farms, that is, state and collective farms. Large farms were expected to provide the country with most of its food, and as the previous chapter demonstrated, these farms were in fact the primary food producer for most types of food production in the post-Stalin period. As a result, the procurement system fell on the shoulders of large farms.

Generally speaking, the Soviet food system was centralized and administered by Gosplan, the State Planning Committee, and implemented by a number of different ministries. The Ministry of Agriculture oversaw the growing of food according to plans enumerated by Gosplan. State and collective farms were supplied with machinery from the Ministry of Tractors and Farm Machinery, and received fertilizer from the Ministry of Fertilizer Production. From the 1950s into the early 1980s, state purchases of food from farms were conducted by a Ministry of Procurement. In the early 1980s responsibility for food purchases was shifted to a department within the Ministry of Trade. The Ministry of Trade also was responsible for food distribution to regions and cities, all the way down to individual retail stores, restaurants, and dining halls. Suffice it to say that state and collective farms received procurement orders specifying quantities to be delivered to food processors and at what price. Processors were regulated as to which retail outlets processed goods would be delivered, and at what price their processed food would be sold to retail stores. Retail food stores similarly had their prices fixed by state planners.

Soviet food policy strategy was intended to regulate the flow of food from the countryside to urban consumers, to control food supplies so that certain segments of the population and regions of the country benefited, and to keep food prices artificially low, thereby ensuring broad access to food by protecting Soviet consumers from market-level food prices. The centralization of the Soviet domestic food market produced four main characteristics: (1) state control over wholesale food trade through a system of state procurements; (2) high percentages of food trade occurring through state-controlled channels of trade; (3) state control over food procurement prices; and (4) state regulation of retail food prices in a network of food stores and cooperatives.

The Soviet Procurement System

The state procurement system evolved significantly during the 1920s and 1930s, starting with a contract system which then evolved to a system of obligatory deliveries. During the New Economic Policy (NEP), which extended from 1921 to 1928, state procurement prices were essentially market based. Private dealers dominated the wholesale market, there was no state monopoly, and deliveries were not obligatory. The contract system was intended to be voluntary, with obligations on both sellers and government buyers. Sellers were to benefit from advance payments, guaranteed supplies of goods and productive inputs, and loans. In return, they were to sell certain quantities of grain, with bonuses for above-contract deliveries. Neither the signing of contracts nor the sale of grain was compulsory.[1] Beginning in the winter of 1927-1928 various steps were taken by the government to curtail private trade and to direct more grain to state buyers. The campaigns of 1927-1928 and 1928-1929 set the stage for collectivization and led to the introduction of a contract system. After 1932, contracts and deliveries became obligatory, and the system of state procurements meant that state and collective farms received targets and quotas, from which they were to plan their production and deliveries to the state. In 1947, differentiated farm quotas were introduced for stronger and weaker collective farms, replacing the uniform rates that had been introduced during 1939-1940.

Allowing for some policy changes during World War II,[2] the Ministry of Agriculture and its local organs specified production plans to collective farms until 1955, and procurements remained the responsibility of the Ministry of Procurement until 1956, and then of the Ministry of Agriculture until 1959. In 1958 a complete reorganization of the procurement system was undertaken. Under this reform, the different types of procurements were combined into one system with a single price for each commodity within a region. Second, the method of calculating compulsory deliveries was reformed. Previously, deliveries were based on the sown area of land, from which calculations were made as to expected yield per hectare, and from that basis, for deliveries to the state. First Secretary Nikita Khrushchev reformed the system so that deliveries were based on actual output. Purchase quotas were established for a five-to-seven-year period, subject to an annual review. New purchase prices were introduced that were close to or exceeded the old above-quota price.[3] After the procurement system was reorganized, procurements became the responsibility of Gosplan and various state committees, including the Committee on Grain Products and the Committee on Meat and Dairy Industry.[4] While a general procurement plan was adopted by the central government, republican governments were largely responsible for supplying their own populations with resources from their own areas. State grain procurements thus tended to come from high-production/low-cost areas, and many oblasts in central and northern Russia, as well as the Baltics, were wholly or partially exempt from grain deliveries.[5]

After Khrushchev, the first few years of the Brezhnev regime ushered in changes in the procurement system, although the essential features of the procurement system remained intact from the past. Plans for production and purchases were established down to the raion level with specific targets assigned to farms.[6] One new wrinkle to the procurement system occurred at the March 1965 plenum when stable procurement plans for agricultural products were introduced that were to run for five years. Firm purchase plans were worked out according to a region's natural and economic conditions, zonal specialization, the presence and location of processing plants, and the composition of labor resources.[7] The basis for this system were "contracts" that were concluded between the farm and the local procurement organization. In reality the contracts were obligatory and there was little that was negotiable. As one source noted: "The purchase plan is obligatory for all. It cannot be changed and it is not permitted not to fulfill it."[8] The purpose for stable purchases was to allow farms to plan their obligations, knowing that above-plan sales could lead to substantial bonus monies. At the same time, penalties for late or nondelivery were established. Farms were required to pay 1 percent of the value of the food product to procurement organizations for late delivery, a penalty that increased to 2 percent of the value if the delivery was more than ten days late. Procurement organizations were obligated to accept food products according to existing contracts. Failure to accept food would result in a penalty of 3 percent of the value of the product, payable to the farm.[9]

Above-plan sales were planned as well, and the July 1970 plenum adopted regulations that no less than 35 percent of above-plan grain and no less than 8-10 percent of above-plan production of animal husbandry products would be sold to the state.[10] In order to encourage above-plan sales, the bonus system for above-plan production was reintroduced.

An Inside View of How the Procurement System Worked

I would be remiss if the discussion of the procurement system ended without acknowledging that in reality the procurement system did not work nearly as smoothly as mass publications indicated. Several interesting aspects of the procurement system were discovered when researching archival documents in Kostroma oblast that permit a view of how the system really worked.

In the archives, there were numerous letters from farm chairmen and subsidiary farms to the *oblispolkom* (oblast executive committee, a nonparty governing body) complaining about the refusal of procurement agents (usually food processors) to accept their produce (in some cases it concerned above-plan produce).[11] In one case a state farm director sent a telegram to the deputy chairman of the *oblispolkom*, stating that "the Kostromskoi meat factory categorically refused to accept [our] poultry. I ask you to take urgent measures toward the meat factory."[12] Why did such instances occur? First, several documents suggested that the quality of produce was often low. In fact, a common correspondence was from collective farm chairmen asking for relaxation of food quality standards for a certain quantity of produce (mainly milk products).[13] I found no records in the archival documents in which such requests were not granted. Following approval of delivery of "substandard" products, further instructions were then issued indicating exactly how many liters of milk would be delivered to which organizations. Interestingly, sub-standard milk invariably was delivered to children's schools.[14]

Another factor in the refusal to accept raw food products was an inability of procurement organizations to pay for above-plan produce, suggesting that timely receipt of credits or other financial resources was a problem.[15] Last, there was evidence of personal conflicts between farm chairmen and heads of procurement agents to the extent that the latter would simply refuse to accept the farm's production. Letters were found from both collective and state farm chairmen who complained about the "rudeness" of certain procurement bosses.[16] I found no evidence in the archival record that procurement organizations were fined for non-acceptance of food products.

Archival documents also shed light on how the procurement system operated in areas where the plan was chronically underfulfilled. One tactic of farm chairmen was to request that the farm's output quota be lowered for a variety of reasons. Perhaps the year before the farm had an unusually good year and could not possibly fulfill the higher standard in the present year. Perhaps there was bad weather which affected the harvest. A favorite complaint was to assert that the farm's infrastructure, mechanization, and quantity of skilled personnel simply did not allow the farm to meet the plan. How did the system treat chronic underachievers? Two examples in separate raions in Kostroma oblast illustrate how weak farms in poor regions fared.

The first example is from Makar'yevskii raion, located in the south-center part of Kostroma oblast. It shares a similar climate with Kostromskoi and Nerekhtskii raions, which are the most favorably located in the oblast. In short, agricultural shortcomings were not due solely to weather; Markar'yevskii was relatively well situated in the oblast. A report issued by the Executive Committee of the Oblast Council of People's Deputies in August 1980 stated that "the raion *ispolkom* [executive committee] in Makar'yevskii is unsatisfactorily fulfilling the decision of the oblast *ispolkom* from February 27, 1978 'On Increasing Procurement Discipline in the Oblast.' Many collective and state farms in the raion are systematically not fulfilling state purchase plans for agricultural products."[17] In particular, it was noted that twelve of the fifteen farms in the raion did not fulfill their plan for flax in 1979, and plans for food products had gone underfulfilled as well during the first four years of the five-year plan. Among the problems that were cited were "the possibilities for increasing purchases of animal husbandry products are poorly utilized." Specifically, the document cited the fact that food products were being distributed for intrafarm consumption instead of being sold to the state. One collective farm, "Rodina," underfulfilled its plan for cattle by 6.6 tons but distributed among its workers 14.3 tons; a similar situation occurred in the collective farm "Na strazhe," which underfulfilled its plan for meat but distributed 16.2 tons for internal farm purposes. In other cases farms were not selling sufficient quantities of high-quality milk; three farms were named whose milk sales comprised between 2 to 7 percent of "first quality" milk.

The blame for this situation was placed upon the chairman of the raion *ispolkom*, A. A. Okhlopkov. At the direction of the chairman of the oblast *ispolkom*, K. V. Dontsov, several agricultural leaders of the raion, including Okhlopkov, met to discuss the situation. The record from that meeting was extraordinary. One participant, Mr. Balanshin, when speaking about the milk deficit, stated that there was an increasing tendency to feed young calves milk. He then revealed that on one farm, according to farm accounts, one calf had consumed 624 kilograms of milk. He asked, "How can one calf drink so much milk?" Mr. Kuznetsov then remarked that this tendency—decreases in milk production and purchases by the state—are the fault of Mr. Okhlopkov. "He should have personally investigated where the 624 kilograms of milk went." Mr. Riabtsov, the head of the procurement inspectorate in the raion, defended food processors in the raion. "Existing factories are in bad condition. They were built in 1960 with poor quality bricks." He also claimed there "are no refrigerators in the raion." Mr. Balanshin then retorted that Mr. Raskin, the head of a milk-processing factory, "should go to Makar'yev to see his poor factories, which he had not seen in two years." At the same time, Mr. Riabtsov accepted blame for not fining farms: "We are guilty for not fining farms that systematically underfulfilled their plan for the delivery of milk." Mr. Peretiagin revealed that the same situation existed for cattle sales: "[Farms] have until August 10th to fulfill their plan for deliveries of cattle. After that we will fine them."[18]

The criticism/self-criticism meeting adjourned after the participants "pointed out the shortcomings" of the work by comrades Okhlopkov, Raskin, and Peretiagin. In a follow-up report to the oblast *ispolkom* in early 1981 (required by the oblast *ispolkom* decision of August 8, 1980), Okhlopkov reported: (1) that more milk was being purchased from "the population," (private plot operators), and that 42 points existed where the population could sell their milk; (2) that "a raion socialist competition" was being held for collective and state farms and rural soviets in order to increase the level of procurement discipline; and (3) that for "violations of state discipline and poor work in the organization of purchases" one collective farm chairman, one director of a state farm, and two chairmen of rural soviet *ispolkoms* were "punished," and one director of a flax factory was fired.[19] He promised that "the forces of the *ispolkom* of the raion Soviet, rural soviets, farm leaders and agricultural specialists will be directed at increasing procurement discipline in the raion and eliminating the existing large shortcomings." A little over a year later, in March 1982, he submitted his final report in which he claimed previous decisions had been fulfilled, and he cited increased state purchases (although only the targets for hay, flour, and cattle and pig skin were met in 1981), and he listed the decisions that had been adopted by the raion bureau of the CPSU and the raion *ispolkom* to remedy the problems that had been identified.[20]

A second example comes from Mezhevskii raion, which is located in the far northeast of the oblast in a region that has a short growing season and poor soil. For this reason animal husbandry products comprised the bulk of farm activities. A report from the oblast *ispolkom* in June 1981 cited the chairman of the raion *ispolkom* and the head of the agricultural administration for "extremely unsatisfactory work in organizing the production and purchase of animal husbandry products. . . .Year after year production and purchases of animal husbandry products decline. . . .The majority of farms do not fulfill their plan for sales of milk and almost a half do not meet their plan for sales of cattle. . . .the raion *ispolkom* and raion agricultural management have dealt with the basic task of animal husbandry—the creation of a firm feed base—in an exceptionally poor way, have permitted serious shortcomings in production, and have not undertaken the necessary work to improve the situation."[21] The chairman of the raion *ispolkom* was required to submit two reports to the oblast *ispolkom* indicating the steps that had been taken to address the shortcomings indicated in the oblast report. The first report was submitted after half-year results were known in July 1981 (one month after the oblast report was written) and the second in January 1982.

What do these examples reveal about the way the procurement system operated? There are a number of interesting insights to note. It appears that, in these cases at least, the shortcomings in farm production and sales to the state had been going on for some time, thus suggesting that chronic underachievers were singled out for reprimand.[22] Attention from oblast officials was rather short lived, often extending no more than six months, although in the case of Makar'yevskii raion a follow-up report was submitted almost eighteen months after oblast officials' initial report. Once oblast officials focused on a raion, their demands were specific. That is, in their decisions oblast officials would specify output and sales level that the raion was to meet. But the whole process seemed formalistic. The required documents were submitted to oblast officials, but in the cases I read the targets indicated in the oblast decision were not met, although raions did achieve production and sales increases. Once the required report was filed, attention from oblast officials ended, even in cases where targets had not been met.

The historical record raises a series of questions: What really motivated these production and procurement discipline campaigns? Was the purpose to fulfill the plan or simply to increase production? Were production and procurement discipline campaigns, or did they become "standard operating procedure"? Were they triggered automatically by the quantitative monitoring of underfulfillment of norms, much like a late payment notice if a person forgets to pay a bill? Or were they something extraordinary, requiring special attention and procedures to cope with?

There are no simple answers. On the one hand, even though the volume and detail of party interventions in agriculture often exceeded party supervision in industry,[23] the system seemed overly formalistic. Oblast officials were doing their job by identifying shortcomings and requiring corrective action in raions. Raion officials were doing their job by complying with *oblispolkom* instructions (democratic centralism), by overseeing corrections, and by reporting on their outcome. But the impression is inescapable that generating decisions (*reshenii*) and responses to them seemed to be an end in itself. There was no follow-up even in cases where directives went unfulfilled. Furthermore, not much happened to weak farms (or their directors) for underfulfilled norms. As indicated above, only two farm managers were "punished" (the nature of the punishment was not defined), but mostly farm managers did not appear to suffer personally from plan underfulfillment, a fact that supports Peter Rutland's conclusion about managers and party officials in industry.[24]

On the other hand, discipline campaigns could not have been triggered automatically, or else chronic underfulfillment of norms could not go undetected. Raion officials were responsible to oblast officials, but it would appear that individual farms could get away with chronic underfulfillment as long as other farms' output in the raion covered the shortfall. Was nonpunishment of chronic underfulfillment a systemic function *not* to penalize weak farms? Or was it a function of party weakness in the countryside?

It may be too strong to argue that raion leaders deliberately ignored underfulfillment of farms' norms because individual farms were economically weak, or to suggest that weak farms were allowed to avoid plan fulfillment. Indeed, efforts were made to improve economic conditions so that weak farms could increase their production. But it would also be wrong to argue that by the late 1970s-early 1980s farm underfulfillment occurred because the party was still weak in the countryside, that is, as some kind of resistance to party rule.

By the 1980s, party strength had increased considerably, measured by the following: (1) about one-third of the party was employed in the countryside in the 1980s; (2) there was approximately one party organization per farm; (3) nearly all state and collective farm chairmen were party members; and (4) the educational level of state and collective farm chairmen had improved significantly. In Kostroma oblast in 1980, only 12.5 percent of collective farm chairmen did not have a higher or specialist education, while less than 10 percent (9.6 percent) of state farm directors did not have a higher or specialist education. The most common background for collective farm chairmen was agronomist (39 percent) followed by engineer (24 percent). Among state farm directors, 29 percent were agronomists and another 29 percent engineers.[25] Thus, farm managers were well-trained and skilled, suggesting that farm underfulfillment was not due to a lack of rural party strength or to the educational level of farm management, but perhaps to natural conditions, unrealistic plans for poor agricultural areas, poor quality or insufficient inputs, inadequate infrastructure, labor, or mechanization, or some combination thereof.

The Soviet Procurement Price System

A central aspect of the state procurement system was the use of procurement, or purchase, prices. In general, procurement prices were established by the government for specific products and were differentiated by geographic region. When Josef Stalin was in power, procurement prices were set below production costs, and thus it became uneconomical to produce food. Procurement prices became a large tax on the countryside. For this reason, one of the earliest acts of the post-Stalin regime was to increase agricultural procurement prices, which prior to their increase in September 1953 were still at their 1929 level.[26]

During the early Khrushchev period, procurement prices were increased and delivery quotas were reduced. In addition, above-quota prices were revived. With this set of multiple prices, there were four main types of procurements. The first type was compulsory deliveries, for which purchase prices were the lowest. The second type was above-quota prices which were much higher, an arrangement that benefited stronger collective farms. The third type of procurement price was used for industrial crops, such as cotton and sugar beets. These procurements were characterized by large premiums above the basic price for deliveries in excess of quotas. Last were payments in-kind to machine tractor stations for services provided to collective farms, which increased over time until the dissolution of Machine Tractor Stations in 1958. From this system of internal trade, state and collective farms received the overwhelming majority of their income, industrial workers were provided cheap food through their factory dining hall or factory store, and the growing urban population was ensured a reliable source of inexpensive food.[27] After the 1958 reform, above-quota prices were abolished and single regional commodity prices were used, as noted above.

Brezhnev reversed the 1958 Khrushchev reform of the procurement price system. By the mid-1970s the Ministry of Procurement was once again responsible for food procurements and storage. Above-quota prices were reintroduced, meaning that a two-tiered system of prices existed; and the reintroduction of zonal prices abolished uniform commodity prices by region. Zonal pricing meant that low-cost areas received lower prices with higher profitability, while high-cost areas received higher prices but had lower profitability.[28] Thus, during much of the post-Stalin period procurement prices were established for specific products and were differentiated by geographic region, with zonal prices reflecting different production costs and implicit land rents.[29]

After 1965, a two-tiered premium system of prices was used whereby one procurement price was paid to the farm for quota deliveries, and a 50 percent higher price was paid for above-plan deliveries for wheat, rice, cattle, poultry, milk, wool, and eggs.[30] Perhaps as a result of the bonus system, state purchases of animal husbandry products increased each of the first 10 years of Brezhnev's rule with the exception of 1969 (meat and milk purchases declined); and for grain, potatoes, and vegetables the average level of state purchases during the

Eighth Five-Year Plan (1966-1970) and Ninth Five-Year Plan (1971-1975) increased as well. At the July 1978 plenum special price supplements of 50 percent were added to the purchase prices for above-quota produce sold to the state in order to stimulate sales of basic agricultural products.[31] In general, however, state procurements accounted for a larger and larger share of agricultural output.

Reforms in the Food Procurement System under Gorbachev

A variety of economic factors suggested that when Mikhail Gorbachev assumed the position of general secretary in March 1985 he might be a reformist leader who would prioritize the agrarian sector. Buttressing this belief was the fact that Gorbachev was the best educated Soviet leader since Lenin, one who had given clear indications that he was reform minded and not satisfied with the state of agriculture long before coming to power.[32] Just a few months before coming to power, for example, as second party secretary under Konstantin Chernenko, Gorbachev argued in a speech in December 1984 before party ideological workers that it was necessary to reform the economy by searching for "new ideas," adopting "new views" and "refusing old approaches and methods."[33]

Second, Gorbachev was acutely aware of the problems and needs of the state agricultural sector due to the fact that he was Communist Party secretary in charge of agriculture from 1978 to 1985. A final reason for the belief that Gorbachev would pursue agrarian reform was that at that time the political climate in the Soviet Union was more conducive to policy innovation than at any time in the recent past. Even though prior to becoming general secretary Gorbachev had displayed "relatively conformist" behaviors, he also brought a "zeal for change" to the Secretariat and his party duties.[34]

In the economy as a whole, it is well known that as part of perestroika Gorbachev advocated a new approach to "social justice" in order to overcome excessive egalitarianism within the economy as a whole.[35] In early 1986 Gorbachev signaled his sentiment when he devoted a section of his speech before the 27th Party Congress to social justice, commenting that "payment of unearned money and unmerited bonuses, setting 'guaranteed' pay rates unrelated to the work contributed by the worker, are impermissible. On this theme it should be said quite emphatically: when the work of a good worker and a careless worker are paid the same, this is a gross violation of our principles."[36] Gorbachev continued to pound away at this theme over the years by arguing that differences between good and poor workers should be encouraged, that earned wealth by individuals in general was not harmful, that economic activity outside the social sphere benefited society, and that individuals should be able to earn more money and to spend it as they please.

Within the agricultural sector Gorbachev hoped this new approach would promote the emergence of strong farms which in turn would affect food production in a positive way. Because the goal of his reforms was to instill higher efficiency and production at lower cost, Gorbachev moved on a series of fronts concerning planning and procurement.

To begin, Gorbachev's early efforts were designed to make the existing system work better, much as his *uskorenie* campaign was intended to do in the economy at large. One of his first acts was to centralize oversight over the entire agroindustrial complex by merging five ministries into one "superministry" called *Gosagroprom* that had local committees and a national organization. This reorganization (the tenth in postwar Soviet history) of agriculture was important because it transferred responsibility for state procurements to *Gosagroprom*, which existed until being disbanded in April 1989. The dissolution of *Gosagroprom* meant that the State Commission on Food and Procurements within the USSR Council of Ministers became responsible for food procurements. The purpose was to centralize responsibility in the hope that efficiency and oversight would improve.

Planning reforms were introduced on an experimental basis in several Russian oblasts and krais during 1986-1987, testing many of the elements contained within the March 1986 decree. Thus, in Stavropol' krai, farm autonomy was expanded, and farms were transferred to a self-financing basis. In Kuybyshev oblast, production, procurements, processing, and sales of products were put under a single unified management. As a result, the oblast's agricultural management staff was reduced to forty-nine persons (from sixty-three), its wage fund decreased, and the nature of its functions changed to "economic methods of management."[37]

What the use of "economic methods of management" meant in practice was the use of norms to plan the work of agricultural enterprises. Farm production was planned according to "resource-norms" which took into account the quality of land and available labor resources. The goal was to standardize production in regions with similar land and climate and to end the Brezhnev system where literally every farm had its own output plan and purchase prices, a system that had been unfair to stronger, more productive farms. Resource norms were also used for expenditures of labor, and in Stavropol' krai piece rate payments (*akkordnaia oplata*) were tied to final production output.

Experiments were also carried out in other branches of the agroindustrial complex to improve efficiency and productivity. For example, in Kursk oblast, a "financial-accounting center" was established to coordinate payments and accounts between agricultural enterprises and organizations. Together with *Gosbank* this financial center planned the financial and credit activities of enterprises within the agroindustrial complex and in doing so "was an effective instrument of influence on the financial status of enterprises and organizations." This was accomplished by unifying the credit system so that the financial center was the single source of credit to farms. In turn, by using a unified credit system, oversight of farm repayment was strengthened and nonrepayment by farms of their debt was reduced.[38]

Another early reform in the agricultural sector was Gorbachev's liberalization of the conditions under which farms could market their produce. In March 1986, the Central Committee of the Communist Party defined state policy in food procurements, farm wages, labor organization, and farm finances.[39] Through these policies, Gorbachev attempted to introduce flexibility into the state procurement system and allow farms more freedom in marketing after meeting their state quota. Gorbachev announced that after farms met their planned quotas they would be allowed to sell up to 30 percent of their surplus on the open market. The other 70 percent of the surplus had to be sold to the state, at prices that were higher than the base procurement price, but lower than market prices. In reality, however, it turned out that quotas were simply raised so as to preclude any "surplus."

A further area of reform by Gorbachev was procurement prices. During 1986-1989 procurement prices rose almost 6 percent a year, while retail food prices rose by less than 1.5 percent a year. In 1989, the USSR government relinquished control over retail and wholesale prices of potatoes and vegetables, and stopped paying subsidies for them.[40] In addition, the number of price zones was reduced (procurement prices were differentiated according to zone). For meat, the number of zones was reduced from 49 to 5, and for milk from 98 to 4 or 5 (depending on quality). Uniform national prices were established for most grain and oilseeds.

Gorbachev also introduced both inducements and higher procurement prices in order to attract higher production and deliveries. For example, as an inducement, in August 1989 a two-year experiment was announced in which high quality grain sold to the state, above the average levels procured during the Eleventh Five-Year Plan, would be paid for with hard currency and credited to the farm's account.[41] Other inducements included allowing farms to sell up to 30 percent of their state-ordered produce at contract instead of obligatory prices; and up to 50 percent of the grain sold over and above state orders would be paid for in hard currency. In order to provide farms with further incentives to sell their produce, in July 1991 the USSR Council of Ministers adopted a resolution that recommended to republican governments that they increase the availability of automobiles, tractors, and other machinery, as well as consumer goods for sale.[42]

In addition, there were procurement price increases. In May 1990 all grain purchase prices were increased an average of 50 percent. In August 1990, purchase prices were raised for sunflower seed, sugar beets, cotton, tea, tobacco, poultry, livestock, and milk, to become effective January 1, 1991.[43]

Regarding procurement policy, on the one hand it appeared that Gorbachev was trying to make the system more contractual and less obligatory. As described by one source, for food goods covered by state orders the procurement system worked thusly. No later than March 15 buyers (processors) were to comprise a list of suppliers (farms) with which they are able "to conclude contracts" for the delivery of food goods. Buyers were to choose from a list provided by planning bodies. Within a ten-day period, buyers reported back to planning agencies with a specific list of suppliers with whom they would like to trade. "Negotiations" stipulated a detailed list of the assortment, quality, and quantity of goods, the date of delivery, and the price—these elements were obligatory or the agreement was considered invalid. The agreement could be in force for up to five years, one year, or some other term that was mutually agreeable. The buyer's order could include a quantity that exceeded the state order. The contract was considered accepted and finalized if within a twenty-day period the supplier did not report objections to the terms or conditions. If the contract was finalized, it was signed by both sides with each side retaining a copy. Buyers retained the right to refuse delivery and collect for losses if quality levels did not correspond to those stipulated in the contract. The buyer could also be released from the contract, in which case planning bodies would direct the buyer to a different supplier.[44]

On the other hand, the compulsory nature of the procurement system remained clear. The state order (*goszakaz*), on which the procurement system was based, was retained, despite Gorbachev's efforts to reform it. One source characterized state orders as follows:

> The state order has the goal of satisfying priority needs of society. It defines the type and quantity of products that should be sold to the state. The fulfillment of the state order in the plan is obligatory. The state order and control figures are given to raion agroindustrial enterprises and agroprocessing plants, which on that basis conclude agreements for the delivery of products to state and collective farm procurement organizations and other agricultural enterprises.[45]

However, to be fair, it should be noted that the procurement system under Gorbachev did contain some flexibility. The same source noted that, "with the permission of the USSR *Gosagroprom*, the agroindustrial committees within the Council of Ministers of union republics could introduce correctives that were linked to changes in demand by the population and needs by trade organizations."[46]

As central authority declined, the food procurement system under Gorbachev became less effective each year, coinciding with broader economic reforms.[47] In 1987, for example, the state purchased 38 percent of the gross grain harvest. By 1991, the last year of the Soviet procurement system, the state was able to purchase only 24 percent of the gross grain harvest.

Within the Russian Republic, the government adopted a two-pronged strategy to compensate for falling procurement levels.[48] As noted above, "carrots" were offered to farms in the form of higher purchase prices. "Harvest '90" and "Harvest '91" campaigns offered to transfer hard currency to farm accounts for above-quota sales and to allow farms to purchase scarce farm machinery with these monies. In reality, these and other incentives failed, largely because the state often did not pay for the grain that was "sold" to it. For example, of the 1.2 million tons of grain that were to be purchased with hard currency in 1991, only about one-half of it had actually been paid for by March 1992.[49] Despite repeated promises in 1992 by the Yeltsin administration to pay for grain that had been delivered during the 1989-1991 experiment, by early 1994 the state still owed farms more than 600 million rubles.

These "carrots" were only partially successful, and therefore carrots were combined with sanctions for noncompliance, and thus the "stick" was also used as part of the procurement system. For example, a RSFSR Supreme Soviet resolution fined farms that did not fulfill their quota. In principle, farms could be fined up to 10,000 rubles, but in reality farms had little to fear once party *raikoms* were abolished following the August 1991 coup. Farm managers who "dis-

rupted" the harvest (did not fulfill their quota) would be held personally responsible.[50] After the August coup, however, farms themselves were responsible for
plan fulfillment and it was unlikely that farm managers would fine themselves.
As a result, state procurements of many foodstuffs, in particular grain, declined
significantly as shown in table 2.1.

Table 2.1. Grain Production and State Procurements, USSR, 1985-1991

	Gross Harvest, (million tons)	State Purchases, (million tons)	% of Harvest Purchased by State
1985	191.7	73.5	38
1986	194.0	78.8	40
1987	193.8	73.3	38
1988	180.2	61.4	34
1989	196.7	58.9	30
1990	218.0	68.0	31
1991	160.0	39.0	24

Source: Stephen K. Wegren, "Two Steps Forward, One Step Back: The Politics of
an Emerging New Rural Social Policy in Russia," *The Soviet and Post-Soviet
Review*,19, nos. 1-3 (1992): 11.

As "carrots" were unsuccessful and "sticks" increasingly ineffective, the
RSFSR government adopted a food tax (*prodnalog*) for 1991 that was to be fulfilled in addition to the state order. The purpose was to assure adequate food
reserves for the central fund. The size of the state order averaged around 30 percent of production, and the food tax added another 40 percent.[51] The tax was
assessed to state and collective farms and other agricultural enterprises. Newly
created private peasant farms were exempt from this food tax. In order to enforce this tax, penalties for nonpayment to the central fund consisted of with-
holding of fuel, machinery, and other needed inputs.

As government and party authority and power to enforce orders declined,
however, neither state orders nor the food tax was successful in fulfilling state
reserve targets. By the fall of 1991 newspapers carried threats of starvation.
Food rationing was introduced in several cities for the first time since World
War II during the winter of 1991.[52] The Soviet procurement system had broken
down.

Channels of Food Trade in the USSR

In the Soviet Union there were three main channels of food trade. The dominant
channel was state-managed trade through state-owned retail stores, supplied by
state orders and the state procurement system. This system was supplied by food
from state and collective farms, and accounted for about 70 percent of food trade
in the 1980s. The state retail outlets that belonged to this system were located
primarily in urban areas.

The second main channel of food trade consisted of consumer cooperatives which operated primarily in rural areas and accounted for about one-quarter of food trade in the 1980s. Retail stores within the consumer cooperative system (*Tsentrosoiuz*) were state managed and owned, and as such were supplied by the state procurement system.

Table 2.2. Volumes of State Procurements for Selected Food Products, 1970-1987 (in million tons unless otherwise noted)

	Cattle/ Poultry (live weight)	Milk/Milk Products	Eggs (billion pieces)
Purchases from State and Collective Farms			
1970	11.5	44.2	16.1
1980	15.0	54.0	41.7
1985	17.8	67.4	49.7
1986	19.4	71.4	52.8
1987	21.3	74.1	54.7
Purchases from the Population			
1970	1.3	1.5	2.0
1980	.9	3.2	1.4
1985	.6	.7	1.0
1986	.6	.4	.8
1987	.5	.2	.8

Source: *Sel'skoe khoziaistvo SSSR: statisticheskii sbornik* (Moscow: Finansy i statistika, 1988), 337.

The third channel of trade was a small but important source of food and food trade—so-called collective farm markets. The primary contributor to collective farm markets' produce was that grown by individuals on their "private plots," dacha plots, or in some collective garden setting. State and collective farms, once they fulfilled their plans, could sell surplus food to food cooperatives or through collective farm markets. However, the main source of food for collective farm market trade was from households' private plots.

Food grown on private plots was not subject to state procurements or planning, although citizens could and did sign contracts with processors and procurement agents to sell their output directly to them. However, the percentages of output sold to processors was low. In 1987, for example, of produce grown by households or individuals, only 10 percent of meat, 1 percent of milk, and 4 percent of eggs were purchased by the state.[53] The vast majority of production was either consumed by the household or sold at collective farm markets. Because privately grown food was not explicitly regulated by the state, this type of food trade was considered to be nonstate trade. In the 1980s, about 5 percent of food flowed through collective farm markets, which were located in large urban areas as well as in nearly every medium and small town. Table 2.2 illustrates trends in state procurements by category of farm. Food from state and collective farms was channeled into state wholesale and retail networks, while food produced by households was channeled through farmers' markets.

Private plots were small-scale land holdings (usually about 200 square meters), and too small to grow commercial crops in large quantities.[54] In aggregate, for a variety of reasons private plots were large contributors to the nation's total food supply for selected products. One reason had to do with the assistance that they received from nearby large farms. Another reason had to do with the amount of time spent tending the plots. For example, males in the RSFSR spent an average of 4 hours per weekend, and about 6.5 hours during the week, tending the household plot. Females spent almost 3 hours on the weekend and almost 5.5 hours during the week working on the family plot.[55]

However, the volume of trade turnover through collective farm markets was small compared to state channels of trade.[56] Overall, a long-term decline was evident in the volume of produce sold on the urban collective farm market, dating from the 1960s to the late 1980s.[57] Surveys showed that a main motivation for operating a private plot was to provide food for the household.[58] For these and other reasons, in 1988 collective farm market trade accounted for just 2.5 percent of food sales in the USSR (calculated in 1988 prices). Moreover, an index of the physical volume of food sales at collective farm markets in the RSFSR showed that by 1988 the index had declined to 88 percent of the 1980 level, with meat at 61 percent its 1980 level, milk and milk products at 71 percent its 1980 level, vegetables and eggs at 89 percent their 1980 level, and potatoes at 73 percent their 1980 level. Only grain, fruits, and berries were equal to or exceeded their 1980 level.[59] With the decline in sales at collective farm markets, the percentage of household income derived from private plot sales also decreased, from nearly one-half of a collective farmer's income in 1940 to less than one-quarter by 1986.[60] Likewise, during this same time period, households that operated private plots possessed fewer head of livestock, although there was considerable variance by region and size of family.[61] Volumes of produce sold through collective farm markets for selected products are shown in table 2.3.

In general, therefore, from the 1960s until the late 1980s, private plots and their relative contribution to the nation's food supply, and their position in domestic food trade, declined. In 1990, however, a revival in private plot production became evident. The aforementioned trends began to reverse and more rural households became engaged in small-scale plot operations. As a result, output increased, and in 1991 there were more than 38 million private plots encompassing 8.2 million hectares of land. Private plots contributed more than 30 percent of the nation's meat, 28 percent of its milk, and 27 percent of its eggs, as well as nearly two-thirds of its potatoes and one-third of its vegetables.[62] During 1990-1991, however, even as household output began to increase, this production was either consumed or sold at collective farm markets, as official statistics do not indicate an increase in state procurements from the population.

Table 2.3. Volumes of Food Produce Sold at Collective Farm Markets, 1970-1988

	1970	1980	1985	1986	1987	1988	1988 sales as % of 1988 production
Grains (thous. tons)	154.7	86.8	72.8	69.7	65.1	69.2	.04
Potatoes (thous. tons)	1,199.3	974.0	959.2	900.7	814.6	777.2	1.24
Vegetables (thous. tons)	1,067.7	1,157.9	1,239.9	1,208.3	1,163.8	1,187.8	4.06
Meat and Poultry (thous. tons)	199.1	223.0	205.5	200.5	185.0	179.7	.91
Milk (million liters)	35.4	11.0	9.3	7.7	6.7	6.4	NA
Butter (thous. tons)	1.5	.8	.8	.7	.6	.6	.03
Eggs (million)	393.7	202.9	195.6	206.1	178.1	186.6	.22

NA=data not available.
Sources: *Torgovlia SSSR* (Moscow: Finansy i statistika, 1989), 317; *Narodnoe khoziaistvo SSSR v 1989: statisticheskii ezhegodnik* (Moscow: Goskomstat, 1990), 436, 442, 443, 467, 468; *Sel'skoe khoziaistvo: statisticheskii sbornik* (Moscow: Goskomstat, 1991), 101; and author's calculations.

Food Consumers: Retail Price Policy

So far the analysis has concentrated on policy, but without politics. It should be acknowledged that the changes in the procurement system, as well as other changes that were being introduced in agriculture such as land leasing, the principle of *khozrashchet* (self-financing) for farms, and reform of collective and state farms, were subjects of intensive debate in the highest circles of the political leadership. There certainly was resistance to change, as reflected by Yegor Ligachev, who served as second secretary of the CPSU under Gorbachev and was in charge of ideology and, during 1988-1990, of agriculture.

> In their aggregate, the false democrats, the anti-Communists. . .want to disorganize the national economy, bring it to the brink of collapse, and then blame the socialist system for this disorder. The reallotment of land and the ruin of collective and state farms were only part of this general strategy. It was also evident in the evolution of the creators of the "500-Day" Program. . . .What in the "500-Day" Program attracted President Gorbachev, who once proclaimed his adherence to it, remains a mystery.[63]

Perhaps no issue was more contentious than retail food price policy. For decades, a dominant feature of Soviet food policy was the subsidization of retail food prices which protected consumers from true market prices. Authorities such as D. Gale Johnson noted that retail price policy was probably the single most distorting element in Soviet agriculture. Incorrect retail prices undermined in fundamental ways the functions that prices should fulfill, namely, sending signals to consumers and producers, and acting as a rationing mechanism. Below-market clearing prices led directly to excess demand and long lines for food products.

Why were prices maintained at levels that were uneconomical? It should be understood that Soviet agricultural policy was, for its last twenty-five to thirty years, really an urban policy.[64] The political strategy underlying the regime's agricultural policy was twofold: first, to provide inexpensive food supplies to the urban population; and second, the regime attempted to meet increased expectations as to variety, selection, and quality of food products supplied to the urban population. Historically, the Soviet regime performed rather well on its first objective, but much less so on the second.

Thus, the Bolsheviks always were a party of urban interests, and as Soviet society urbanized, the primary beneficiary of Soviet retail price policy was the urban consumer.[65] Urban consumers were protected from true market prices in two of the three main food trade channels: state food stores and consumer cooperatives (in the latter retail prices were negotiated and controlled administratively). Only in collective farm markets were retail prices freely set, reflecting quality, seasonal availability, and demand. For this reason, collective farm market prices were higher than in state retail stores, and as the command economy withered, dependence on the market for food increased, a fact that helped food prices on the *kolkhoz* market to increase even more rapidly.[66]

While it is well known that Soviet agriculture was heavily subsidized, it is often forgotten that the single largest category of "agricultural" subsidies went to food consumers. Overall, in 1985, retail food subsidies accounted for 14.5 percent of state expenditures, rising to 20 percent in 1990. Meat, milk, and bread products were the most heavily subsidized commodities.[67]

Control over retail prices was an inherent part of the overall regulation of the Soviet food system. Retail prices in state stores were fixed by the state. Retail prices were differentiated across three broad geographic zones in the former USSR. State-determined retail prices in state food stores did not reflect quality differences, were changed only marginally during different seasons of the year, and were basically stable for several decades starting in the 1960s. The decision to maintain stable retail food prices, of course, was entirely political and had nothing to do with economics. In fact, the political decision to not change retail food prices became increasingly uneconomical as production costs increased as a result of higher purchase prices, higher labor costs, higher production costs associated with increased mechanization, greater use of mineral fertilizers, and widespread reclamation and irrigation projects.

As food subsidies increased and accounted for more and more of the state's budget, price reform was the only option. But governmental unwillingness to break the "social contract" with urban dwellers, and fear of "social tension" prevented the implementation of previous price reform. For example, the head of a department in the State Commission on Economic Reform, Evgenii Iasin, when speaking about a centralized price increase, revealed in February 1991 that "it [the increase of state purchase and retail prices] was ready for implementation three years ago, but only insufficient persistence (*uporstvo*) on the part of the government prevented it from being carried out."[68]

Concern over social tension and the lack of persistence were evident in May 1990, when Prime Minister Nikolai Ryzhkov announced that food prices would increase dramatically effective July 1, 1990, thus setting off panic buying. The Moscow city council reacted by passing a measure which required consumers to prove they were citizens of Moscow in order to shop in state food stores. There was such an outcry over the price proposals that in mid-June the government cancelled the increase in bread prices even though it had raised the purchase price of grains the month before. Gorbachev himself remarked that, "any noticeable increase in retail food prices was resolutely rejected. The problem was totally divorced from economic considerations, and regarded as a purely political issue."[69]

After the Soviet government retreated from its plan to increase retail food prices in May 1990, a big change in retail prices finally came in April 1991 when retail prices were increased for the first time in several decades.[70] Meat and meat products rose an average of 200 percent, milk and dairy products 130 percent, eggs and egg products 100 percent, and bread, flour, cereal, and pasta were to increase an average of 200 percent. Due to leadership fears over public backlash, much of the increase was compensated back to consumers through higher wages. This price increase, however, was administrative and not an overall price liberalization. Following the April 1991 retail price increase, retail food prices continued to be regulated by the state (even if greater volumes of food found their way to the black market).

The ultimate reversal of consumer protection from market-based retail food prices came on January 2, 1992. By freeing all but a handful of food prices (bread prices remained regulated until the fall of 1993), President Yeltsin exposed Russian consumers to the effects of a market. In one fell swoop, federally subsidized price protection was ended, although regions could continue to subsidize retail prices from their own budgets if they desired.

Soviet Foreign Trade

The second dimension of Soviet food policy to be examined concerns foreign trade and patterns of international food trade. Several main characteristics about Soviet foreign trade were distinctive from capitalist nations. First, foreign trade in the USSR—both imports and exports—were state regulated and organized under the jurisdiction of the Ministry of Foreign Trade, which had control over the day-to-day management of foreign trade. Within the Ministry of Foreign Trade there were foreign trade "corporations," or organizations, that traded in specific goods or commodities. These corporations were, of course, state owned and regulated. For example, in the food sector, *Prodintorg* was responsible for trade in dairy products, beef, cattle, and poultry. The corporation *Soiuzplodoimport* had responsibility for fruits, vegetables, and coffee. The corporation *Traktoroeksport* had responsibility for the export of tractors and agricultural machinery. The most notorious foreign trade organization was *Eksportkhleb*, which exported grain and grain products. Most foreign trade organizations were under the jurisdiction of the Ministry of Foreign Trade, although there were exceptions. Trade organizations were to plan the import and export of their types of goods, fulfill the plan, and ensure the quality of both exports and imports.[71] This type of system meant that a given state or collective farm had no control over what happened to its production—whether it was exported or not, and at what price—nor did it have control over the acquisition of foreign agricultural machinery and equipment.

A second main aspect was that foreign trade, as with all economic activity, was subject to planning. The key institution was the State Planning Committee, or Gosplan, which planned both the domestic economy and foreign trade.[72] In foreign trade, although the strategic directions of foreign trade were made by the Politburo, Gosplan would set targets for imports and exports for the foreign trade companies.

A third main aspect was that Soviet enterprises were not run on the profit principle, nor were foreign trade corporations. Although in theory at least foreign trade corporations were to be self-financing, in reality this often was not the case. For example, in the case of exports, a foreign trade corporation would place an order with an enterprise. The good would be "purchased" from the enterprise with rubles, and then sold abroad at world market prices. The proceeds from the sale would be deposited in state reserves and would not directly benefit either the enterprise that produced the good or the foreign trade corporation. In the case of imports, the foreign trade corporation would be authorized to buy a commodity abroad, paying for it using state hard currency reserves, and then would sell the commodity to domestic enterprises at prevailing ruble prices. Any resulting loss (the difference between the international and domestic price) was borne by the state, not the foreign trade corporation.[73]

A final characteristic of Soviet foreign trade was the relative isolation of the Soviet economy from the world economy. Foreign trade was not as significant an economic activity compared to the size of the economy as in Western nations, and this fact was a reflection of the general avoidance of international integration and world trade. In general, the USSR put greater emphasis on autarky, and later on intrabloc trade, than other developed industrial nations. For a variety of reasons, many of them having to do with ideology, the Soviets eschewed foreign trade contacts with the West. For example, in 1985, even including trade with other socialist nations, Soviet exports amounted to only $58.2 billion—3 percent of world trade—or just a little more than Belgium-Luxembourg.[74] Most of the Soviet Union's exports to the nonsocialist world in 1985 came from energy (73 percent), and the only substantial manufactured export from the USSR was weapons. In short, Soviet economic protectionism was very significant, freeing domestic producers not only from foreign competition but from domestic competition as well. Soviet enterprises were isolated from any information about the value or scarcity of their products on world markets. Without signals about their products, Soviet enterprises produced goods that were not competitive on the world market, and without competition, Soviet enterprises remained hopelessly inefficient. A summary of USSR foreign trade by regional grouping is presented in table 2.4.

Table 2.4. Soviet Foreign Trade, 1955-1989 (in billion rubles)

	Total Foreign Trade (imports and exports)	Net Trade to World	Net Trade to Socialist Nations	Net Trade to Western Nations	Net Trade to Developing Nations	Dollar per Ruble
1955	5.9	0.3	0.3	0.1	0	1.11
1960	10.1	-0.1	0.2	-0.1	-0.2	1.11
1965	14.7	0.1	0	-0.2	0.3	1.11
1970	22.1	1.0	0.6	-0.3	0.7	1.11
1975	50.7	-2.7	0.6	-3.6	0.3	1.39
1980	94.1	5.1	3.3	0.2	1.8	1.54
1985	142.1	3.3	2.0	-0.7	2.0	1.20
1986	130.9	5.7	3.8	-2.7	4.7	1.42
1987	128.8	7.4	2.1	0.3	5.0	1.58
1988	132.1	2.1	-0.5	-1.7	4.2	1.65
1989	140.9	-3.3	-2.3	-4.1	3.1	1.58

Source: OECD, *The Soviet Agro-Food System and Agricultural Trade: Prospects for Reform* (Paris: OECD, 1991), 183.

From the mid-1950s onward Soviet foreign trade increased significantly. In 1955, foreign trade totaled 5.9 billion rubles; in 1989, foreign trade reached 140.9 billion rubles. The fastest expansion in foreign trade occurred during the 1980s, rising by almost 47 billion rubles. The table shows that over time, trade with other socialist nations dominated, although trade with the West and developing nations also increased during the 1980s. Until the end of the Soviet period, however, socialist nations remained the primary trading partner of the Soviet Union. The table also shows that the USSR more frequently ran a trade surplus with socialist nations and developing nations, while having a trade deficit with Western nations.

The Soviet Foreign Trade System

Over time, the system of foreign trade that existed in the Soviet Union underwent a number of reorganizations, the details of which need not concern us here. As noted above, foreign trade was conducted through, and monopolized by, foreign trade organizations, many of which were originally created in the 1930s. The number of these organizations varied over time, with a proliferation after Stalin died. Foreign trade organizations had responsibility for the import or export of specific goods or resources.

The centralized nature of the Soviet Union's foreign trade system allowed the regime to pursue a relatively protectionist import policy that was applied regionally, thereby sheltering whole branches of industry and agriculture, including farms, from direct foreign competition, particularly from Western products. Toward this end, most trade took place within the socialist bloc, although foreign trade ties did increase with the West over time, in particular Germany in the latter 1970s. By the mid-1980s about two-thirds of all Soviet foreign trade was still conducted with other socialist countries.[75] Foreign trade, of course, had political as well as economic functions, and was used as an instrument to maintain integration among socialist nations.

Official Soviet goals were for a high degree of self-sufficiency, and the principle of comparative advantage was not usually pursued in foreign trade. Despite efforts to restrict economic ties with the outside world, the Soviets ended up with an economy that was dependent on global trade in several areas. Soviet imports accounted for 12 percent of the GNP in 1988,[76] and significant levels of imports occurred in select categories of food, consumer goods, light industry, machine building, and chemical industries.[77] Even in cases where Western technology was imported, it often was assimilated and diffused ineffectively. Negotiations were long and drawn out because foreign trade organizations were instructed to obtain the lowest price and best credit terms possible; this meant that equipment might be dated by the time the contract was fulfilled. Moreover, once purchased, installation of new equipment was slow, and foreign trade organizations often lacked contact with end users of the equipment being imported. Foreign trade organizations often did not take into account the requirements of the end users because their performance was not judged by those standards, and as a consequence sometimes imported equipment could not even be used.[78]

Change in Soviet Foreign Trade Policies and Strategies

Under Gorbachev, an important attempt was made to break the monopoly of the Foreign Trade Ministry by decentralizing foreign trade. In August 1986, the State Commission for Foreign Economic Relations was formed (and existed until the spring of 1991). The formation of this State Commission, followed by subsequent decrees and regulations on foreign trade in January 1987, led to a significant decentralization of decision-making rights over foreign trade. Under this reform, foreign trade organizations that imported and exported manufactured goods, which previously were almost exclusively under the supervision of the Ministry of Foreign Trade, were reduced in size. In addition, responsibility for manufactured goods was put under the jurisdiction of twenty domestic ministries. Furthermore, about seventy associations and enterprises were given the right to import and export directly with foreign firms.[79]

These twenty ministries and seventy associations were given the right to retain a portion of their foreign currency earnings in special accounts, which they could use without interference from Gosplan or the Ministry of Foreign Trade.[80] These proceeds could be used to purchase imports, although only for high-priority capital goods.[81] Included in the list of ministries given rights to engage directly in trade was *Gosagroprom* (an amalgam of five ministries created in November 1985 and existing until spring 1989), although it was indicated that the Ministry of Foreign Trade would continue to control trade in raw materials, food, and most machinery imports.[82] Furthermore, a September 1987 decree gave tax breaks on foreign venture profits, reduced some prior approvals for imports, authorized hard-currency loans for imports, and allowed local governments to retain earnings and allocate some of those earnings to import consumer goods.[83]

However, offsetting these reforms was another decree that required enterprises, associations, and ministries to obtain licenses for the export and import of many commodities. The ability to import was constrained by difficulties obtaining hard-currency allocations from central authorities. As a result, even after reform of the foreign trade system, the state retained control over about 80 percent of foreign trade through the regulation of direct imports and exports, registration and licensing, and allocation of hard currencies.[84] Trade of food commodities remained as controlled and centralized as in the past.

Despite the fact that reform of foreign trade did not go as far as reformers had hoped, the general trend under Gorbachev was to reduce the barriers of Soviet protectionism and to increase, albeit marginally, the integration of the Soviet economy into the world economic system. Toward this end, Gorbachev began discussions with the World Bank, the International Monetary Fund (IMF), and the G-7. As a consequence of opening to the West, by 1990 the Soviet Union had borrowed itself into a financial crisis, with an estimated $50 billion debt to Western banks.[85] A hard-currency crisis was precipitated when Western banks began to refuse to roll over short-term credits.

The resolution of the hard-currency crisis led to a closer relationship with Western institutions. In a quest for economic advice, during the fall 1990 annual meeting of the IMF/World Bank, a delegation from the Soviet Union attended as "special invitees." A separate delegation from the Russian Republic also attended. At its 1991 annual meeting, the leaders of the G-7 invited the Soviet Union to enter into "special association" with the IMF and World Bank in lieu of full membership, a move that was unprecedented. In October 1991, finance ministers of the G-7 and representatives of 8 Soviet republics, including Russia, signed a memorandum of understanding which provided for a moratorium on principal payments on Soviet debt owed to the G-7. The Memorandum could not be extended beyond March 31, 1992 without IMF approval of a "shadow" economic program, so-called to distinguish it from borrowing programs of IMF members.

The shadow program was intended to provide IMF technical assistance in the restructuring of its economic reforms.[86] The program was also seen as a way to expedite negotiation of a reform program that could be used to obtain IMF loans once IMF membership was approved. Approval of the shadow program was not a precondition to IMF membership, but was, as noted above, important for other financial reasons. A shadow program on economic reform and policy was officially adopted by the Russian government at the end of February 1992, and approval from the IMF came March 31, 1992, opening the way for aid and membership.[87]

As late as July 1991, at the London summit, the United States had expressed opposition to granting the Soviet Union full membership into the IMF and the World Bank, arguing that such a move was "premature." However, by January 1992, the United States changed its position and supported admission into those bodies. On April 27, 1992, the interim committee of the IMF approved membership for fourteen of the former Soviet Republics, including Russia. On June 1, 1992, Russia signed the documents granting full membership into the IMF, making it eligible for loans and technical assistance. Membership in Western international organizations would affect patterns of foreign trade during the remainder of the 1990s, particularly for food, as is shown in a separate section below.

Soviet External Food Trade, 1980-1991

Although food imports vastly exceeded food exports in the latter Soviet period, there is some misunderstanding about the role of imports. During the 1980s, food exports constituted less than 2 percent of all Soviet exports annually, while food imports were more than 20 percent of all Soviet imports in the first half of the decade and over 15 percent in the second half of the decade. During the latter Soviet period, grain trade (mostly wheat) was especially important, being the single largest volume of imported food.

The Soviet Union first imported grain in the 1960s, and it was a small importer as late as 1970. It was only in 1972 that the Soviet Union turned to the West to meet large-scale grain import needs, as part of a deliberate strategy to use imported grain to increase domestic meat production. Therefore, most grain imports were comprised of feed grains for cattle. That year witnessed the beginning of a two-decade relationship of large grain shipments. Beginning in 1976, the United States and USSR entered into long-term grain agreements which bound the Soviets to buy a certain minimum quantity of grain each year, thus assuring the Soviets access to the U.S market and stabilizing U.S. export sales.

Soviet grain imports in the 1980s were utilized to compensate for losses incurred in getting food from the field to the retail market, as well to compensate for drought and poor performance. The 1980s witnessed a significant increase in imported grain, and during this decade the Soviets became consistently large grain importers, averaging nearly 35 million tons of imported grain per year during 1980-1990.[88] Soviet grain imports averaged 38 million tons from 1980 through 1985, and 29 million tons from 1986 through 1991. The Soviet Union thus was an important market for U.S. agricultural exports. Despite the U.S. grain embargo imposed during 1980-1981 in protest of the Soviet invasion of Afghanistan, U.S. agricultural exports to the Soviet Union totaled $34.9 billion over the twenty-year period 1972-1992, and represented nearly three-quarters of U.S. agricultural exports.[89]

During the 1980s, other significant volumes of food imports consisted of Cuban sugar, which comprised more than 25 percent of sugar supplies; dried fruits and berries, which comprised more than 60 percent of supplies; and butter, which comprised between 10 and 15 percent of supplies.[90] In contrast, the Soviet Union was not a significant food exporter during the 1980s and through 1991. For example, food exports averaged $1.4 billion during 1990-1991, while imports averaged $14.5 billion.[91] The Soviet Union did export some wheat, but exports were a fraction of the imported grain levels. Primary commodity exports were fuels and electricity, as well as machinery.[92]

The last years of the Soviet Union, 1989-1991, witnessed the peak of agricultural production in the RSFSR and then the beginning of production declines that were to last nearly a decade. During 1989-1990, the Russian Republic reached its peak in meat production, average food consumption per capita, livestock herds, and grain production. Beginning in 1991, livestock herds were declining (cattle, cows, pigs), meat production began to fall, grain production decreased, and per capita consumption began to decline.[93] It is precisely during this time that food imports as a percentage of all imports began to increase. In 1980, for example, food imports were nearly one-quarter of all imports into the Soviet Union, declining to 21 percent in 1985 and 17 percent in 1986.[94] However, in the Russian Republic, food imports increased to 20 percent of all imports in 1990 and to 28 percent in 1991.[95]

Conclusion

When applying criteria about food marketing systems to the Soviet food marketing system, it is clear that this was not a competitive system. The chapter demonstrated that the Soviet food system lacked market competition, shared market knowledge, and efficient price formation. There was one dominant buyer, the state, which obliged food producers to sell to it at prices determined by the state. There was no balance of market power, as the state held all market knowledge and defined "market" conditions. Food prices not only were not formed efficiently, but sent the wrong signals to producers and consumers.

In particular, in domestic food policy this chapter demonstrated the following:

(1) The procurement system deprived producers (large farms) of the freedom to find the highest bidder for food. At the same time, the procurement system provided farms with secure outlets for the sale of their produce.

(2) The procurement system locked farms into certain production modalities.

(3) The procurement price system did not reward the efficient and sent the wrong signals to producers.

(4) Over time, state channels of trade accounted for a greater percentage of domestic food trade, until perestroika began dismantling the command economy.

(5) The retail price system was political in nature and was intended to protect urban consumers from the true cost of food. As such, retail prices sent the wrong signals to consumers and producers.

At the same time, we should note that the Soviet procurement system served two important functions. First, the system provided farms with a reliable buyer for their produce. Farms were not required to expend time or money marketing their produce. During the Stalinist years, procurement prices were below production costs, but by the end of the Brezhnev period, subsidies and price supplements provided an attractive "price floor." High-cost farms, which received higher unit prices after factoring in price supplements, benefited from an array of subsidies, as well as having a domestic buyer for produce that was otherwise not cost competitive. More efficient farms benefited as well: their efficiency would not lead to a decrease in unit prices, they benefited from a secure domestic buyer, and they had surpluses to sell to the state at above-quota prices or through the collective farm market. From a political perspective, this system was useful in "buying off" the rural sector.

The second function was to supply "consuming regions" with food from surplus regions. In particular, the far northern areas of the Soviet Union, as well as Moscow and Leningrad (now St. Petersburg) were primary recipients from this procurement-and-distribution system. More generally, Western economists have concluded that the Russian Federation was the principal generator of agricultural outflows (as well as other resources) to the other fourteen republics. The magnitude of resource dependence (deficits) varied by republic, with Ukraine the least dependent and the Baltic states the most resource dependent.[96] Thus, it would be fair to conclude that food was used as part of a strategy for creating and maintaining dependencies (and presumably loyalty) to Moscow.

In international food policy, during the Soviet period, any policy dilemmas surrounding food trade could be easily managed because urban and rural wages, farm purchase prices, and food retail prices were centrally administered. The Soviet Union attempted a policy of autarky. Food imports were limited to commodities of critical need, domestic producers were protected, and domestic retail prices were artificially manipulated. The planned nature of foreign trade and the use of trade to achieve political ends meant that neither producers nor consumers had much input or influence over food trade policies. In the 1980s, foreign trade increased, and Gorbachev attempted some moderate reforms of the foreign trade system in order to decentralize it. Gorbachev also laid the groundwork for increased integration into the world community of international organizations, and by the early 1990s Russia had either obtained membership or was given observer status. In food trade, Russia was primarily a food importer, not exporter, and the primary import was grain. The United States was a primary supplier of grain to the USSR, despite ups and downs in the political relationship.

Notes

1. Moshe Lewin, *The Making of the Soviet System* (New York: Pantheon Books, 1985), 144-45.
2. Lewin, *The Making of the Soviet System*, chap. 6; and see Zhores A. Medvedev, *Soviet Agriculture* (New York: W. W. Norton, 1987), 136-41, 162-67 for Soviet procurement policies before the war and immediately thereafter.
3. Lazar Volin, *A Century of Russian Agriculture: From Alexander II to Khrushchev* (Cambridge, MA: Harvard University Press, 1970), 382-99.
4. Alec Nove, *The Soviet Economy: An Introduction* (New York: Frederick A. Praeger, 1961), 88.
5. Nove, *The Soviet Economy*, 88.
6. During the Brezhnev period, the general trend was for the state to purchase larger percentages of production with the exception of vegetables and potatoes.
7. A. Kosynkin, "Tverdyi plan zakupok v sel'skom khoziaistve," *Voprosy ekonomiki*, no. 10 (October 1970): 61-62.
8. Kosynkin, "Tverdyi plan zakupok," 61.
9. *Ekonomika sotsialisticheskogo sel'skogo khoziaistva* (Moscow: Kolos, 1970),159-60.
10. I. V. Popovich, *Ekonomika sel'skogo khoziaistva* (Moscow: Kolos, 1975), 223.
11. For an explanation of party and non-party structures from the national to the local level, see Jerry F. Hough, *The Soviet Prefects: The Local Party Organs in Industrial Decision-Making* (Cambridge: Harvard University Press, 1969), chap. 2.
12. Telegram to V. I. Toropov, KGA, f. R-1538, o. 11, d. 752, l. 112.
13. Due to a shortage of refrigeration capacity. Often refrigerators that existed did not work. For example, one document noted that six of 17 milk refrigerators in the raion did not work. Kostromskoi oblastnoi Sovet narodnykh deputatov Ispolitel'nyi komitet reshenie ot 8 avgusta 1980 goda no. 287, "O neudovletvoritel'nom vypolnenii resheniia ispolkoma oblsoveta ot 27 fevralia 1978 goda no. 62 'O povyshenii zagotovitel'noi distsipliny v oblasti' Makar'yevskim raiispolkomom,'" KGA, f. R-1538, o. (10 dop.), d. 156, ll. 2, 6.
14. KGA, f. R-1538, o. 11, d. 625.
15. For example, one document stated that "The Ispolkom of the Oblast Soviet believes that these shortcoming exist because the oblast inspectorate (the chief inspector comrade Riabtsov) does not deeply analyze the situation with food and purchases of agricultural products, does not show proper exactingness toward farm managers or procurement organizations for the fulfillment of state purchase plans, works poorly in finding supplementary reserves for replenishing state reserves of agricultural products, seldom introduces suggestions to eliminate shortcomings to directive organs and organs of people's control." Kostromskoi oblastnoi Sovet narodnykh deputatov Ispolitel'nyi komitet reshenie ot 25 avgusta 1981 goda no. 320, "O merakh po uluchsheniiu raboty oblastnoi gosu-

darstvennoi inspektsii po zakupkam i kachestvu sel'skokhoziaistvennoi produktsii," KGA, f. R-1538, o.10 (dop.), d. 223, l. 4.
16. KGA, f. 1538, o. 11, d. 752.
17. Kostromskoi oblastnoi Sovet narodnykh deputatov Ispolitel'nyi komitet reshenie ot 8 avgusta 1980 goda no. 287, "O neudovletvoritel'nom vypolnenii resheniia ispolkoma oblsoveta ot 27 fevralia 1978 goda no. 62 'O povyshenii zagotovitel'noi distsipliny v oblasti' Makar'yevskim raiispolkomom,'" KGA, f. R-1538, o. 10 (dop.), d. 156, l. 1
18. KGA, f. R-1538, o. 10 (dop.), d. 156, ll. 5-10.
19. "Informatsiia o vypolnenii reshenii ispolkoma Kostromskogo oblastnogo Soveta narodnykh deputatov ot 8 avgusta 1980 goda no. 287, 'O neudovletvoritel'nom vypolnenii resheniia ispolkoma oblsoveta ot 27 fevralia 1978 goda' no. 62 'O povyshenii zagotovitel'noi distsipliny v oblasti' Makar'yevskim raiispolkomom,'" KGA, f. R-1538, o. 10 (dop.), d. 156, l. 12.
20. "Informatsiia o vypolnenii reshenii ispolkoma Kostromskogo oblastnogo Soveta narodnykh deputatov ot 8 avgusta 1980 goda no. 287, 'O neudovletvoritel'nom vypolnenii resheniia ispolkoma oblsoveta ot 27 fevralia 1978 goda' no. 62 'O povyshenii zagotovitel'noi distsipliny v oblasti' Makar'yevskim raiispolkomom,'" KGA, f. R-1538, o. 10 (dop.), d. 156, ll. 15-16a.
21. Kostromskoi oblastnoi Sovet narodnykh deputatov Ispolitel'nyi komitet reshenie ot 11 Iyunia 1981 goda no. 200, "O neudovletvoritel'nom rukovodstve Mezhevskogo raiispolskoma proizvodstvom i zagotovkami produktov zhivotnovodstva," KGA, f. R-1538, o. 10 (dop.), d. 160, ll. 1-5.
22. This is not a hard and fast rule. Other documents showed that the head of one raion *ispolkom* was reprimanded because his raion had underfulfilled its plans during one six-month period. Kostromskoi oblastnoi Sovet narodnykh deputatov Ispolitel'nyi komitet reshenie ot 27 Iyulia 1981 goda no. 262, "O neudovletvoritel'nom khode proizvodstva i zakupok moloka v kolkhozakh i sovkhozak Parfen'yevskogo raiona v letniy period," KGA, f. R-1538, o. 10 (dop.), d. 161, ll. 1-5.
23. For the party's role in agriculture see Peter Rutland, *The Politics of Economic Stagnation in the Soviet Union: The Role of Local Party Organs in Economic Management* (Cambridge: Cambridge University Press, 1993), chap. 7, and compare with the party's role in industry, chaps. 2 and 3.
24. Jerry Hough analyzed the tenure patterns of collective farm chairmen, but no one has correlated job tenure with farm performance, so we lack both systematic data and analysis on the security of farm chairmen. See Jerry F. Hough, "The Changing Nature of the Kolkhoz Chairman," in *The Soviet Rural Community*, ed. James R. Millar (Urbana: University of Illinois Press, 1971), 103-20. Cynthia Kaplan also discusses the changing characteristics of farm chairmen and tenure patterns, arguing that tenure patterns correlated with the region's agricultural potential. See Cynthia S. Kaplan, *The Party and Agricultural Crisis Management in the USSR* (Ithaca: Cornell University Press, 1987), 79-85. In Kostroma oblast, in 1980, 39.5 percent of collective farm chairmen, and 46 percent of state farm directors had held their post five or more years. "Otchet o chislennosti i sostave po obrazovaniiu rukovodyashchikh rabotnikov v kolkhoze," KGA, f. R-1951, o. 15, d. 680, ll. 1-2; and "Otchet o chislennosti i sostave po obrazovaniiu rukovodyashchikh rabotnikov v sovkhoze," KGA, f. R-1951, o. 15, d. 680, ll. 3-4.
25. "Otchet o chislennosti i sostave po obrazovaniiu rukovodiashchikh rabotnikov v kolkhoze," KGA, f. R-1951, o. 15, d. 680, ll. 1-2; and "Otchet o chislennosti i sostave po obrazovaniiu rukovodiashchikh rabotnikov v sovkhoze," KGA, f. R-1951, o. 15, d. 680, ll. 3-4.

26. Medvedev, *Soviet Agriculture*, 164. During the remainder of the Khrushchev period procurement prices were raised in 1958, 1962, and 1963, and as a result the percentage of food produced that was procured by the state increased.

27. L. V. Zaverniaeva, ed., *Osnovy ekonomiki sotsialisticheskogo sel'skogo khoziaistva* (Moscow: Economic Literature, 1963), 319. The same source noted that "the increase in the production of agricultural products, the growth of procurements, and the lower cost of producing agricultural products is the economic basis for lowering the retail price for food goods in wide demand and for increasing the standard of living for workers, employees, for the entire Soviet people" (319).

28. See Morris Bornstein, "Soviet Price Policies," *Soviet Economy*, 3, no. 2 (April-June 1987): 110-18.

29. For an excellent discussion of Soviet procurement price policy, see V. S. Pavlov, *Radikal'naia reforma tsenoobrazovaniia* (Moscow: Finansy i statistika, 1988), 70-80; and see Stephen K. Wegren, *Agriculture and the State in Soviet and Post-Soviet Russia* (Pittsburgh: University of Pittsburgh Press, 1998), 29-33.

30. The original bonus rate of 50 percent for food products, announced at the March 1965 plenum, was followed by a 100 percent bonus to collective farms for above-plan sales of sunflower seeds and a 50 percent bonus for above-plan sales of cotton.

31. V. A. Matusevich, *Rynok sel'sko-khoziaistvennoi produktsii* (Moscow: Ekonomika, 1988), 119-20.

32. For example, 1978 was a very good year for agriculture, and Brezhnev had every reason to think that his strategy of industrializing agriculture within a collectivist structure was correct. This attitude was reflected in Brezhnev's report to the CPSU July 1978 plenum, in which he spent nearly a quarter of his speech reviewing the achievements his policies had engendered during the past twelve years. Brezhnev's speech stood in sharp contrast to a memorandum (*zapiska*) that the young first secretary from Stavropol' krai, Mikhail Gorbachev, sent to the Central Committee in May 1978. In his report Gorbachev was extremely critical of the agricultural situation in Stavropol'. He complained that *kolkhoz* profitability had declined from 28 percent during 1966-1970 to 10 percent during 1971-1975; and for *sovkhozy* from 42.1 percent to 18.2 percent. The terms of trade continued to discriminate against agricultural products. In 1966 a ton of metal was equivalent to 14.7 centners of wheat, but in 1977 the cost had risen to 23 centners. During 1966-1977 the consumption of fuel oil for machines had decreased 14 percent, but the price of fuel oil had increased 56 percent. In 1978 alone the price went up 84 percent from its 1977 level. The cost of machinery outstripped the growth of its productivity. The cost of producing grain was increasing much faster than the gains in productivity. There were problems with planning, with some regions virtually unplanned while others were chronically over planned with no hope of fulfillment. There also remained a problem with attracting and retaining high-quality cadres in the countryside. A large part of the demographic problem was due to low living and cultural conditions, and Gorbachev complained that while capital investments during the Eighth and Ninth five-year plans had increased 2.5 times over the previous ten years, expenditures on improving living conditions had risen only 16 percent. M. S. Gorbachev, *Izbrannye rechi i stat'i*, vol. 1 (Moscow: Politizdat, 1987), 180-200. Although Gorbachev spoke at the July 1978 plenum, his speech was not published. After the plenum, on July 17, 1978, Secretary for Agriculture Kulakov died suddenly. Neither Brezhnev, Kosygin, nor Suslov attended the funeral. After a delay of a few months, in November 1978 Gorbachev was appointed Central Committee secretary with responsibility for agriculture, thus taking over Kulakov's responsibilities. See Zhores A. Medvedev, *Gorbachev* (New York: Norton, 1986), 67-93.

33. M. S. Gorbachev, *Izbrannye rechi i stat'i*, vol. 2 (Moscow: Politizdat, 1987), 75-108.

34. Archie Brown, *The Gorbachev Factor* (Oxford: Oxford University Press, 1997), 57.
35. See David S. Mason and Svetlana Sydorenko, "Perestroyka, Social Justice, and Soviet Public Opinion," *Problems of Communism*, 39, no. 6 (November-December 1990): 34-43.
36. M. S. Gorbachev, *Izbrannye rechi i stat'i*, vol. 3 (Moscow: Politizdat, 1987), 225-26.
37. A.Okhapkin and M.Ratgauz,"Rezul'taty eksperimenta po sovershenstvovaniiu sistemy upravleniia i khoziaistvennogo mekhanizma v APK RSFSR," *APK: ekonomika, upravlenie*, no. 5 (May 1989): 12.
38. I. Efremov, "Sovershenstvovanie upravleniia proizvodstvom raiona," *APK: ekonomika, upravlenie*, no. 3 (March 1990): 13.
39. *Pravda*, 29 March 1986, 1-2.
40. The World Bank, *Food and Agricultural Policy Reforms in the Former USSR: An Agenda for the Transition* (Washington, DC: The World Bank, 1993), 120.
41. *Sel'skaia zhizn'*, 11 August 1989, 1.
42. *Sel'skaia zhizn'*, 16 July 1991, 1.
43. *Pravda*, 10 August 1990, 1. Despite higher purchase prices, livestock was withheld from sale to the state, which forced the RSFSR government to move up the implementation date to 15 September 1990, and the central government followed suit, moving up the date of new prices to 1 October 1990.
44. P. G. Goncharov, ed., *Organizatsiia torgovli prodovol'stvennymi tovarami* (Moscow: Ekonomika, 1989), 186.
45. I. G. Ushachev, *Khozrashchet i samoupravlenie v trudovykh kollektivakh kolkhozov i sovkhozov* (Moscow: Profizdat, 1988), 85.
46. Ushachev, *Khozrashchet i samoupravlenie*, 85.
47. Ironically, the deterioration accelerated as procurement prices rose.
48. This discussion draws from Stephen K. Wegren, "Two Steps Forward, One Step Back: The Politics of an Emerging New Rural Social Policy in Russia," *Soviet and Post-Soviet Review*, 19, nos. 1-3 (1992): 7-9.
49. *Zemlia i liudi*, 27 March 1992, 3.
50. *Rossiiskaia gazeta*, 27 September 1991, 2.
51. *Sel'skaia zhizn'*, 9 February 1991, 2.
52. William Moskoff, *Hard Times: Impoverishment and Protest in the Perestroika Years, The Soviet Union 1985-1991* (Armonk, NY: M. E. Sharpe, 1993), 35-55.
53. Stephen K. Wegren, "Private Agriculture in the Soviet Union under Gorbachev," *Soviet Union*, 16, nos. 2-3 (1989): 130.
54. Private plots were not actually "private," in that the land was not owned by the operator. The Soviet term for this form was *lichnoe podsoboe khoziaistvo*, or personal subsidiary farming.
55. *Biudzhet vremeni naseleniia SSSR: statisticheskiy sbornik* (Moscow: Goskomstat, 1989), 28.
56. See Karl-Eugen Wadekin, *The Private Sector in Soviet Agriculture* (Berkeley: University of California Press, 1973). Partly because food prices at collective farm markets were determined by market forces, private plots were ideologically anathema and came under periodic attacks by the leadership throughout the Soviet period. In particular, the late Stalin period and the Khrushchev period after 1958 witnessed attempts by the Soviet leadership to restrict private plot output by constricting supplies of inputs, limiting opportunities for sale of output, and imposing various taxes. Nonetheless, private plots were permitted because of their large contribution to the nation's food supply.
57. Wegren, "Private Agriculture in the Soviet Union Under Gorbachev," 128-33.
58. Wegren, "Private Agriculture in the Soviet Union Under Gorbachev," 116.

59. *Narodnoe khoziaistvo RSFSR v 1988 g.*, 113.

60. *Narodnoe khoziaistvo SSSR za 70 let: iubileinyi statisticheskii ezhegodnik* (Moscow: Finansy i statistika, 1987), 445.

61. *Lichnoe podsobnoe khoziaistvo naseleniia v 1988 godu* (Moscow: Goskomstat, 1989), 29-33, 72-77.

62. "O lichnom podsobnom khoziaistve semei kolkhoznikov i rabotnikov sovkhozov," *APK: ekonomika, upravalenie*, no. 2 (February 1992): 66-67.

63. Yegor Ligachev, *Inside Gorbachev's Kremlin: The Memoirs of Yegor Ligachev* (New York: Pantheon Books, 1993), 326-27.

64. In general, perestroika was also characterized by concern for urban interests first and foremost. This fact was explicitly admitted by a member of the Presidium of the RSFSR Supreme Soviet when he said: "The defense of the interests of the country and the state through a defense of the interests of workers—such an approach dictates our attitude to the problem of the transition to a market in general." *Ekonomika i zhizn'*, no. 14 (April 1991), 4.

65. An oddity of the Soviet system was that retail food prices were lower than wholesale food prices, with the difference subsidized by the national government to the benefit of the consumer. Pavlov, *Radikal'naia reforma tsenoobrazovaniia*, 72.

66. Throughout 1990, prices on the urban kolkhoz market increased an average of 21 percent for all types agricultural produce during the first half of the year above 1989 prices. Meat prices in particular rose dramatically. For example, beef prices rose 21 percent and pork 25 percent over their level in 1989. *Ekonomika i zhizn'*, no. 36 (September 1990), 12.

67. World Bank, *Food and Agricultural Policy Reforms in the Former USSR: An Agenda for the Transition* (Washington, DC: The World Bank, 1992), Table 8.1, 218.

68. *Izvestiia*, 15 February 1991, 2.

69. Mikhail Gorbachev, *Memoirs* (New York: Doubleday, 1996), 121.

70. Retail prices for bread and bread products, sugar, eggs, and vegetable oil had not been raised since 1954. Retail prices for meat, butter, milk, and cheese had not been increased since 1962. Valentin Pavlov, *Overhauling the Entire System of Prices* (Moscow: Novosti Press Agency Publishing House, 1987), 13.

71. See Glen Alden Smith, *Soviet Foreign Trade: Organization, Operations, and Policy, 1918-1971* (New York: Praeger Publishers, 1973), 74-107.

72. See Eugene Zaleski, *Stalinist Planning for Economic Growth, 1933-1952* (Chapel Hill: University of North Carolina Press, 1980), 42-48.

73. See Paul R. Gregory and Robert C. Stuart, *Soviet Economic Structure and Performance* (New York: Harper and Row, 1974), 272-74.

74. Ed A. Hewett with Clifford Gaddy, *Open for Business: Russia's Return to the Global Economy* (Washington, DC: Brookings Institution, 1992), 10-11.

75. *Narodnoe khoziaistvo SSSR za 70 let*, 640.

76. Hewett and Gaddy, *Open for Business*, 16.

77. Hewett and Gaddy, *Open for Business*, 17.

78. Joan F. McIntyre, "Soviet Efforts to Revamp the Foreign Trade Sector," in Joint Economic Committee, *Gorbachev's Economic Plans*, vol. 2, Joint Committee Print, 100th Congress, 1st session (Washington, DC: Government Printing Office, 1987), 492.

79. For early analysis and background on the ideological and personnel changes that underlie Gorbachev's new approach to foreign economic relations, see Jerry F. Hough, *Opening up the Soviet Economy* (Washington, DC: Brookings Institution, 1988), chap. 4. For the institutional evolution see Hewett and Gaddy, *Open for Business*, chap. 3.

80. Hewett and Gaddy noted that the amount retained could range from 2 to 97 percent, but in practice seldom exceeded 30 percent. Hewett and Gaddy, *Open for Business*, 62.

81. OECD, *The Soviet Agro-Food System and Agricultural Trade: Prospects for Reform* (Paris: OECD, 1991), 184.

82. McIntyre, "Soviet Efforts to Revamp the Foreign Trade Sector," 498.

83. OECD, *The Soviet Agro-Food System and Agricultural Trade*, 184.

84. OECD, *The Soviet Agro-Food System and Agricultural Trade*, 184.

85. Unless otherwise noted, this section draws from Patricia A. Wertman, "Russian Economic Reform and the IMF: Financing Economic Adjustment," *CRS Issue Brief*, Report No. IB92128 (Washington, DC: Congressional Research Service, Library of Congress, 1993); and Curt Tarnoff, "U.S. and International Assistance to the Former Soviet Union," *CRS Issue Brief*, Report number IB91050 (Washington, DC: Congressional Research Service, Library of Congress, 1993).

86. As a backdrop to contacts with the IMF, at their June 1990 meeting, members of the G-7 decided to commission a study of the Soviet economy by the World Bank, which in its study recommended a comprehensive reform of the Soviet economy, including a decontrol of prices, a restructuring of the financial system, a system of property rights, privatization of the industrial sector, and trade liberalization.

87. *New York Times*, 1 April 1992, 1, 7.

88. In 1991, grain imports fell sharply due to an excellent harvest, but still totaled over 19 million tons. Grain imports rose to 29.5 million tons in 1992. Economic Research Service, *International Agriculture and Trade Reports: Former USSR, Situation and Outlook Series*, RS-93-1 (Washington, DC: United States Department of Agriculture, 1993), 32.

89. See Remy Jurenas, "U.S. Agricultural Exports and Assistance to the Former Soviet Union," in Joint Economic Committee, *The Former Soviet Union in Transition*, vol. 2 (Washington, DC: Government Printing Office, 1993), 543-44.

90. *Narodnoe khoziaistvo SSSR za 70 let*, 644.

91. *Rossiiskaia Federatsiia v 1992 godu: statisticheskii ezhegodnik* (Moscow: Goskomstat, 1993), 52-53.

92. *Vneshnie ekonomicheskie sviazi SSSR v 1989g.: statisticheskii ezhegodnik* (Moscow: Finansy i statistika, 1990), 20.

93. Jaclyn Y. Shend, *Agricultural Statistics of the Former USSR Republics and the Baltic States*, Statistical Bulletin no. 863 (Washington, DC: Economic Research Service, 1993), 176, 232; *Narodnoe khoziaistvo RSFSR v 1989g.: statisticheskii ezhegodnik* (Moscow: Goskomstat, 1990), 452-53, 517; *Narodnoe khoziaistvo Rossiiskoi Federatsii. 1992: statisticheskii ezhegodnik* (Moscow: Goskomstat, 1992), 419-20, 475.

94. *Narodnoe khoziaistvo SSSR za 70 let*, 647.

95. *Rossiiskaia Federatsiia v 1992 godu*, 53.

96. Stuart S. Brown and Misha V. Belkindas, "Who's Feeding Whom? An Analysis of Soviet Interrepublic Trade," in Joint Economic Committee, *The Former Soviet Union in Transition*, vol. 1 (Washington, DC: Government Printing Office, 1993), 176.

Chapter Three

Domestic Food Policies in the Post-Soviet Period

Having examined food production trends, Soviet-era food policies, and Soviet-era patterns of domestic and foreign food trade, this chapter turns its attention to domestic food policy in the post-Soviet period. The previous chapter demonstrated that the domestic Soviet food system lacked market competition, shared market knowledge, and efficient price formation. Instead, the majority of food trade was dominated by a network of state wholesale agents and retail outlets that operated according to plans generated by party bureaucrats and political considerations instead of the forces of supply and demand. Domestic food policies influence Russia's transition away from communism and are important in a number of ways. First, domestic food policies are an integral part of the market infrastructure that must exist if broader market reforms are to be consolidated. Privatization alone is not sufficient to create a market economy, and instead requires supporting domestic policies.

Second, domestic food policies affect and reflect the role of the state and its degree of regulation over food production and distribution, thereby defining the policy environment in which food producers operate. This larger policy environment affects production and distribution decisions. Thus, food policies are a key variable in understanding producers' motivations, as well as the incentives and disincentives that they face. The nature of food policies, therefore, directly affects the responses of food producers to purchase prices and marketing opportunities. Food policies that are too restrictive for producers will decrease motivations to increase production, or will lead them to withhold sales.

Third, food policies are important to marketing agents and the development of a marketing strategy by defining the freedom and latitude marketing agents have to operate.[1] The role food marketing agents play in food trade can either alleviate or exacerbate food shortages. In this respect it is useful to remember that food shortages in the Soviet Union had less to do with inadequate production than with the way in which domestic food policies were defined.[2] As suggested by the previous chapter, Soviet food policies were characterized by an inefficient and unresponsive trade and distribution system. As one USDA analyst noted, "The main cause of the growing food shortages. . . was not a fall in production, but rather disruption in the distribution of what was produced."[3]

Delegations of U.S. officials who visited post-Soviet Russia to survey the agricultural situation concluded that among the chief causes of agricultural crisis was "an overemphasis on production agriculture without commensurate investment in post-harvest food handling facilities."[4] The importance of post-harvest processes is witnessed by the fact that during the first half of the 1990s grain imports were estimated to be roughly equal to harvest losses.[5] By reducing or eliminating losses, imports could be significantly cut, thereby freeing up hard currency for other urgent needs.[6]

Finally, food policies are important to consumers because government policies affect the retail price for food, with ripple effects on households' budgets, standards of living, and disposable income. With the liberalization of retail prices, the cost of food has accounted for a greater share of the household budget. In the post-Soviet period, households with multiple children, even among working families, are most likely to be malnourished. To protect the most vulnerable segments of the population, municipal and regional governments have had to offer programs of social protection.

To investigate changes in domestic food policies, the chapter is organized as follows. The first section below defines some basic analytical and conceptual criteria about food marketing systems by which we can judge reform progress in Russia. The second section examines change in procurement policy that affects domestic food marketing channels and marketing agents. A third section analyzes change in procurement price policy. Within this section, impediments to free trade within Russia are analyzed, and the growing importance of regional restrictions on food trade are discussed. This section also presents a case study of the grain market and illustrates the contemporary approach to price policy and the changed role played by the federal government. The fourth section investigates changes in retail food price policy affecting food consumers. The second through fourth sections show that an enormous amount of change has taken place in terms of state policies and behaviors compared to the Soviet period. Changes in food policy and the role of the federal government have led to the rise of numerous rural interest groups which try to influence food policy and the implementation of policy. A fifth section surveys these groups, and their goals and activities, and assesses their influence in the policy process.

A Conceptual Approach to Domestic Food Policies

Having briefly discussed the impact of domestic food policies on different actors in the agricultural economy, the pertinent question now is, how do we compare food marketing systems? Analytically, food marketing systems may be distinguished by applying the following criteria.[7] The first, and most important, criterion is the degree of competition in food marketing. Competition is important because it is the force that guides private self-interest into serving social welfare. For competition to guide private interests, however, the exchange relationship must be balanced so that no one agent can influence the outcome of the exchange. The clearest example of the principle of competition occurs when there is only one participant either on the selling or buying side. But numbers alone do not determine competition. Two sellers can provide competition if they compete. Likewise, a number of sellers may not be competitive if they are guided by mutual understanding as to their expected market behavior—think of the four gas stations situated on each corner of an intersection who sell their gas for exactly the same price. Only very large numbers of market participants (either sellers or buyers) guarantee competitiveness.

A producer is motivated to receive the highest price for his produce that he can. The greater the number of agents competing to buy his produce, the more information the farmer has about prevailing prices and the easier it is for him to switch to the buyer with the higher price. Identifying the farmer's range of choices at the initial point of sale is a crucial consideration in understanding how competitive the market is (and thus how accurate the prices generated by the market will be).

A second consideration is the balance of market power, or put differently, market knowledge. Market knowledge is market power. Whoever has more information or greater market knowledge can use that as an advantage in setting the initial price of a product. One of the most important market interventions that governments can make is to improve the fairness of market information so that less discrimination takes place against the small farmer. Alternatively, market knowledge can be provided by private commercial structures.[8] Such information allows sellers to bargain more equally with purchasing agents. Thus, a second criterion is how well the food system balances market information and provides a more equal distribution of the gains from market price formation.

A third criterion is how efficiently prices are formed, and how accurately prices send signals to both buyers and sellers.[9] Efficient price formation is particularly important for the efficient allocation of resources in a market economy. Prices are formed when buyers and sellers agree on a basis for exchange, a price. A price then signals to buyers the cost of obtaining that resource or good, and to sellers it signals the willingness of consumers to buy that resource or good at that price. Prices are also important for signaling opportunity costs to society. When prices do not signal opportunity costs, serious misallocations of resources can result, resulting in disruptions of food supplies to consumers. When markets fail, participants with inside information and economic power are able to exploit both consumers and producers.

These three criteria—competition in food marketing, the balance of market power, and how efficiently and accurately wholesale prices are formed—form a basis from which we are able to measure change from the Soviet food system and its food policies. These criteria allow us to understand the nature of domestic food policies in post-Soviet Russia.

Food Marketing Agents: Change in Procurement Policies

After food is produced, the producer is faced with three central questions: how much to sell and how much to consume or use; at what price will he sell; and who will buy it?[10] These considerations took on importance in post-Soviet Russia. The collapse of the Soviet Union brought significant changes to the food procurement system, the most immediate of which was organizational and institutional, as state planning bodies were abolished. Other reforms were introduced as well in the policy realm, although several of those changes took several years to evolve. As the domestic food trade system was reformed, the most notable changes included:

(1) the liberalization of foreign trade which allowed the import and export of food through nonstate channels;

(2) the reduction and then elimination of obligatory deliveries of food products to state delivery points;

(3) the establishment of competitive marketing channels for food trade, namely the emergence of commodity exchanges and private food traders;

(4) the ending of federal-level consumer food subsidies in retail stores.

As a result of these reforms in the food system the federal government became less able to control the nation's food supplies, less able to regulate the food import/export balance, and less able to manage the domestic food trade system. The highlights of those changes are surveyed before concentrating on the effects of those changes. Some of the most important legislation marking the changes in procurement policy and procurement price policy are shown in table 3.1.

Table 3.1. Procurement Policy and Procurement Price Legislation

Name of Legislation	Date Adopted
On the Formation of State Food Funds in 1992	January 1992
On the Formation of Federal and Regional Food Funds in 1993	February 1993
Law on Grain	May 1993
On the Liberalization of the Grain Market	December 1993
On Purchases and Deliveries of Agricultural Products	December 1994
On State Regulation of Agroindustrial Production	July 1997
On Price Policy in the Sphere of Agroindustrial Production	March 1999

During the first half of the 1990s, state intervention and regulation of the domestic food system decreased significantly. In 1992 the unsuccessful food tax was eliminated, and in its place a different procurement system arose. In early January 1992, Russian President Boris Yeltsin signed a presidential decree that instructed landholders and land users engaged in agricultural production to deliver defined percentages of their crop and animal husbandry production, based upon average annual production attained during 1986-1990.[11]The new procurement system differed from the Soviet system mainly in that percentages of production to be sold to the state were much lower than before.

In early 1993, the Russian government announced that obligatory food deliveries to the state had officially ended.[12] To replace obligatory deliveries, in February 1993 the Russian government established federal and regional food funds in order to ensure reserves of basic foodstuffs to meet the food needs of large cities and regions that were not grain sufficient, to feed the military and its subdivisions, and to supply Moscow and St. Petersburg.[13] The federal food fund was established to replace the Soviet-era "state orders" or obligatory deliveries of food products to the state. As such, the establishment of food funds represented a reduction in state intervention in domestic food supplies, and the quotas were at greatly reduced levels. The declining role of state procurements in the first half of the 1990s is shown in table 3.2.

Table 3.2. Food Sales to State Procurement Organizations, 1991-1996 (in percent of volume produced)*

Product	1991	1992	1993	1994	1995	1996
Grain	63	64	63	34	34.5	29
Potatoes	69	60	52	37	13	11
Vegetables	84	73	70	59	43	32.5
Cattle and Poultry	83	80	79	70	57	50
Milk	98	96	96	93	78	71

*"State" is defined as both federal and regional food fund purchases.
Sources: *Sel'skoe khoziaistvo Rossii* (Moscow: Goskomstat, 1995), 88; *Osnovnye pokazateli agropromyshlennogo kompleksa Rossiiskoi Federatsii v 1999 godu*, (Moscow: Goskomstat, 2000), 41.

In late February 1994, a government resolution repeated the instruction that various ministries and agents were to use "contracts" for sales to the federal food fund.[14] In order to stimulate sales to the federal food fund, monetary advances of "not less than 50 percent of the value of these products" were to be offered to food producers. Advances were to be paid "not less than 30 days from the moment the contract was signed."[15] In reality, the state had little money to fulfill either advances, or even to pay for purchases.

During the rest of the 1990s, the amount of food procured by federal and regional food funds decreased. (Trends in food trade away from state purchases for the duration of the 1990s and into the early twenty-first century are presented in the following chapter. In addition, channels of domestic food trade are discussed in more detail in the following chapter.)

Even with reduced delivery quotas, the federal food fund was only a partial step away from state control of the wholesale food market. Essentially, the federal food fund was organized at the national level, like a broad umbrella organization, with separate organizations that procured different food commodities. Most federal food organizations had regional subdivisions. The food organizations were funded out of the federal budget and the money was to be used to purchase food for state needs, as indicated above. The federal government licensed purchasers who acted as agents on behalf of the state to purchase, store, and distribute specific food commodities. In most cases only one federal organization was licensed to purchase a specific food commodity, and thus these purchasing organizations acted as monopolies. For example, the organization to buy grain for state needs was called *Roskhleboprodukt*. State-licensed food organizations were not privatized until 1994.

The federal food fund did not operate in every oblast. During interviews in Kostroma oblast, in the early and mid-1990s, agricultural officials indicated that farms in the region did not have federal food fund quotas for grain. Officially, food fund quotas were said to be contractual (allegedly based on negotiations between two equal sides). The government treated quotas ambiguously, at times suggesting that contributions to food funds was voluntary, while simultaneously emphasizing the importance of supplying food funds for national needs and reserves. It never was entirely clear how voluntary or obligatory the quotas were.

Quotas were disaggregated to the farm level, although interviews in Kostroma revealed the fact that enforcement of quotas was minimal and few, if any, sanctions were applied if farm quotas were not met. The primary attraction to sell to food funds was the fact that transportation to the point of sale was paid for by the state, and for some time in the early 1990s state procurement prices were higher than those offered by commodity exchanges. While federal quotas diminished, regional funds' food quotas, which obtained food to feed the region's population, became more important.

From 1994 onward, state procurements declined significantly for most food products. The primary achievement may be said to be the withdrawal of the state from a high level of procurements which allowed producers to sell more food through nonstate channels. As a result of state withdrawal, producers have had choices about food trade. On the one hand, producers may sell on the internal market for prices that the market will bear. The "internal" market refers to sales to private processors, which are not state-licensed purchasing agents, through private retail networks, through urban markets, or to commodity exchanges (*birzhi*). Producers may arrange barter trade, an option that was quite popular during the 1990s. In addition, producers may export their produce, with some limitations. The second choice is to sell to state procurement agents. Although declining in importance, the state retains a presence in domestic food trade. Producers may sell to state-licensed purchasing agents for state needs.

Thus, during the first half of the 1990s the federal government purposely attempted to reduce its intervention in food trade by reforming the Soviet-era procurement system. In its place, a minimalist approach arose, based upon food funds as national and regional reserves. These food funds purchased food, but at much lower levels than Soviet-era procurement policies had done. As a result, much more food was traded through nonstate channels as chapter 4 demonstrates. For example, whereas state procurement agents purchased 63 percent of harvested grain in 1993, in 1999 they purchased only 19 percent, and in 2000 only 15 percent. Milk products, due to the need for refrigeration, remained a common state purchase, declining from 97 percent to 60 percent, but this was an exception.[16]

In summary, by 1996, the basic parameters of the liberalization of procurement policies were in place. These policies charted a course toward a reduction in the role of the state, particularly at the federal level. However, we should be clear that liberalization of food marketing did not necessarily equal a competitive food market. Nor did state withdrawal necessarily lead to true market relations in the countryside as privatized monopolies continued to dictate purchase prices. In addition, regional administrations and governors often dictated fixed prices. Nonetheless, despite deformations in the Russian food market, policy reforms in the procurement system set in motion changes in the way that domestic food was purchased and distributed.

Food Producers: Change in Procurement Price Policy

Changes in procurement policy led in turn to deregulation of the procurement price system and its pricing policies.[17] Procurement price policy is central to broader domestic food policy because it is the most direct economic signal that is sent to food producers. As such, procurement price policy affects in fundamental ways producers' profitability and, for large agricultural enterprises, their ability to fulfill social functions in the rural community. For these reasons, the evolution of procurement price policy is traced below. The remainder of this section focuses on the formation of procurement prices used by state purchasing agents. The formation of wholesale prices in general, that is, in the "free market place" is not considered because those processes are a function of supply and demand. Our concern here is with the role of the state in wholesale state policy.

In the post-Soviet period, a twofold price system emerged. On the one hand, federal withdrawal from direct control over domestic food markets led to a market based price system in which wholesale prices are determined, or at least influenced, by factors of supply and demand (at least in theory—impediments will be examined). On the other hand, while federal control over domestic purchase prices declined dramatically, state-licensed purchasing agents continue to exist and to purchase food from farms in order to fulfill the needs of federal and regional food funds. These food funds have different purposes: the federal fund allocates food to the military, hospitals, orphanages, and schools. Regional funds are defined at the regional level in terms of their size and composition, and are intended to ensure adequate food supplies for the population. Thus, as a whole, the procurement system, based upon procurement prices, has changed substantially, but has not disappeared altogether.

When the Soviet Union ceased to exist in December 1991, Russian President Boris Yeltsin followed through on the promise he made in late October 1991, and on January 2, 1992 the liberalization of retail prices for almost all food goods was enacted, accompanied by an end to federal subsidies for food at the retail level (see below). A few days later in January 1992, Yeltsin signed a presidential decree stipulating the state would pay "market" prices for food produce sold to the state. Moreover, if contracts with the state were concluded, the state would pay transportation and storage costs. If actually implemented, this would have been an enormous benefit to large farms. Farms would have obtained a secure market for their produce, sold at fair market value, without having to expend time, energy, or resources in searching out buyers.

The reality was quite different, however. Because private farmers, state and collective farms, and other agricultural enterprises often had little storage capability of their own, state procurement agencies were able to dictate wholesale prices to food producers. The problem in trying to liberalize wholesale prices was that producing farms were victimized by a lack of storage options—grain farms did not have their own elevators and cattle farms did not have their own refrigerators. Moreover, at least in the case of grains, all producers came on the market at essentially the same time. This was due to the fact that financial regulations often require that credits and loans be repaid by December 31 of the year in which they were received. Purchasing agents were thus able to take advantage of their monopoly position by offering purchase prices that were firm (not negotiated), too low (below internal market value), and did not allow for a profit to producers.

Therefore, it is important to note that price liberalization did not immediately translate into liberalized wholesale prices. In fact, agricultural purchase prices remained largely defined by the state during 1992 and 1993. This meant that even as procurement policy was changing and state intervention lessening, state control over prices in the early post-Soviet period reflected a distrust of market forces. This reality—an outcome of deliberate policy choice—also meant that while inflation was soaring in the economy as a whole (more than 2,600 percent in 1992 and 940 percent in 1993), agricultural wholesale prices remained artificially low and state regulated. The financial squeeze for large farms and private farmers was twofold: fuel, fertilizers, and agricultural machinery and equipment increased more than twice as much as procurement prices during 1992. For grain producers, if they did not accept the firm purchase prices they were offered, they ran the risk of losing large portions of the harvest, thus aggravating their financial situation even more. Table 3.3 illustrates the terms of trade among agricultural products, industrial goods, and the consumer price index. The table shows that for most years wholesale prices for agricultural goods lagged behind increases in the consumer price index and prices for industrial goods.

Beginning in 1994, the purchase price system moved away from state-mandated purchase prices to price "recommendations" made by licensed agents which purchased food for federal and regional food funds. These recommendations were calculated by the Ministry of Agriculture, taking into account the product, inflation, and quality standards. Recommended state prices were said to be "indicative" rather than obligatory and were intended to guarantee a minimum level of profitability to the producer. In reality, price recommendations were often ignored by monopolistic food purchasing agents, which in turn motivated food producers to use other channels of trade.

In response to the fact the state had difficulty stimulating sales for its needs, in early December 1994 a federal law, "On Purchases and Deliveries of Agricultural Products, Raw Materials, and Food for State Needs," was adopted that established "guaranteed minimum purchase prices" for products sold to the state.[18] The intent was to create a price floor for grains and other products sold to the federal food fund. In order to ensure adequate food supplies, purchasing agents were given quotas for the purchase of foodstuffs at guaranteed prices. Food not sold to state-licensed purchasers through other channels of trade was sold at whatever level the market would bear, with some constraints. Similar to price recommendations, guaranteed purchase prices "were not obligatory" but were to be used "as the lowest guaranteed level of freely negotiated prices" of agricultural products sold to the federal food fund. However, few efforts were made to enforce the system of guaranteed purchase prices, and federal funds were not made available to purchasing agents.[19] Sanctions were neither elaborated nor applied in instances of noncompliance. Monetary advances envisioned in the law were often not provided. In short, guaranteed purchase prices were seldom used because market prices were higher, due to underfunding of food fund accounts, and due to monopolistic practices by purchasing agents. [20]

Table 3.3. Terms of Trade for Agricultural Products, 1992-2002 (in percent)

	1992	1993	1994	1995	1996	1997	1998	1999	2000	2001	2002
Consumer Price Index	2,600	940	320	230	22	11	84	36.5	20	19	15
Industrial Goods Price Index	3,380	1,000	330	270	26	7.5	23	67	32	11	17
Agricultural Goods Price Index	940	810	300	330	43.5	9	42	91	22	17.5	8

Industrial price index uses wholesale prices; agricultural price index uses farmgate prices.
Data are for percentage increase in retail price compared to previous year.
Sources: *Rossiiskii statisticheskii ezhegodnik* (Moscow: Goskomstat, 2001), 583; *Rossiiskii statisticheskii ezhegodnik* (Moscow: Goskomstat, 2003), 611.

In July 1997, the law "On State Regulation of Agroindustrial Production," was signed by President Yeltsin.[21] This law introduced a series of different price interventions by the federal government, including special-purpose prices and guaranteed prices for agricultural production. The law stipulated several important aspects. Article 5 of the law guaranteed free (unregulated) sales of agricultural products, raw materials, and foodstuffs. Article 10 provided for "market" (negotiated) and guaranteed prices for agricultural products. Article 13 provided for federal-level subsidies of certain inputs used by producers who sold to state-licensed agents to meet state needs. Article 7 provided for state intervention when "market prices" fell below a "minimum level," or in cases when difficulty arose in selling production due to a drop in demand. The intent was to emulate Western practices of price supports: if market prices dipped below the state minimum price then farms would receive the guaranteed price. If market prices were higher, farms would receive those prices.

However, similar to other laws, enforcement was often lacking, as indicated by the fact that four years after the guaranteed minimum purchase price policy was adopted, the Russian government continued to urge the use of this price policy. A government resolution issued in March 1999, "On Price Policy in the Sphere of Agroindustrial Production," instructed the Ministry of Economics to use guaranteed procurement price levels for purchases of agricultural production intended for state use.[22] In much the same vein, in early 2000, three years after the adoption of the law "On State Regulation of Agroindustrial Production," the Fifth Congress of the Agroindustrial Union of Russia called on the federal government to ensure compliance with that legislation. The congress called on the government to provide guaranteed procurement price levels, to purchase surplus production from domestic producers, and to ensure the validity of contracts.[23] Based on the previous discussion, official state policy since 1995 has been to guarantee minimum purchase prices for products sold to federal and regional food funds. The key variable has been the degree to which federal policy has been implemented and enforced.

An interesting question is the relationship between "market" prices and state-guaranteed prices. Prices are a key signal to producers and as such producers have a strong incentive to seek out the highest bidder. In theory, the federal government no longer sets procurement prices directly, leading to a system of "negotiated" prices that were to be market based (reflective of supply and demand).

In this respect, two closing sets of remarks are in order. First, under Putin, there is a greater willingness to use state intervention, particularly for grain, by using purchase price supports, as is shown in the case study of grain that is presented below. In this respect the policies that were adopted earlier are being used. The intent of state intervention, of course, is to benefit producers by increasing chances of profitability. The long-term effect of state intervention and price supports on the domestic food market remains to be seen, but it should be recognized that the state under Putin has reemerged as something of a competitor with the private market.

Second, it should be noted that the relationship between food supply and procurement prices is not always clear. "Market" manipulations, or at least distortions, are sometimes evident. For instance, in 1998, when the grain harvest was the lowest in 40 years and when drought ravaged southern grain-growing regions, procurement prices were lower than they had been during relatively good harvests of 1996 and 1997.[24] Lower wholesale prices, of course, did not prevent higher retail prices, and in fact several regions and cities imposed price controls to protect consumers.[25] Moreover, despite depleted state reserves and Western food aid to prevent hunger, Russia exported more than 1 million tons of grain in 1998.[26] Conversely, in 2000, when the harvest was almost 20 million tons more than in 1998 and about 10 million tons greater than in 1999, domestic grain prices increased about 40 percent over their 1999 level.[27] Therefore, while the procurement price system has been deregulated, it probably has more deficiencies and distortions than other aspects of the food system. Some of the impediments to a fully market-based procurement price system are discussed next.

Impediments

To say that procurement price policy has been decentralized is not to say that market competition has arisen. Several impediments account for this occurrence. An important impediment to market-based purchase prices is the continued existence of monopoly purchasing agents, which, even though privatized, did not usher in market competition. Three monopoly pressures were felt by food producers: (a) state purchasing agents which ignored federally established "guaranteed prices" at the wholesale level; (b) the replacement of federal intervention with regional intervention and the establishment of regional food markets which used "state orders" to purchase food; and (c) the use of dictated prices by regional authorities in the purchase of food. As state purchasing representatives, these monopolies, which are issued state licenses, act "rationally" by dictating the lowest possible purchase prices to producers. Absent of competition, purchase prices are, in reality, fixed. Thus, "contracts" between buyer and seller have little meaning if the terms are largely dictated by the buyer. True, "fixed" prices apply to a smaller percentage of food trade than during the Soviet period. Animal husbandry production is affected the most, contributing to the fact that "animal husbandry is the most unprofitable branch of agriculture" and has been slower to recover.[28]

Thus, state control over procurement prices has been supplanted by privatized monopoly control. As a result, food producers, particularly large farms, are not significantly better off than before. Why has the liberalization of the procurement price system not benefited large farms? Many of the benefits that Soviet-era farms received to compensate them for low purchase prices have evaporated. Today, farms derive a much greater percentage of their income directly from purchase prices, and much lower percentages of income from credits, subsidies, and loans. Thus, farms are more dependent on "fair" domestic purchase prices, and fair prices are more the exception than the rule.[29]

A second impediment has been a lack of market knowledge by food producers, reflecting the absence of a market infrastructure, although that situation is changing. As was noted previously, market knowledge is important because it provides accurate, reliable information about market conditions and prevailing prices, without which the food market is not able to function as efficiently or effectively as it might. A lack of market knowledge undermines the use of market channels of trade and gives an unfair advantage to state purchasing agents.

To address that problem, the Russian Ministry of Agriculture and the United States Department of Agriculture worked jointly for several years to develop a system of market information to disperse to food producers in Russia.[30] At the beginning of 1998 this system was operating in thirty-two regions in Russia, and during 1998 it was introduced into four more regions.[31] Unfortunately, by spring 2003 the information system was no longer operative, a victim of administrative reform. When it was functional, the market information system, as it was called, operated at the federal, regional, and district levels. This system was state owned and intended as a nonprofit service. The system was designed to provide individuals, organizations, and agricultural managers with analytical reports and information on wholesale prices and price trends, news on supply and demand, and reports on volumes of purchases. Market information was gathered for four categories of food products: (1) milk and milk products, (2) meat and meat products, (3) potatoes, vegetables, and fruits, and (4) cereals. Information on market conditions, including weather, is gathered weekly at the district level and then forwarded to the regional and federal levels, the latter maintaining a federal database.[32] The information was disseminated at the district level, and access to market information is available at the district level through newspapers, radio, and television, or through answering machines, and, where possible, through the Internet. The original scope of the program was to introduce the service to all regions of Russia, but financial constraints allowed only about one-third of regions to participate. However, documents and software applications for the program were sent to nonparticipating regions if they wished to fund the program themselves. In addition, the World Bank provided a loan of $200 million to help expand the system of market information for domestic producers, a program that continued through 2000.[33] This type of program was extremely important to balance the playing field between producers and purchasers, providing producers with information about market conditions. Finally, various food unions distribute information about wholesale prices and market conditions to their members. Some unions distribute information weekly, others monthly. Although this information is useful, the relatively small number of members in most food unions means that most producers/processors do not have access to this information and must depend upon state sources.

Several consequences flow from the incentive structures created by procurement price reform during the 1990s, although the situation is improving for producers under Putin: (1) During much of the 1990s, large farms were motivated to curtail production because procurement prices did not cover production costs. This in turn affected farm profitability and regional food supplies. (2) Producers are motivated to search out higher purchase prices through nonstate channels of trade, but often operate with insufficient market knowledge. (3) During the 1990s, market-based outlets were insecure and disadvantageous, meaning that transaction costs for farms have risen, reinforcing motivations to consume production or use it for payments in-kind.

One recent change has been the willingness of the state to intervene in the domestic food market by offering price supports when market-based prices fall below certain minimum levels. As was shown before, the basis for this policy was laid during the Yeltsin period but never enforced. Under Putin, the situation has changed and the section below offers a case study of the grain market to illustrate state intervention.

Case Study: State Intervention and the Grain Market

Grain is one of the most politically sensitive of all food products because of the importance of bread and bread products to the Russian diet, even more so during the 1990s as standards of living dropped and consumption patterns shifted to a higher intake of carbohydrates and less protein. In this respect, it is interesting to chart state policies toward the grain sector. The discussion below shows an evolution of policy toward grains, from the use of threats, to ineffectual policies and laws under Yeltsin, to a more vigorous attempt to provide tangible support for grain producers under Putin. In general, state policy toward grain reflects broader attitudes toward the agricultural sector by the Russian government.

During the 1992 harvest season, the financial squeeze on producers, which was shown above, worsened. Farms withheld their produce in response to procurement prices that they felt were disadvantageous. Even more ominous, rural district strike committees organized around the country. By mid-August 1992, the Russian government had obtained only about one-half the volume of grain as in August 1991. In early August 1992, a government resolution instructed farms to sell their grain at state-established prices to procurement enterprises and forbade farms from selling their grain until their state delivery quota had been met.[34] If a farm violated this decree, the government could confiscate the proceeds from that illegal sale.[35] In order to bring an end to farm strikes, a compromise between farms and the government was reached. In mid-August 1992, the government increased grain procurement prices by an average of 20 percent and offered various other financial concessions, although these increases were far below the level of inflation.[36] Over the next nine months state grain prices were raised repeatedly in an attempt to keep up with inflation. But it is important to note that the price increases were administrative and not set by market forces. As such, grain prices were at least in part a function of what the state could afford to pay.

In order to avoid a repeat of the 1992 experience, in May 1993 the Law on Grain repeated the promise that the state would buy grain from producers at "negotiated market prices."[37] The Law on Grain stipulated that the government would select, on a competitive basis, purchasers who, acting as state representatives, would buy grain from producers.[38] State purchase agents were responsible for delivering the required volume of grain to the federal fund from their region.[39] Not all regions were required to contribute, and most grain came from grain-producing southern areas of Russia.

However, once again there was a gap between policy and reality. Procurement prices continued to be defined by state purchasing agents and were not negotiated. *Roskhleboprodukt* controlled state grain elevators, received state credits to buy grain, and in turn offered state-set prices to grain growers, much as in the past. As a result of disadvantageous terms of trade, by the summer of 1993 *Roskhleboprodukt* was having a difficult time purchasing the volume of grain established for the food funds because farms would not honor their contracts. The main problem was the price for grain, which producers argued was too low.[40] Thus, during the crucial years of 1992-1993 when inflation was rampant, the state continued to control procurement prices for grain, as well as other agricultural products. Even though the events of July 1993 showed the government was susceptible to unified political pressure by agrarian conservatives and liberals, the overall effect of the state's control was to exacerbate the financial condition of large farms.

In December 1993, Yeltsin signed another decree entitled "On the Liberalization of the Grain Market in Russia."[41] According to the decree, federal and regional food funds would continue to exist, and regions had the right to define the needs for their fund. Deliveries to these funds were to be voluntary, and purchases were to be at market prices. The goal of the decree was to achieve freer domestic food trade than had previously existed. Toward this end, the decree stipulated that "all enterprises for the purchasing, primary processing, storage of grain and production of bread products" that were state property were to be auctioned before April 1, 1994.[42] Furthermore, according to the decree, any local decision by an organ of executive or representative power that in any way limited or forbade the free trade of grain was declared invalid. The penalties for violating free trade were "the stopping of all forms of federal support to agricultural enterprises located in the territories of the corresponding subjects," and "ceasing to send food and agricultural products from the federal funds."[43] In early 1994, a government resolution attempted to stimulate sales to the federal food fund by offering monetary advances of "not less than 50 percent of the value of these products" to food producers. Advances were to be paid "not less than 30 days from the moment the contract was signed."[44] In reality, advances were seldom offered because the government lacked the money to implement this policy.

The lack of enforcement of state purchase price policy during the Yeltsin period was indicative of the low priority placed upon agriculture by the president. More generally, the lack of enforcement was symptomatic of Yeltsin's "weak state" and lack of desire to follow through on legislation. For example, in 1994 the Federal Food Corporation (FCC) was created and was charged with regulation of the food market through purchase intervention. However, the funds that were allocated—several billion rubles—disappeared and were never accounted for, and the FCC was abolished amidst scandal. In 1997, a successor organization was created with the same goals, called the Federal Agency for the Regulation of the Food Market. A government resolution of July 10, 1998, established procedures for purchase intervention, but those procedures were never put into practice and the resolution was abolished.[45] The situation regarding state intervention changed when Vladimir Putin became president in 2000. During the early period of Putin's rule, the political will to intervene in food policy rose, as shown by state intervention in the domestic grain market.[46]

The background to federal government intervention in the domestic grain market was a very good grain harvest in 2001 (85 million tons, up from 65 million tons in 2000). In addition to a good harvest, a number of other factors contributed to the need for state intervention. Those factors included a domestic grain market in which higher demand did not necessarily lead to higher purchase prices, and limited export capacity: a shortage of ships, storage, and adequate ports constrained exporters' ability to ship abroad. Even though Russia exported more than three million tons of grain in 2001, the "surplus" grain depressed domestic grain prices. As a result the federal government intervened in order to help prop up wholesale prices and to benefit producers.

Based upon optimistic forecasts for a good harvest, the 2001 budget had allocated two billion rubles for purchase price intervention.[47] However, as news about the size of the harvest came in, it became evident that the original allocation would be insufficient, and by late September Minister of Agriculture Gordeev revealed that Putin had approved an increase in this sum so that "the state may more actively influence the situation in the grain market."[48] In November 2001, a government resolution established a range in purchase prices for state intervention, from a minimum of 2,300 rubles per ton for class 3 soft wheat up to a maximum of 2,700 rubles per ton for class 3 soft wheat.[49] It is interesting to note that purchase intervention reflected not only the attempt by the government to influence domestic wholesale prices, but also signaled the reintroduction of minimum purchase prices that had been in place, at least in theory, since the mid-1990s. However, as state purchases of grain decreased, the practice of establishing minimum purchase prices for grain sold to the state had gone by the wayside. In 2000, for example, the state purchased only 15 percent of domestic grain, and therefore for 2001 the government had not originally even established minimum purchase prices.[50]

The method of state intervention used under Putin was purchase price support, as practiced in the West. This meant that if average purchase prices fell below a defined minimal level, the state would offer a higher purchase price, and purchase grain in order to support the purchase price level. The intent was to offer better prices to producers and to use "the market" to ease some of the oversupply of grain available to other purchasers. The intervention was conducted through three purchasing channels: through commodity exchanges, through the state purchasing agent Federal Agency for the Regulation of the Food Market, and through fifteen grain elevators located in eight regions of Russia.[51] The purchase intervention would continue until either "market" purchase prices reached the minimum level or until the funds allocated to intervention were expended.[52] Eventually, the government expended more than five billion rubles to purchase grain on the domestic market during the 2001-2002 agricultural year.

State purchase intervention came under sharp criticism from several sides. Liberals decried the reentry of the state into the domestic food market. The motives of the intervention were doubted, raising questions as to who really benefited. Given the lack of specificity about the purchase procedure, concerns about corruption were raised.[53] Some criticized the plan as offering prices that were too low compared to average domestic prices and world prices for wheat.[54] Still others stated that the allocated sums were simply too small to have much of an effect.[55]

In 2002, with a harvest of 86 million tons, state price intervention again was again provided in the domestic grain market. The procedure was much the same as in 2001, except on a broader scale. For example, this time more grain elevators were involved, 138.[56] In November 2002, seven commodity exchanges were licensed for the state purchases, and these were listed on the website of the Ministry of Agriculture.[57] Intervention began on November 13, and the first transactions for rye occurred on November 20. The government established the following prices: 2,300 rubles per ton for class 3 soft wheat, 1,800 rubles per ton for class 4 soft wheat, and 1,400 rubles per ton for group A rye; these prices were inclusive of delivery to the elevators, reception, thrashing, drying, and insurance. Further, the state issued regulations for price protection for services and commodities from natural monopolies.[58] During fall 2002/winter 2003 "up to six billion rubles for financing state purchase intervention" were allocated by the Russian government.[59] An analysis of purchase intervention showed that it had an effect on prices, as purchase prices were set 10-30 percent higher than average purchase prices in several regions. The option to accept state purchase prices was more popular to the east of the Urals and in Siberia, where low demand led to grain surpluses, where few opportunities for exports exist, and where domestic regional barriers for the export of food are highest.[60]

This example of state purchase intervention in the grain market is indicative of a willingness to use state levers to improve the financial condition of domestic producers. It is interesting to note that the government was willing to trade off higher purchase prices at the expense to the consumer, who saw retail prices for bread and bread products increase as a result of purchase intervention.

Moreover, state intervention following the 2001 and 2002 harvests was not an anomaly. In early 2004, a draft law entitled "On Regulation of Agriculture and the Agrofood Market in 2005-2007" was circulating in Moscow.[61] The draft law, with 33 separate articles, envisioned a wide range of state support for various producers and purposes during 2005-2007. Among the provisions is Article 17, "The State Program of Regulating the Grain Market." This article, which spans some eighteen subpoints, lays out the basis for future purchase price intervention in the event that the average monthly market price falls below the minimum guaranteed prices offered by the state. The draft specifies minimum and maximum purchase prices, and allows for price variation by 15 percent either up or down from indicated levels according to market conditions. In the event of state purchases exceeding ten million tons, the government may allow grain exports from the intervention fund. Thus, it appears that state intervention in the form of price supports, at least for grain, will continue to be a characteristic of Russian agriculture as long as Putin is president.

Food Consumers: Change in Retail Price Policy

Having examined state procurement policy and changes in the procurement price system, this section turns to a third dimension of domestic food policy, retail prices. For decades the Soviet consumer experienced either no or very low inflation in food prices, a deliberate policy pursued by the state to ensure political tranquility. The consequences of that policy were chronic shortages, long lines, and high subsidies. The introduction of retail price liberalization in January 1992 signified the removal of the central government from direct consumption subsidies. For the first time consumers in Russia were exposed to market forces, even if at times the market was distorted by various machinations.[62]

Through price liberalization, Russian food consumers experienced "sticker shock." Although food price increases lagged inflation in the economy at large and the cost of industrial products in particular (see table 3.3), retail food prices increased an average of 5 percent a week throughout 1992, and about 3 percent a week during 1993. Overall, during the early reform period a monthly basket of nineteen basic food items rose in price from 1,500 rubles during January-February 1992 to 48,500 rubles in May 1994. The relationship between increases in monetary income and the price of a basket of food goods during the decade of reform is shown in table 3.4. It should be noted that the data for retail food prices is an index using a consumer basket of nineteen common food goods that the government estimates represents buying patterns of a typical Russian family.

The consequences of retail price liberalization were considered in chapter 1, showing a general trend in which individuals ate less, changed the structure of their consumption, and spent more on food. There were variations, of course, by place of residence (urban/rural), region, and size of family. By the end of the 1990s, according to official statistics, the urban consumer ate a bit more than the average rural dweller, southern regions had higher consumption levels, and large families ate significantly less per capita than families with fewer children.[63] Under Putin there has occurred an increase in per capita consumption, although consumption has yet to reach pre-reform levels. Despite skyrocketing prices and reduced consumption, the feared—and widely predicted—political turmoil did not occur over the price of food. Why?

There are two reasons that explain the tolerance of the Russian consumer for higher prices. First, the food supply has improved, and improved most notably in small and middle-sized cities. The Soviet "food problem" always was less in Moscow or Leningrad—those cities received preferential status in the food system dating from the Stalin period. The critical problem was the almost complete absence of food in state stores in second- and third-echelon cities. It is precisely the Russian consumer in medium cities and small towns who can see a significant difference from the pre-reform period. Granted, the selection and quality may not be as high as in large cities, and certainly Westerners would not

Table 3.4. Relationship between Increases in Monetary Income and Retail Food Prices, 1992-2002

	1992	1993	1994	1995	1996	1997	1998	1999	2000	2001	2002
Monetary Income	53	16	12	-16	1	6	-16	-13	11	10	10
Food Goods Price Index	2,630	900	310	220	18	9	96	36	18	17	11

Data are for percentage increases from December to December.

Sources: *Rossiiskii statisticheskii ezhegodnik* (Moscow: Goskomstat, 2001), 171, 587; *Rossiiskii statisticheskii ezhegodnik* (Moscow: Goskomstat, 2003), 169, 616.

be impressed, but for Russian consumers the improvement is real and tangible. The basic criterion today for the consumer is no longer what can be found to buy, but whether the product fits into the family budget.

The second reason is closely related, but more psychological, less tangible, and has been repeated to the author many times in conversations with Russians. For years in Soviet Russia, even if a person was successful, there was little to buy—a basic disincentive to work hard. In post-Soviet Russia, the situation is reversed. The shelves are full of goods, but prices are often prohibitive for the average Russian. Psychologically, however, there is the prospect of attaining those desired goods through hard work, savings, and perhaps some luck. Thus, in two important respects, retail price reform has given hope and optimism, even in the face of present difficulties. Present supply conditions are better than what they were, and for the future, there is the hope that conditions will improve further.

Moreover, it is important to note that despite price liberalization the consumer was not entirely without social protection.[64] In post-communist Russia social protections are directed at specific segments of the population and are not available to the population at large as state policy. Two main sources of consumer protection continue to exist. The first source of consumer protection is the local or regional administration which uses limits on prices. For example, in January 1992, various attempts were made by officials in Kostroma oblast to protect consumers from the full effects of price liberalization. From July 1992 to July 1993, the Kostroma oblast soviet (later renamed "administration") imposed ceilings on price markups that wholesalers and retailers could pass on to consumers. These limits were reintroduced in July 1994 but rescinded again in 1995.

This practice of ceilings on price markups extended well beyond Kostroma oblast. Limits on wholesale price markups for flour existed in the Republic of Karelia in 2000, as well as ceilings on profit margins for bread and grain products. The disastrous harvest of 1998 and collapse of the ruble dramatically showed how food remained a politically sensitive issue. In autumn 1998, city and regional administrations acted to regulate retail prices. Immediately after the collapse of the ruble in August 1998, several oblasts, krais, and cities announced steps to protect consumers from skyrocketing retail food prices. For example, Primorskii krai, Saratov oblast, Kemerovo oblast, and Kursk oblast announced that price increases would be "forbidden" and created price control departments to oversee this edict. Individual cities also took action: limits on retail price increases were established in Nizhnii Novgorod, Ekaterinburg, St. Petersburg, and even Moscow.[65] Even in 2000, about one-half of all of Russia's regions regulated the price of bread, and many regions placed controls on primary food products such as milk, flour, and bread.[66]

Oblast and city administrations also have special programs to help pensioners and low-income families. In the city of Kostroma, this program is administered by the city department for the social defense of the population during the 1990s. Since 1992, monetary resources from the oblast budget have been allocated to low-income families, invalids, the chronically sick, orphans and children of soldiers, and pensioners. These funds are not large and are limited by budget constraints, but they do indicate an effort to assist the very poorest.[67] The monies are used to subsidize food purchases of animal husbandry products. In addition, the city rents land from landowners or large farms and distributes it to pensioners and low-income families to allow them to grow potatoes that will supplement their diet. In the 1990s, the city also offered advantageous terms for pensioners who wished to purchase municipal land for agricultural purposes.[68] Other oblasts, such as Ulianovsk and Belgorod, maintained retail price subsidies for their populations which resulted in lower food prices than in other regions during the 1990s.

A second source of protection in the form of subsidized food comes from the place of employment, as during the Soviet period. Interviews with managers of agricultural enterprises in Rostov oblast revealed that lunch meals are provided at extremely low cost to farm members and that employees are able to purchase food products "at cost." In the city of Kostroma, food processors provide advantages in the form of subsidized food sales to employees at enterprise stores, either attached or separate from the processing plant. For example, in the mid-1990s employees at the Kostroma milk factory were able to purchase the plant's products at a 1 percent markup over the cost of production, and the meat plant allowed its employees to purchase its products at a 5 percent markup.[69] Employees in restaurants are also able to purchase their main meal of the day at a discount. Finally, many retail food stores have a section called *otdel veteranov* where pensioners and war veterans can purchase food at reduced prices. This system has been retained as a social protection measure. Thus, in retail food policy, we see continuity and change, both of which are significant. Consumers are no longer protected by direct federal subsidies of retail food, yet they are not completely exposed to full market prices because of protections offered by local governments and places of employment.

The Rise of Rural Interest Groups

Changes in the procurement price policy, in procurement policy, and in retail food policy were introduced from above, that is, by the Russian government. However, once reforms were in place, they did not operate in a vacuum. A significant change was the fact that the deregulation of domestic procurement policy and the withdrawal of direct federal regulation over the domestic food market gave rise to the creation of various food interest groups. Therefore, what is new to Russia and domestic food policy is the rise of non-governmental interest groups and the attempt by these groups to influence the formation and implementation of domestic food policies. Although some interest groups trace their origins to the Yeltsin period, the basic goals of rural interests often faced either opposition or indifference during the Yeltsin years.

Rural interest groups function in Russia as elsewhere, with defined goals and permanent bureaucratic structures. Some of them have their own websites or other means of communicating with members and dispersing their views. In general, rural interest groups, particularly those that are commodity specific, favor domestic food policies that: (1) facilitate the free trade of food commodities; and (2) limit competition from foreign imports.

Today in Russia there are many rural interest groups. In February 2000, President Putin sent a letter to twenty leaders of organizations and movements that are oriented toward "market development of the countryside."[70] Rural interest groups may be categorized into two different types: (1) broad groups with diverse memberships, combining political orientations with general economic policy preferences, and focusing on improving the general economic environment for its members; and (2) narrow commodity specific that are largely apolitical and which concentrate on influencing policy for that commodity. A summary table of some of the more important groups in these two categories is presented in table 3.5, followed by a more detailed discussion of each group in the sections below.

Table 3.5. Rural Interest Groups, Organizations, and Food Unions

Name of food union	Year created	Name of leader in 2004	Main constituent in APK
Agroindustrial Union	1990	N. Kharitonov	Workers, Processors
Agrarian Party of Russia	1993	V. Plotnikov	Workers
Union of Landowners	1994	V. Bashmachnikov	Landowners
AKKOR	1990	V. Bashmachnikov	Private farmers
Russian Agrarian Movement	2002	A. Gordeev	Workers
Grain Union	1994	A. Zlochevskii	Processors
Union of Sugar Producers	1996	L. Nesterenko	Processors
Poultry Union	2001	V. Fisinin	Processors
Meat Union	1998	I. Rogov	Processors
Dairy Union	1999	V. Kharitonov	Processors

Broad Groups

• The Agroindustrial Union.[71] This organization was formed in April 1990 and is second only to AKKOR in duration of operation. In 2004 its leader was Nikolai Kharitonov, who succeeded the longtime leader of the union, Vasilii Starodubtsev.[72] The influence of the union is suggested by the fact that its main office is located in the Ministry of Agriculture. The political orientation of the Agroindustrial Union is leftist, and the union often works in concert with the Agrarian Party of Russia and the Trade Union of Workers in the APK in order to organize protests against the government's rural policies, to publish policy statements, or to publish open letters addressed to the president.[73]

The union is said to represent some fourteen million workers in both agricultural production and processing. The goal of the present union is "to unite all producers of goods, employed in the sphere of agricultural-industrial production and related branches, independent of which party, union, or organization to which they belong."[74] Today, the Agroindustrial Union is a spokesgroup for higher state expenditures in the agroindustrial complex, social development of the countryside, state regulation of certain aspects of the rural economy, and protection of domestic producers from foreign competition.[75]

• The Agrarian Party of Russia.[76] Perhaps the best known rural interest group is actually a political party, the Agrarian Party of Russia, or APR.[77] The party had been headed by Mikhail Lapshin since its founding, although as the party has faltered at the polls his leadership was increasingly assailed.[78] The criticism became especially harsh in the run-up to the APR's 12th Party Congress in May 2004. At the 12th Party Congress Lapshin was replaced as chairman of the party by Vladimir Plotnikov, who was the chairman of the Committee on Agrarian Questions in the State Duma during 1999-2003.[79] In the present Duma (2003-2007) he is the deputy chairman of that committee.

The Agrarian Party held its first meeting in Nizhnii Novgorod in December 1992. Its founding congress was held in February 1993, and since its inception the APR has held regular congresses. Party membership was highest in the early 1990s, increasing from around 100,000 in late 1993 to an estimated 300,000 members by mid-1995, before dropping to 60,000 in 2002.[80] During the first half of the 1990s the party published its own newspaper called *Zemlia i trud*, but this paper stopped publication after 1995. In April 1996, a new newspaper, called *Rossiiskaia zemlia*, was registered and is published on a weekly basis.

The Agrarian Party primarily represents state and collective farm interests and food processing workers in the agroindustrial complex, even though the party claims to represent all rural dwellers and workers, including private farmers. Instead of lobbying for specific commodity support, the APR attempts to improve the financial and social condition of the rural sector through policy positions that are more protectionist of domestic producers, more regulatory to protect domestic producers from price disparities, and less market oriented in general. Thus, the APR attempts to influence policy for improving the general production environment and the social sphere in the countryside.

The Agrarian Party is explicitly against the "uncontrolled" sale and purchase of agricultural land, against the return of land to former owners, against landlessness of the peasantry, and against foreign ownership of land by foreign individuals or businesses. Its party program proceeds from the principle "that land first and foremost is for those who work it." Further, "the party is against the rise of large private land owners—so called latifundia."[81]

• Union of Landowners. At the liberal end of the political spectrum, a smaller group that represents mainly private farmers and small landowners is called the Union of Landowners. This organization was created in December 1994. Similar to the APR, the Union of Landowners attempts to improve production, trade, and social conditions for private landowners of all types (private farmers and small individual land users). The Union of Landowners is an organization that was created out of a larger organization, the Association of Peasant Farmers and Agricultural Cooperatives of Russia (AKKOR). One might argue that the Union of Landowners is basically the political wing of AKKOR.[82] Taken together, these two organizations have political and economic functions, although separately the Union of Landowners is more political and AKKOR is more economic.

• The Association of Peasant Farmers and Agricultural Cooperatives of Russia (AKKOR).[83] The private farming movement in Russia began in 1989 in accordance with the federal law on cooperatives and private entrepreneurial activities. In January 1990, AKKOR was created, and in that same month its first congress was held in which 314 delegates from 57 regions of the USSR attended. From the beginning AKKOR's president has been Vladimir Bashmachnikov. In 2004, the vice president was Andrei Morozov. Following the founding congress, regional and raion associations were created and began to operate in the first half of 1991.[84] Thus, by the beginning of 1992 AKKOR had a three-tiered structure: federal, regional, and raion. In 2004, AKKOR had farmers' associations in 56 regions of Russia and more than 500 raions. AKKOR holds annual congresses each year, the latest being its 15th Congress held in February 2004. AKKOR publishes a monthly press bulletin with information about developments in the private farming movement, speeches, news about AKKOR, results of conferences, congresses, etc. The press bulletin is called *Fermerskoe samoupravlenie* and is distributed to regional AKKOR associations, the administration of the president of Russia, and offices of presidential appointees in federal okrugs, leading members in the Ministry of Agriculture, leading members of other economic ministries, and deputies of the State Duma.

From the beginning, AKKOR became the primary rural supporter of reform policies. Already in the fall of 1990 it "actively participated in working out strategies" for several landmark pieces of early reform legislation, for example the 1990 laws "On Land Reform" and "On Peasant Farming." Thus, during the early 1990s AKKOR was the only rural interest group to explicitly advocate and support land privatization, land distribution from large farms, and the development of a strong private farming stratum. In return for this symbiotic relationship with reformers in Moscow, when the "Russian Farmer" program was introduced in 1992, state monies and credits were channeled through local branches of AKKOR offices with the goal to expand the private farmer movement and increase the number of private farms.[85] This program was initially successful, leading to a substantial increase in private farms during 1992-1993, during which time more than 220,000 private farms were created, reaching a total number of 270,000 private farms by January 1994.[86] However, there were abuses in the distribution of money, and toward the end of 1994 the program was terminated.[87]

More broadly, it may be argued that AKKOR has not been very successful in obtaining financial resources for its constituents. In 1993, the average private farm received about $100 of state support, rising to only $179 in 2001. Importantly, since 1996 a separate budget line in the federal budget has not existed for direct subsidies to private farmers, and their primary source of support comes from regional budgets. Private farmers are eligible for federal programs such as the leasing program that allows rural producers of all types to lease agricultural machinery with the state covering some of the costs. However, this leasing program is not specifically directed at private farmers. As a consequence, private farms remain undercapitalized and in need of mechanization, although larger private farms are much better equipped than smaller farms.[88]

Today, AKKOR is the primary spokesgroup for improving the production and social spheres of private farming, for protecting their economic interests, for increasing state support to private farmers, and for the development of market relations in the countryside.[89] It speaks on behalf of 263,886 private farms that existed in January 2004. Through successful lobbying, AKKOR was able to establish budgetary quotas in regional budgets to subsidize the interest rate for loans obtained through commercial banks. These budgetary quotas went into effect for the first time in 2002, but were fully used in only thirty regions.[90] At the 14th Congress of AKKOR, held in February 2003, it was noted that many farmers find it difficult to actually receive this form of state support. In 2003, only 1,000 private farmers were able to receive state loans; and only 1,000 obtained crop insurance.[91] In general, AKKOR's lobbying strength is weak at both the federal and regional levels. In May 2004, only eight people work in the apparatus at the federal level, and regional offices are usually staffed by one to ten persons, with considerable variance.

Nonetheless, AKKOR is a firm supporter of Putin, as indicated in the materials at its 15th Congress. For this reason its fortunes might be improving. Article 16 of the 2004 draft law "On Regulation of Agriculture" envisions fifteen year loans to private farmers for obtaining livestock, equipment, and machinery, and for purchasing, constructing, or repairing farm buildings. Moreover, the draft law suggests federal budget allocations of 1 billion rubles in 2005 and 1.2 billion rubles in 2006.[92]

• Russian Agrarian Movement (*Rossiiskoe agrarnoe dvizhenie*), or RAD. This is the most recently created broad rural interest group.[93] RAD held its founding congress in May 2002, electing Minister of Agriculture Aleksei Gordeev as its chairman.[94] Its vice chairman is Valentin Denisov, who is also a member of the Duma Committee on Agrarian Questions. Unlike the APR or AKKOR, RAD has direct access to policymakers, indicated by the fact that Denisov is a member of the Duma; to President Putin, indicated by his meeting with leaders of RAD following its opening congress; and by the fact that Gordeev is a member of Putin's cabinet.

In an interview, Denisov described RAD as neither a leftist nor rightist organization, but rather as an organization working "for the unification of all those who contribute their participation and responsibility for the creation of a highly effective agroindustrial complex, for ensuring the food security of the country, for the revival of the countryside, and for the creation of a worthwhile life for the peasantry."[95] Denisov further indicated that RAD was ready to work with other political organizations such as the APR, AKKOR, or the Agroindustrial Union. In a published "declaration" following its founding congress, a general promise was made to the rural sector: "Our organization provides an opportunity for all participants in agrarian production to determine their position on important questions, to carry that position to the leadership, and to begin constructive cooperation."[96]

RAD shares many of the same goals as the organizations surveyed above, differing primarily in the fact that its political orientation is explicitly pro-Kremlin. For example, RAD favors support for domestic producers and their interests in the areas of trade tariffs, finances-credit, and tax policy, encouraging domestic investment in the agrarian economy, reforming land relations, improving social development of the countryside, including rural standards of living, rural employment, and rural educational and health facilities, and promoting integration in the agroindustrial complex.[97]

Whether RAD can be successful in uniting broad agrarian interests, or whether it represents the further splintering of agrarian interests, remains to be seen. On the one hand, with Gordeev as leader, RAD will enjoy access to the Kremlin, and implicitly the organization is the primary intermediary between the government and the countryside by being the mouthpiece for rural interests and in turn supporting state policies. On the other hand, cooperation with other rural interest groups and parties remains problematic, as previously existing organizations are unlikely to be willing to subsume their goals and constituencies to a new organization that claims to unite all agrarian interests—a claim made as well by the APR and the Agroindustrial Union. When RAD was first formed in mid-2002, Lapshin indicated that the APR was ready to cooperate.[98] However, by the end of 2002 signs of discord became evident, as press reports indicated that Lapshin felt his leadership position was threatened by the emergence of RAD.[99]

Commodity-Specific Interest Groups

In Russia today there are more than thirty commodity-specific interest groups. These groups—referred to as unions or associations—attempt to influence policy in support of their commodity, and therefore are more focused in their efforts than are broad rural interest groups. Among the most notable are the Grain Union, Dairy Union, Meat Union, Union of Sugar Producers, Poultry Union, and Union of Exporters of Russian Food Products.

In addition, in April 2000, an "Association of Branch Unions of the APK" was created in an effort to coordinate the activities and jointly defend the interests of these various commodity groups. Viktor Semenov, former minister of agriculture, was elected chairman. Semenov stated that the association was intended to form a constructive agrarian lobby, so that the "voice of agrarian business would be better heard."[100]

Several important, and interesting, aspects should be noted with regard to these commodity specific interest groups. The first is that, in interviews with several union heads, it was repeatedly asserted that unions operate "democratically"; what that may mean in reality is not clear. But more importantly, union heads stressed that their unions were actively consulted by the government concerning the formation of policy and the drafting of legislation. The exact form of participation varies, of course, but ranges from being consulted in the policy/law formation stage to commenting on policy/legislation already drafted. Thus, interviews yielded a strong sense that food unions participate actively in the policy process and are not thrust into a role whereby they react to policies delivered from above without their input.

Second, the fact that there are so many different unions, whose various goals are to protect food producers, food processors, domestic food traders, and food exporters, means that the "agrarian lobby" is in fact fractured along many lines. This fact belies the impression of a monolithic agricultural lobby that resists reform and frustrates policy implementation. Producers have different interests and goals than do processors. Exporters and importers have different interests. Different commodities compete for market share, consumer preferences, and, of course, for state support. Moreover, the fact that so many different agricultural interests exist and compete provides an important impetus to adapt and adjust to market relations. During interviews with union heads I did not have the feeling that unions were attempting to resist reform as much as they were trying to find ways to influence policy and market conditions in a way that was advantageous to them.

Finally, the common assumption of an agrarian lobby, acting as an outside lobby group that exerts strong pressure on policymakers, is not quite accurate. This view suggests a situation in which outside groups (food unions and rural interest groups) attempt to influence insiders (policymakers). The perception of outside actors trying to influence policymakers and the policy process is closer to the American model, whereby interest groups do not have direct representation in governing bodies and therefore try to influence decision-makers through contributions and other forms of lobbying. Interviews with participants in the Russian policy process suggest that instead of an outsiders-insiders policy dynamic, the reality is somewhat different. Instead of an American model of interest groups and group influence, the reality is closer to the German model, whereby relevant interest groups are actively consulted by decision-makers for their expertise and input. Moreover, key members of interest groups may be recruited to serve in government legislative committees. In Russia, it is often the case that heads of unions served in a ministry and maintain contacts there. It is also the case that union officials may have dual membership, one in a governmental capacity of some sort and one in a rural interest group or food union. Thus, the Russian policy process is built upon insider contacts, expertise, and insider influence. In this respect, the differences between the American and Russian models of interest group influence and policy process are fundamentally different.

A brief survey of some of the commodity-specific interest groups is provided below. Unless otherwise noted, the information about these groups was obtained from their websites or from interviews conducted in Moscow by the author during May 2004.

• The Grain Union.[101] The Grain Union is a voluntary noncommercial organization formed in November 1994, which means that it is the oldest of the main food unions, and was created at the initiative of Western advisers for the purpose of breaking the monopoly held at the time by *Roskhleboprodukt.* (*Roskhleboprodukt* subsequently became a member of the union and continued its membership as of May 2004.) Its noncommercial status means that the union is not permitted to buy or sell grain and does not own any grain elevators. In short, it does not engage in market transactions, and its primary funding comes from the dues that members pay. As such, its primary role is as a lobby for grain interests. In May 2004 its president was Arkady Zlochevskii, who was a co-founder of private grain trading company in the mid-1990s and subsequently he worked in the Ministry of Agriculture for a few years. In September 2003 Zlochevskii assumed the position of acting president of the Grain Union, and at the 9th Conference of the Grain Union in November 2003 he was elected president of the Grain Union. Before that, Zlochevskii was the chairman of the board of Directors of the Grain Union. The union's main office is located in Ministry of Agriculture. Approximately twenty persons work in the union's apparatus at the federal level, with one representative in each of the federal okrugs. The union has six departments, or working groups: infrastructure, defensive measures, exports, technological regulation, biotechnology, and the development of commodity exchanges and grain trade.

Membership in the union was about 300 in 2004, in addition to about twenty-five to thirty holding companies. The number of members fluctuates because there is annual turnover as some members leave the union and new members join. Individuals may not be members of the Grain Union; only enterprises, firms, and businesses that are engaged in the purchase, storage, processing, and sale of grain, or legal entities that are engaged in business operations related to the trading of grain, such as commodity exchanges, are eligible to join the union.

In the past the union published a regular insert in *Krest'ianskie vedomosti* several times a year on the status of the grain market and issues relevant to grain trade. Today, members—who pay annual dues—receive weekly information on prices and market conditions sent by e-mail. They also receive a monthly publication called *Vestnik Rossiiskogo zernovogo soiuza*. This publication contains regional data on the grain market, market conditions, prices, and statistics on production, imports, and exports. In addition, members receive free legal advice from on-staff legal consultants, discounted registration fees for exhibitions and conferences, and free advertising in agricultural journals such as *Torgpreg*, *Agrorynok*, or *Agrobiznes*.

The basic goals of the union are to assist in the formation and development of a national grain market in Russia; to create the necessary organizational, economic, legal, and social conditions for interaction among participants in the grain market; to represent and defend the interests of participants in the grain market inside of Russia and in world markets; to assist in the training of skilled professional personnel for participation in the grain market; and to assist in supplying information to participants in the grain market.

The Grain Union has benefited less from direct import quotas or tariffs than other food unions, primarily because grain imports have comprised such a small percentage of the nation's grain supplies—an average of about 3 percent per year since 1994 (with the exception of 1999-2000, when food aid was received—so there has been little reason to erect trade barriers).[102] Recent efforts at influencing policy include protests over limits on imported grain by the European Union (EU), which were not accompanied by reciprocal "defensive" measures by the Russian government on EU meat and meat products imported into Russia[103]; and opposition to tariffs on imported soybeans into Russia.[104]

Moreover, the Grain Union lobbied for an end to export tariffs, which were allowed to expire in May 2004. It also lobbied for and received advantageous rates for the transport of grain from one region of Russia to another. When increases in transportation rates via truck and rail for grain products were introduced, the union protested.[105] The Grain Union and its members also benefit from a range of other indirect support measures which help make Russian grain cost-competitive with foreign imports.

• The Union of Sugar Producers.[106] The Union of Sugar Producers is a voluntary noncommercial organization formed in 1996, which means that it, similar to the Grain Union, is not permitted to buy or sell sugar and does not engage in commercial transactions. In 2004, the chairman was Leonid Nesterenko. In December 2003, union membership consisted of 116 members. The basic goals of the union are to represent and defend the interests of sugar beet growing farms and sugar plants, as well as other participants in the sugar market in legislative and executive bodies; assist in the creation of an effective system of state regulation of the sugar market in Russia; participate in working out the legal basis for the sugar market; and to create a single information system for participants in Russia's sugar market. The union is notable for lobbying for quota restrictions on sugar imports in 1999 and the use of import tariffs on white sugar thereafter.[107] It is a member of the Agroindustrial Union of Russia, and the Union of Food Producers and Food Processing Industry.

• The Poultry Union.[108] The Poultry Union is a voluntary noncommercial organization formed in 2001.[109] In 2004 its president was Vladimir Fisinin, who is also the vice president of the Russian Academy of Sciences.[110] It has its main office located inside the Ministry of Agriculture.

The Poultry Union unites the entire cycle of poultry raising—from the production of feed through the sale of processed poultry products. In 2002 it had more than 200 Russian enterprises and organizations as members, as well as twenty-three foreign firms. Both poultry producers and processors may join the union. The union was created in order to assist in the development of domestic poultry raising; to defend the interests of the poultry sector in legislative and executive bodies; to coordinate the activities of poultry-raising farms; to form production and commercial links to enterprises and organizations that directly influence the development of the poultry sector; and to mobilize the financial resources of members of the union in order to carry out their joint activities in the production, processing, and sale of poultry products. The union is notable for obtaining import quotas on poultry products that were first introduced in 2001.

• The Meat Union.[111] The Meat Union is a voluntary noncommercial organization formed in 1998 on the initiative of the government and of several actors in the domestic meat market, including the Committee on Economic Security of the Meat Market and Meat Products, and the Association of Meat Processors of the Russian Federation. In May 2004 the union's chairman was Iosif A. Rogov, who also serves as rector of the Biotechnology University in Moscow. At the federal level a total of four persons work in the apparatus: the chairman, the executive director, an accountant, and a cashier. The chairman of the union serves without compensation.

As a noncommercial organization, the union neither buys nor sells meat, and does not find buyers abroad for domestically produced meat. In May 2004 the Union had 892 "formal" members, and informally more than 2,000 members. The union represents meat processors, not producers, who have their own union. Members account for 70 percent of the processed meat in Russia, according to Rogov.

The union holds annual conferences, to which foreign heads of processing plants and even ministries are invited, mainly from Europe.[112] In 2002, the union changed its system of dues based upon the value of production. For example, annual production valued at up to 100 million rubles has a membership fee of 500 euro; production from 100-200 million rubles costs 1,000 euro; production from 200-500 million rubles costs 1,500 euro, from 500-1,000 million rubles costs 2,000 euro, and production valued at over 1,000 million rubles costs 3,500 euro annually. Among the unions where interviews were conducted, this was the only union that had a sliding scale of dues based upon production, whereas other unions levied a set fee. For the fee members receive information about health and sanitary standards; for example, in 2004 a main theme was how to avoid mad cow disease. Information is gathered about foreign experiences and technology and disseminated quarterly to members. The union publishes a journal entitled *Vsyo o miase.*

The union has three subcommittees: on the future development of the meat industry, on trade and information, and on animal husbandry and development of raw resources. The union is notable for having advocated restrictions on imported meat and meat products, and then defending those policies once they were announced by the Putin government.

The main goals of the union are to inform processors about and implement better technology and health standards. In other words, the primary task is to assist in the development of meat-processing enterprises, increase the competitiveness of Russian meat products, and to improve their quality through the introduction of modern machinery and the use of highly effective, scientific technology for the processing of raw meat. A second main task is to defend processors by influencing tariff policy.

Other goals include: (a) to assist organs of state power in the implementation of its stated priorities for the development of the national economy and support for producers; (b) to defend the legal rights of producers and consumers during state regulation of production and sale of meat products; (c) to assist in the creation of Russia's food strategy; and (d) to coordinate the activities of members of the union, and to represent and defend their interests in the domestic and world markets.

Membership in the union is open to any corporate entity that participates in or supplies the meat market, and requires the submission of a written application to the chairman of the union, and is subject to the decision by the union's governing council. Upon acceptance, new members enjoy the same rights and responsibilities as founding members. Members have the right to withdraw from the union at the end of a financial year, based upon a written application to the governing council. Members who withdraw are responsible for dues for two years following their withdrawal.

• The Dairy Union.[113] The Dairy Union is a voluntary noncommercial association of milk producers and processors. Its founding congress was held in December 1999 and its registration was completed in August 2000. In May 2004 its president was Vladimir Kharitonov and the chairman of the union's council was Sergei Plastinin. The founders of the union comprised seventeen large milk processors, a series of milk producers, and some leading scientific enterprises in the milk industry. In May 2004 the Union had over 100 members who accounted for about 35 percent of the milk market. The union has four sub-committees: on strategic planning, on integration and cooperation, on the quality and analysis of the milk market and milk products, and on the development of new production technologies.

The basic goal of the Dairy Union is to coordinate the commercial activities of union members, with an eye toward the formation and development of a national market for milk products in Russia. The union also represents and defends the interests of its members in federal and municipal organs of power, in public and other organizations, and in international organizations. The union does not have the right to interfere in the economic plans for development of its members, including questions of production, productive capacity, the sale of milk, or the price of milk. The union is allowed to express its views on the status of the milk market and future forecasts.

Conclusion

The reform of the procurement price system, procurement and marketing policies, and retail food policy were important steps in the transformation of domestic food policy. This chapter showed that during the 1990s the food marketing system was decentralized and liberalized through the elimination of obligatory state orders and a reduction in the level of state procurements. The procurement price system also experienced significant change, with the government today using a price support system to ensure a pricing floor. This price support system was used for the first time during 2001 and 2002 for grain. Policy reform was intended to create a food marketing system that would facilitate the free trade of agricultural products based on prevailing market prices. Several impediments and deformations in the wholesale price system continue to exist, frustrating this policy goal from being realized.

Another significant occurrence in domestic food policy has been the emergence of numerous commodity specific interest groups which represent a potentially powerful voice for domestic free trade and market-based prices. These rural interest groups take an active role in the policy formation and implementation. Several of the commodity-specific groups have been successful in achieving policy protection. The model of lobbying is closer to the German model of peak associations than to the American model of outside groups attempting to influence insider policymakers.

On the whole, state withdrawal from regulation of food procurement facilitated rural change by increasing the range of permissible behaviors. With the liberalization of the food marketing system and the reduction in federal procurements, food producers could choose the channel of food trade they preferred. Thus, not only did policy change, but the effects of policy led to changes in patterns of food trade. These patterns of domestic food trade are explored in the next chapter.

Notes

1. See K. Busultanov, "Sovershenstvovat' sistemu marketinga v otrasliakh APK," *APK: ekonomika, upravlenie*, no. 6 (June 2002): 19-24.
2. During the early period of Russian reform there was a general consensus that distribution problems—broadly defined—constituted a greater obstacle to improving food availability than increases in gross production. See for example, Allan Mustard and Christopher E. Goldthwait, "Food Availability in the Former Soviet Union: A Summary Report of Three Missions Led by the US Department of Agriculture," in Joint Economic Committee, *The Former Soviet Union in Transition*, vol. 2, Joint Committee Print, 103rd Congress, 1st session (Washington, DC: Government Printing Office, 1993), 506-13; and William M. Liefert, "The Food Problem in the Republics of the Former USSR," in Don Van Atta, ed., *The 'Farmer Threat': The Political Economy of Agrarian Reform in Post-Soviet Russia*. (Boulder, CO: Westview Press, 1993), 25-42.
3. Liefert, "The Food Problem in the Republics of the Former USSR," 40.
4. Mustard and Goldthwait, "Food Availability in the Former Soviet Union," 509.
5. Western sources commonly estimate that as much as 30 percent of the harvest is lost annually, which includes losses in the field as well as post-harvest processes. In addition, Russian sources estimated that for a variety of reasons, between 20 and 25 million tons of grain were not harvested in the early 1990s. *Krest'ianskie vedomosti*, no. 18 (9-15 May 1994), 1.
6. Mustard and Goldthwait, "Food Availability in the Former Soviet Union," 509.
7. Unless otherwise noted, the criteria for analyzing domestic food policies are taken from C. Peter Timmer, Walter P. Falcon, and Scott R. Pearson, *Food Policy Analysis* (London and Baltimore: Johns Hopkins University Press for the World Bank, 1983), chap. 4.
8. In one Russian agricultural newspaper, an advertisement published free information on grain prices. Commodity exchanges, state purchasers, private farmers, and private individuals would be able to obtain data on advertised prices for different grain products. The database was to be updated daily and information is available via telephone, fax, or computer from the Russian Company of Commodity Exchange Brokers. "Informatsiia po rynku zerna vesnoi besplatna!" *Krest'ianskie vedomosti*, no. 19 (May 16-22, 1994), 12.
9. Clearly, social goals pursued by governments can distort the price formation process in a market environment, so in part these criteria are theoretical. That is, there is no perfect market. At the same time, these criteria are extremely useful in distinguishing among food systems and in determining if the market is functioning.
10. Food marketing agencies are agents of wholesale food trade and are instrumental actors in food policy. They purchase the raw produce from the farmer, thereby establishing the "market" price for that good in that locale. In turn, these agencies then have a

series of options for use: to resell immediately, to process the product into a form saleable to consumers, or to hold the product and hope for a higher price in the future.

11. "O formirovanii gosudarstvennykh prodovol'stvennykh fondov na 1992 godu," *APK: ekonomika, upravlenie*, no. 4 (April 1992): 3-4. Excluded from the list were private plot farmers, collective gardens and orchards, suburban cooperatives, nonagricultural enterprises, and subsidiary agricultural operations of enterprises and organizations.

12. *Izvestiia*, 28 January 1993, 2.

13. "O formirovanii federal'nykh i regional'nykh prodovol'stvennykh fondov v 1993 godu," *APK: ekonomika, upravlenie*, no. 5 (May 1993): 7-8.

14. The following committees and ministries were defined as state purchasing agents for these products: the Committee on Trade was given responsibility for procuring meat and meat products, milk and milk products, and sugar. The Ministry of Agriculture and Food was responsible for eggs, potatoes, vegetables, and vegetable oil. *Roskhleboprodukt*, previously the state purchase agent for grain but now a joint stock company, was to procure grains and oilseed. The Committee on Fisheries was to procure fish products. In addition, the Ministry of Finance was to form food reserves to supply the regions of Far North and equivalent areas and their localities, and for parts of the cities of Moscow and St. Petersburg. The Ministries of Defense, Internal Affairs, Counterespionage, and Atomic Energy were to form reserves to feed military units and subunits, as well as other sectors dependent on state food such as hospitals and schools.

15. *Sel'skaia zhizn'*, 26 February 1994, 1-2.

16. Data are taken from Stephen K. Wegren, "Neoliberalism and Market Reforms in Rural Russia," in *Dilemmas of Transition in Post-Soviet Countries*, ed. Joel C. Moses (Chicago: Burnham Publishers, 2003), 38.

17. Some of the material on the procurement pricing system and policies is drawn from Stephen K. Wegren, "Building Market Institutions: Agricultural Commodity Exchanges in Post-Communist Russia," *Communist and Post-Communist Studies*, 27, no. 3 (1994): 195-224; and Stephen K. Wegren, "From Farm to Table: The Food System in Post-Communist Russia," *Communist Economics and Economic Transformation*, 8, no. 2 (1996): 149-183.

18. *Rossiiskii fermer*, 3-9 January 1995, 3.

19. I. Glazunova, "Regulirovanie tsen v APK," *Ekonomist*, no. 2 (February 2001): 87.

20. Even had the system been enforced (or fully funded), we should note that as less food was sold to procurement organizations, state-defined minimum purchase prices were applied to smaller percentages of domestic production.

21. "O gosudarstvennom regulirovanii agropromyshlennogo proizvodstva," *Sobranie zakonodatel'stva Rossiiskoi Federatsii*, no. 29 (21 July 1997): 5689-5698.

22. Resolution no. 295, issued March 16, 1999, reprinted in *Ekonomika sel'skokhoziaistvennykh i pererabatyvaiushchikh predpriiatii*, no. 5 (May 1999): 28.

23. *Sel'skaia zhizn'*, 11 July 2000,1, 3.

24. A. I. Altukhov, "Sostoianie i perspektivy zernovogo proizvodstva i rynka zerna v Rossiiskoi Federatsii," *Agrarnaia Rossiia*, no. 1 (2000): 8.

25. See Stephen K. Wegren, "The Russian Food Problem: Domestic and Foreign Consequences," *Problems of Post-Communism*, 47, no. 1 (January-February 2000): 38-48; and Glazunova, "Regulirovanie tsen v APK," 88.

26. D. S. Bylatov, "Gosudarstvennoe regulirovanie vneshnei torgovli zernom," *Agrarnaia Rossiia*, no. 1 (2000): 39.

27. *Sel'skaia zhizn'*, 28 November 2000, 2.

28. E. Kiseleva, "Rynok zhivotnovodcheskoi produktsii v 1991-1997 g.", *APK: ekonomika, upravlenie*, no. 3 (March 1999): 53.

29. Export prices are a close approximation of world market prices. Contemporary price data show that Russian farms are not being paid world market prices, and there is often a significant gap between domestic purchase prices and export prices.

30. See I. A. Glazunova and N. S. Romanova, "Marketingovaia informatsiia v agropromyshlennom komplekse," *Ekonomist*, no. 9 (September 2000): 81-83; and for a description of the program, its goals and functions, see www.aris.ru/WIN_E/ARIS/3/ (6 April 2000).

31. I. A. Glazunova and N. S. Romanova, "Sozdanie sistemy informatsii o rynke v agropromyshlennom komplekse," *Ekonomika sel'skokhoziaistvennykh i pererabatyvaiushchikh predpriiatii*, no. 8 (August 1998): 22-24.

32. Information is gathered by "reporters" who obtain information "voluntarily" over the telephone, at wholesale markets, at collective farm markets, and at stores. The information is forwarded by computer where available, or by fax.

33. Information from Christian Foster, Foreign Agricultural Service, U.S. Government, 17 October 2000.

34. Glazunova, "Regulirovanie tsen v APK," 86-87.

35. Moscow Television, 15 August 1992, translated in Foreign Broadcast Information Service, *Daily Report: Central Eurasia*, 17 August 1992, 11.

36. For example, the government promised to pay farms for the "Harvest '90" and "Harvest '91" experiments which had promised to pay farms hard currency for above-quota deliveries, and that farms would also receive some 600 billion in credits in order to complete the harvest, and would receive compensation for fuels.

37. The law was called "Zakon o zerne," *Rossiiskaia gazeta*, 29 May 1993, 13.

38. "Zakon o zerne," *Rossiiskaia gazeta*, 29 May 1993, 13.

39. "Zakon o zerne," section 3, articles 6-11.

40. Negotiations over grain prices were held between the government and agrarian representatives in mid-July 1993, with no result. A week later, the Agrarian Union officially presented a demand to Prime Minister Viktor Chernomyrdin and Vice Premier Aleksandr Zaveriukha to establish the state price at 110,000 rubles per metric ton. *Izvestiia*, 22 July 1993, 1. One day later, the government raised the starting price for class 3 soft grain to 60,000 rubles per ton, and purchase prices became indexed against the monthly inflation rate. *Izvestiia*, 23 July 1993, 1.

41. *Sel'skaia zhizn'*, 28 December 1993, 1.

42. *Sel'skaia zhizn'*, 28 December 1993, 1.

43. *Sel'skaia zhizn'*, 28 December 1993, 1.

44. *Sel'skaia zhizn'*, 26 February 1994, 1-2.

45. N. Borkhunov, "Zakupochnye interventsii na rynke zerna," *APK: ekonomika, upravlenie*, no. 2 (February 2002): 40-41.

46. See for example *Krest'ianskaia rossiia*, no. 2 (15-21 January 2001), 2. The article is entitled "The Government is Returning to the Grain Market" and talks about state intervention in the grain market. Among other things, guaranteed purchases are discussed.

47. *Krest'ianskaia rossiia*, no. 41 (15-21 October 2001), 2.

48. *Krest'ianskaia rossiia*, no. 38 (24-30 September 2001), 2.

49. "O povedenii v gosudarstvennykh zakupochnykh i tovernykh interventsii na rynke sel'skokhoziaistvennoi produktsii syr'ia i prodovol'stviia," *Sobranie zakonodatel'stva Rossiiskoi Federatsii*, no. 45 (5 November 2001): 9435-9436.

50. Borkhunov, "Zakupochnye interventsii na rynke zerna," 41.

51. *Krest'ianskie vedomosti*, nos. 31-32 (16-31 August 2001), 2.

52. *Krest'ianskie vedomosti*, nos. 35-36 (16-30 September 2001), 2.

53. Borkhunov, "Zakupochnye interventsii na rynke zerna," 43.

54. *Krest'ianskie vedomosti*, nos. 39-40 (16-22 October 2001), 8.
55. *Krest'ianskie vedomosti*, nos. 39-40 (16-22 October 2001), 2.
56. *Krest'ianskie vedomosti*, nos. 1-2 (1-31 January 2003), 2-3.
57. See www.agronews.ru (1 May 2003).
58. "O povedenii v 2002-2003 godakh gosudarstvennykh zakupochnykh interventsii dlia regulirovaniia rynka zerna," *Sobranie zakonodatel'stva Rossiiskoi Federatsii*, no. 42 (21 October 2002): 10013-14.
59. "O povedenii v 2002-2003 godakh gosudarstvennykh zakupochnykh interventsiy dlia regulirovaniia rynka zerna," 10013.
60. See the analysis by E. Serova in the analytical center called Agroprodovol'stvennoi Ekonomiki, "Zernovye interventsii 2002," *Biulleten'* no. 4 (October-December 2002), available at www.iet.ru/afe/bulletin.html (10 July 2003).
61. "O regulirovanii sel'skogo khoziaistva i agroprodovol'stvennogo rynka v 2005-2007 godakh." I thank Allan Mustard, agricultural minister-counselor, in the U.S. Embassy in Moscow, for making this draft law available to me.
62. Early reports in 1992 and 1993 indicated that sometimes large farms withheld food from sale in order to drive up prices, and newspaper articles alleged that food deliveries remained on trains and would not be unloaded.
63. *Potreblenie produktov pitaniia v domashnikh khoziaistvakh v 1999-2000 gg.* (Moscow: Goskomstat, 2001), 11-34.
64. Some of the material in this section is drawn from Wegren, "From Farm to Table: The Food System in Post-Communist Russia," 173.
65. *Kommersant'*, 20 August 1998, 3; and *New York Times*, 23 September 1998, A1, 10.
66. I. Glazunova, "Tsovye aspekty gosudarstvennogo regulirovaniia ekonomiki APK," *APK: ekonomika, upravlenie*, no. 1 (January 2001): 37.
67. In 1995, this budget line equaled only about 1 percent of total oblast expenditures. *Kostromskoi krai*, 31 January 1995, 2; *Kostromskoi krai*, 7 February 1995, 3; *Kostromskoi krai*, 4 March 1995, 2; and *Kostromskoi krai*, 2 June 1995, 1.
68. Interview, Committee on the Agroindustrial Complex in the city of Kostroma, 21 July 1995.
69. It was interesting to note that processing enterprises in the city of Kostroma also continued such Soviet-era practices as providing housing for its employees. In fact the milk factory had used its "dividends" in 1994 to build new, larger apartments for its workers. Another continuation was busing employees to a processing plant, something that was necessary since many processing plants were located in relatively remote sections of the city (industrial zoning) where public transportation was infrequent and irregular.
70. *Krest'ianskie vedomosti*, no. 6 (7-13 February 2000), 2.
71. The Agroindustrial Union's website is: www.catalog.aris.ru/ROS.INF/AGROSZ/.
72. *Sel'skaia zhizn'*, 17-23 July 2003, 2.
73. See, for example, *Sel'skaia zhizn'*, 23-39 November 2000, 1-2; and *Sel'skaia zhizn'*, 23-29 May 2002, 4. Trade Union of Workers in the APK is led by Aleksandr Davydov and concentrates its efforts on the interests of food processors and employees in the food-processing sector.
74. See www.catalog.aris.ru/ROS.INF/AGROSZ/ (22 December 2003).
75. See V. I. Naumov, "Rosagropromsoiuz zashchishchaet interesy tovaroproizvoditelei APK," *Ekonomika sel'skokhoziaistvennykh i pererabatyvaiushchikh predpriiatii*, no. 2 (February 2000): 10-12; and *Sel'skaia zhizn,'* 25 March 2003, 1.
76. The APR's website is: www.agroparty.ru.
77. For an analysis of the APR's political fortunes, see Stephen K. Wegren, "The Demise of the Agrarian Party of Russia," *Radio Free Europe/Radio Liberty Russian Political*

Weekly, 3, no. 47 (27 November 2003), available at www.rferl.org.rpw.archives.asp (20 December 2003).

78. In the Duma elections of December 1993, the APR crossed the 5 percent threshold for party list seats (8 percent), and in total won 45 seats. In December 1995, the APR failed to reach the 5 percent threshold (3.7 percent), but did win 17 single mandate districts, and together with Communist candidates created a faction in the Duma. In December 1999, the APR did not run independently, but rather combined its forces with the party Fatherland-All Russia. In December 2003, the APR ran independently but received only 3.6 percent of the vote for party list seats, and won only 2 single mandate district seats.

79. See *Rossiiskaia zemlia*, no. 17-18 (May 2004), 1.

80. *Krest'ianskaia rossiia*, no. 28 (24-30 July 1995), 2; and www.rferl.org/specials/russian/election/parties/agrarian.asp. (20 December 2003).

81. The APR's program may be found at www.agroparty.ru, following the link to the party program.

82. Further information may be found in Stephen K. Wegren, *Agriculture and the State in Soviet and Post-Soviet Russia* (Pittsburgh: University of Pittsburgh Press, 1998), 222-23.

83. AKKOR's website is: akkor.ru.

84. *Fermerskoe samoupravlenie press-biulleten'*, no. 3 (March 2004): 7.

85. See Wegren, *Agriculture and the State in Soviet and Post-Soviet Russia*, 191-93.

86. V. D. Smirnov, *Fermerstvo v Rossii: chto eto takoe* (Novosibirsk: Russian Academy of Sciences, 2003), 11.

87. Wegren, *Agriculture and the State in Soviet and Post-Soviet Russia*, 193-94.

88. Smirnov, *Fermerstvo v Rossii: chto eto takoe*, 38-39.

89. See the summary of AKKOR's 14th Congress in *Sel'skaia zhizn'*, 4 March 2003, 1.

90. V. I. Kudriashov and M. P. Kozlov, "Integratsiia krest'ianskikh (fermerskikh) khoziaistv v sistemu mnogoukladnoi ekonomiki APK," *Ekonomika sel'skokhoziaistvennykh i pererabatyvaiushchikh predpriiatii*, no. 9 (September 2003): 44.

91. United States' funding initiated insurance for private farming.

92. Draft law, "O regulirovanii sel'skogo khoziaistva." I thank Allan Mustard for making this draft law available to me.

93. This discussion of RAD draws from Stephen K. Wegren, "Putin and Agriculture," in *Putin's Russia: Past Imperfect, Future Uncertain*, 2d ed., ed. Dale R. Herspring (Lanham, MD: Rowman and Littlefield, 2004).

94. See the interview with Gordeev on the creation of RAD in *Sel'skaia zhizn'*, 25-31 July 2002, 3.

95. *Krest'ianskie vedomosti*, nos. 31-32 (23-29 September 23-2002), 7.

96. *Sel'skaia zhizn'*, 14-19 June 2002, 3.

97. *Sel'skaia zhizn'*, 14-19 June 2002, 3.

98. *Krest'ianskie vedomosti*, nos. 25-26 (21-30 June 2002), 2.

99. *Krest'ianskie vedomosti*, (4 November-15 December 15 2002), 2.

100. *Krest'ianskie vedomosti*, no. 17 (24-30 April 2000), 2.

101. The Grain Union's website is: www.catalog.aris.ru/ROS/INF/z_souz1.html.

102. I. Terent'ev, "Sostoianie i perspektivy APK," *Ekonomist*, no. 4 (April 2000): 87, 90.

103. *Krest'ianskie vedomosti*, nos. 39-40 (15-31 December 2002), 2. This protest was in the form of a letter to President Putin.

104. *Sel'skaia zhizn'*, 11 February 2003, 1. The opposition was based on the fact that imported soy does not "negatively effect" domestic production, which is insufficient to meet demand. This opposition was joined by *Roskhleboprodukt*.

105. *Krest'ianskie vedomosti*, no. 3 (17-23 January 2000), 2; and *Krest'ianskie vedomosti*, nos. 15-16 (11-20 April 2002), 3.

106. The Sugar Union's website is: www.rossahar.ru/scdp/page.
107. N. S. Dem'ianov, "Rossiiskii rynok sakhara v 2000-2001 godu," _Ekonomika sel'skokhoziaistvennykh i pererabatyvaiushchikh predpriiatii_, no. 10 (October 2001): 48.
108. The Poultry Union's website is: www.rps.ru.
109. _Sel'skaia zhizn'_, 17-23 May 2001, 2; and "Rosptitsesoiuz—novoe ob'edinenie ptitsevodov Rossii," _Ekonomika sel'skokhoziaistvennykh i pererabatyvaiushchikh predpriiatii_, no. 11 (November 2002): 54.
110. Information from Allan Mustard and Valeri Patsiorkovski, May 2004.
111. The Meat Union's website is: www.meat-union.ru.
112. Rogov noted that invitations for participation from the United States usually went unanswered. Interview by author, 27 May 2004.
113. The Dairy Union's website is: www.dairyunion.ru.

Chapter Four

Domestic Food Trade in Post-Soviet Russia

The previous chapter examined different aspects of domestic food policy, and showed that core elements in Russia's domestic food policies changed in a number of ways from the policies that were pursued in the Soviet Union. Procurement and marketing policies have been liberalized, food producers have more marketing choices, and state procurements capture a much smaller percentage of raw food products than previously. Retail food prices have been decontrolled, exposing the Russian consumer to the market value of the goods he purchases. Nonstate interest groups have arisen that attempt to influence the formation and implementation of food policy, and thus are a component of an emerging civil society. All of these changes are important and represent significant movement toward a more competitive, market-oriented economy.

This chapter explores the effects of policy changes by examining patterns of domestic food trade. Thus, the focus of attention shifts from policy to effects of policy. Specifically, the chapter examines channels of food trade and the use thereof by different actors. The chapter is divided into the following sections. The first section immediately below examines channels of food trade at the national level for the purpose of providing background information regarding where and how food is traded in post-Soviet Russia. The next section uses survey data to explore channels of food trade at the farm level, using survey data to analyze different independent variables. Within this section, an examination of commodity exchanges is provided, showing that commodity exchanges have not realized the impact and economic influence hoped for at the beginning of reform. The third section surveys how food processors have fared during the reform period, showing that processors remain a dominant outlet for food sold by large farms. The fourth section analyzes channels of food trade at the household level using survey data. The final section offers an examination of some questions and dilemmas arising in food trade as a result of the changes in Russia's procurement system. In particular, restrictions on free domestic trade by the federal government, regional governments, and city administrations are examined.

National Channels of Food Trade

As was shown previously, the Soviet domestic food market was dominated by three main channels of wholesale and retail food trade: (1) state-managed trade through state-owned retail stores, supplied by state orders and the state procurement system; (2) the consumer cooperative system; and (3) *kolkhoz* markets (collective farm markets) found in large and most medium-sized cities. The collective farm market network was not a "system" per se in the sense that it was organized, regulated, and operated by a central authority. Nonetheless, collective farm markets numbered several thousand and constituted a loose network that was regulated by local officials at the municipal level.

The first two channels were official state trading channels, meaning that they were supplied by the state procurement system. With the liberalization of the procurement system in the post-Soviet period, food trade through nonstate channels increased. Nonstate food trade assumed a number of different forms, entailing trade through commodity exchanges, regional food markets, sales at urban collective markets, direct sales through producer-owned or leased stores, stalls, or kiosks, or direct sales to various buyers. In addition, a common phenomenon in the post-Soviet period has been the expanded use of barter transactions in which food is bartered for services, inputs, or debt payments.

Declines in state food procurements and reform of the procurement system brought a significant shift in food trade away from state channels. This shift was possible due to decreased levels of federal purchases, thereby freeing up food supplies which gravitate to private channels of food trade where prices are higher, transaction costs lower, or terms of trade more advantageous. Official Goskomstat data clearly illustrate the decline in state purchases (both federal and regional) and the increase in food trade through "other channels."[1] These trends are shown in table 4.1.

The data show a significant change in channels of food trade during the 1990s, continuing into the new century. In 2002 an overwhelming percentage of plant products was sold through nonstate channels. Change was evident in the sale of animal husbandry products as well, although not quite as dramatic as for plant products, due to the perishable nature of meat and milk products. During the 1990s, sales of cattle and poultry (dead weight) through private trade channels increased from 21 to 62 percent of all trade; milk and milk products, from 3 to 29 percent, and eggs, from 8 to 52 percent. One factor restraining animal husbandry trade is that private, nonstate channels of trade were handicapped by the absence of cold storage and refrigerators which state purchasers had. Thus, in large agricultural enterprises, milk and meat products have higher percentages sold to nearby processing plants.

It should be noted that changed patterns of food trade, away from state channels, is not simply a result of a reduction in the percentage of food production that is sold. Of course, a decline in production translated into less food sold in terms of *volume*. But the *percentage* of production that is sold has remained constant or even increased. Recent official statistics show a general increase in the percentage of food sold by different types of producers as agricultural production has rebounded. For example, large agricultural enterprises sold 45 percent of their grain in 1995, rising to 53 percent in 2001. Thus, the shift away from state channels reflects the freedom, and the willingness, to search out channels of trade where the terms are most advantageous. The percentage of food sold by different food producers is shown in table 4.2.

Table 4.1. Channels of Food Trade for Sale of Agricultural Products, 1993-2002 (in percent of total sales)

	Grain	Sugar Beets	Potatoes	Vegetables	Cattle and Poultry	Milk and Milk Products	Eggs
Purchases by Organizations/ Enterprises for State Needs							
1993	63	98	52	71	79	97	92
1994	34	67	37	59	70	93	91
1995	28	21	37	55	62	90	87
1996	26	8	32	45	54	84	83
1997	26	9	29	40	45	81	75
1998	12	19	24	37	41	80	70
1999	19	17	24	32	42	76	61
2001	11	11	19	24	38	71	48
2002	8	7	16	22	34	67	41
Sale of Food Products through Other Channels*							
1993	37	2	48	29	21	3	8
1994	66	33	63	41	30	7	9
1995	72	79	63	45	38	10	13
1996	74	92	68	55	46	16	17
1997	74	91	71	60	55	19	25
1998	88	81	76	63	59	20	30
1999	81	83	76	68	58	24	39
2001	89	89	81	76	62	29	52
2002	92	93	84	78	66	33	59

*Other channels are defined as the sale of food products to industrial organizations, through wholesale trade, at collective farm markets, through farm enterprises' own retail networks, and through barter.

Sources: *Rossiiskii statisticheskii ezhegodnik* (Moscow: Goskomstat, 1999), 358; *Sel'skoe khoziaistvo v Rossii* (Moscow: Goskomstat, 2000), 101; *Sel'skoe khoziaistvo v Rossii* (Moscow: Goskomstat, 2002), 94; *Rossiiskii statisticheskii ezhegodnik* (Moscow Goskomstat, 2003), 407.

Table 4.2. Percent of Food Production That is Sold by Different Producers, 1995-2001

	Grain	Sugar Beets	Potatoes	Vegetables	Cattle and Poultry (live weight)	Milk and Milk Products	Eggs
Sold by Large Farms							
1995	45	11.3	32.5	71.3	100	78.8	91.7
1996	43.8	15.3	34.7	73.8	100	78.3	95.1
1997	45.2	18.2	38.7	72.0	100	80.3	94.2
1998	56.4	37.8	47.4	85.6	100	81.3	95.3
1999	53.1	56.4	43.3	70.8	100	81.1	93.5
2001	53.4	71.5	43	77.1	100	83.7	92
Average, 1995-2001	49.5	35.1	39.9	75.1	100	80.6	93.6
Sold by Households							
1995	NA	NA	11.7	8.5	23.0	18.0	8.2
1996	NA	NA	9.8	8.2	23.3	18.0	8.2
1997	NA	NA	9.7	8.7	22.9	17.4	8.2
1998	NA	NA	10.9	8.9	22.4	17.4	8.2
1999	NA	NA	8.2	7.1	24.1	18.7	8.2
2001	NA	NA	10.1	7.9	19.1	21.0	7.5
Average, 1995-2001	NA	NA	10.1	8.2	22.5	18.4	8.1
Sold by Private Farmers							
1995	44.0	NA	46.9	40.1	94.9	47.0	81.2
1996	46.2	NA	40.2	49.9	94.9	43.6	85.4
1997	30.0	NA	40.2	37.3	94.9	62.8	89.5
1998	39.9	NA	40.2	49.4	79.1	63.5	93.8
1999	52.7	NA	40.2	56.2	94.9	75.2	89.5
2001	34.5	NA	34.9	62.6	92.9	64.5	81.8
Average, 1995-2001	41.2	NA	40.4	49.3	91.9	51.6	86.9

NA=data not available.
Sources: *Sel'skoe khoziaistvo v Rossii* (Moscow: Goskomstat, 2002), 95; and author's calculations.

The data in tables 4.1 and 4.2 lead to the following conclusions:

(1) Changing patterns of food trade and use of nonstate channels of trade suggest an adaptation to new economic opportunities that arose during the 1990s, a direct result of changes in policy and in the procurement system. In particular, large farm producers have shown an ability and willingness to utilize new channels of trade, about which more will be said in a section below. It should be noted, however, that this conclusion is not uniformly applicable. Large farms have not only very diverse financial conditions, but also different survival strategies. Some farms are more able to adapt, and survive, over the longer run than others.[2] One Russian academic grouped large farms into three categories: Group A, which has favorable economic conditions, is adapting to market conditions, and will not only survive but has effective development. Group B comprises farms that are in the initial stages of adaptation. Group C farms are those that have not adapted to new market conditions and are not likely to survive.[3] A different Russian scholar, Aleksandr Petrikov, the director of the Agrarian Institute in Moscow, concluded that 22 percent of large farms were financially solvent and had favorable economic conditions, 17 percent were experiencing "temporary" financial difficulties, and 61 percent were unable to pay their bills or debts.[4] Since Petrikov published that article in 2001, it is likely that the number of solvent farms increased, while those experiencing temporary problems decreased. It is also possible that the percentage of insolvent farms also decreased due to improving financial conditions of large farms since 1999, during which time the financial condition of agricultural enterprises improved, profitability increased, and price disparities diminished.[5]

(2) Furthermore, it is clear that despite the increased importance of household food production during the 1990s, large farms sell more of their production while households consume more of their production. Thus, large farms' production plays a larger role in domestic food trade, and for that reason it is wise to keep in mind the distinction in importance between food production and food trade.

(3) A final conclusion from the data is that the financial crisis and collapse of the ruble, which made imports more expensive and provided an economic boost to domestic producers, does not appear to have had a significant impact on the amount of food that was sold or on the utilization of food trade channels. Comparing 1998 to 1999 shows no significant break in ongoing trends; this is interpreted here as meaning that the process of shifting away from state channels of trade continued. The issue of domestic channels of trade and their use by large farms is considered in more detail below.

Large Farm Enterprises' Channels of Food Trade

In the section above it was argued that large farms' produce constitutes the primary source of food that is traded domestically, while household production is mainly consumed. This section examines wholesale channels of food trade used by large farms to market their produce. A survey of large farm producers provides more detail on changes in food trade by large farms. The survey was taken in two rounds, the first during the first half of 1995, the second in 1997.[6] The survey was conducted in three oblasts in European Russia: Orel, Pskov, and Rostov oblasts. Respondents were asked which channels of food trade they used for the sale of food-quality wheat, milk, and beef. The results for large farms are indicated in table 4.3.

Table 4.3. Channels of Food Sales for Large Farm Enterprises, 1995 and 1997 (in percent)

	Wheat 1995	Wheat 1997	Milk 1995	Milk 1997	Meat 1995	Meat 1997
Large Agricultural Enterprises						
Sales to Processing Plants	39	9	75	94	63	94
Sales to Procurement Agents of Local Administration	5	13.5	6	0	3	0
Sales thru Retail Food Stores	0	0	1	1	1	2.5
Sales on City Market	2	.2	8	3	2	0
Sales to Large Wholesale Intermediary	3	27	0	0	2	0
Direct Sales to Budget Organization	4	0	0	0	2	0
Barter	16	25	0	.7	4	1
Use as Wage Payment	4	8	1	.2	1	.1
Use as Dividend Payment	0	6	0	0	0	0
Direct Sales to Population	9	1	2	.3	15	2
Sales to Other Agricultural Enterprises	3	11	0	0	1	.1
Other Channels*	15	0	7	.2	6	0

Notes: *Other channels are not defined.
Source: E. Serova and I. Khramova, "Struktura i funktsii agroprodovol'stvennykh rynkov v Rossii," *Voprosy ekonomiki*, no. 7 (July 2000): 49-50.

For large agricultural enterprises in 1995, the two main channels of wheat trade were sales to processing plants (39 percent) and barter (16 percent).[7] Processing plants were the primary outlet for sales of meat and milk products in the 1995 survey, increasing to 94 percent of commodity trade in the 1997 survey. Wheat, due to its nonperishable nature, had more outlets and in some respects became a substitute currency. In the 1997 survey, wheat sales to processing plants fell significantly, while three other channels became more significant. In 1997, sales to procurement agents of local administrations accounted for 13.5 percent of wheat sales, up from 5 percent in 1995. Sales through large wholesale intermediaries accounted for 27 percent, up from 3 percent in 1995. And sales to other agricultural enterprises accounted for 11 percent in 1997, up from 3 percent in 1995. Interviews at food processing plants in the city of Kostroma revealed that farms and processors often established or maintained pre-existing direct trading contacts. Evidence is presented below that shows this pattern is not unique to Kostroma.[8]

An interesting aspect shown by the table is the importance of wheat purchases by local administrations. Why are local administrations active in regional wheat trade? One answer, of course, is to ensure adequate supplies in their regional food funds. One might even be tempted to argue that certain regions and cities strive for local autarky, and distrust market based trade to supply their populations. City and regional administrations provide some financial assistance to purchasing agents to ensure the region has sufficient reserves. But that is not the full answer. During 1994-1997, the federal government provided "commodity credits" to agricultural producers. Commodity credits were essentially input supplies—fertilizers, seeds, oils and fuels, etc.—which producers could not afford to pay for up front. Thus, the government advanced input supplies as a loan, to be repaid with food produce by the end of the year. In 1997, the federal commodity credit system was abolished, but regional governments continued to provide commodity credits from their own budgets. The repayment of these credit loans took the form of sales to the regional food fund. Regional governments became more interventionist in food trade in order to receive repayment.

The consequences of regional government involvement were twofold: (1) Regional governments had an interest in paying as low a price as possible for food, or to have the most advantageous exchange between input supplies and food products. This fact depressed farm incomes and affected profitability. (2) Regional governments in turn used wheat (as a nonperishable) as a source of revenue to the regional budget. Wheat (or other products) which had been obtained at a low price could be sold through market channels, resulting in a profit to the administration. Thus, while food production became increasingly unprofitable for farms, food trade became even more profitable for regional and local administrations.

Of interest as well is the increase in the prevalence of barter transactions used by large farms. Some analysts characterized barter trade as a form of resistance to reform, but in reality it is much more likely that barter represents adaptation to economic conditions and the economic environment.[9] In the 1997 survey cited above, the use of wheat in barter transactions increased from 16 to 25 percent in comparison with 1995. National statistics support these survey data. Comparing 1995 to 2001, barter transactions conducted by agricultural enterprises doubled for grain, more than doubled for sugar beets, meat and poultry, increased by more than three times for milk, and rose fivefold for eggs.[10]

To add more recent insights into channels of food trade by large farms, a team of researchers from the Netherlands surveyed a sample of large farms in two regions of Russia (Pskov and Rostov). They found that during 2001 and 2002 (the two waves of the survey), large farms increasingly tended to sell through private, not state, channels, although in general large farms used a multiplicity of channels: an average of two to three outlets per farm. Moreover, large farms are not locked into specific trading partners, but have changed trading partners since reform was begun. The primary reason for changing partners is problems with payments or low prices offered by the buyer. Of particular interest is the relationship between farm profitability and its business networks. It was discovered that profitable or highly profitable farms are much more likely to have trading networks in other regions. Unprofitable or low-profit farms tend to have networks that are concentrated in their region, and specifically in their raion (district).[11] Although the authors were not able to indicate the causal arrow between profitability and the scope of business networks, this finding has enormous implications for stratification among large farms and the viability of low-profit or unprofitable farms.

A different survey, headed by the author, of 800 households in five regions of Russia asked respondents about their farm enterprise: its financial state and a host of other questions about its economic conditions.[12] The relevant question here concerns the factors that influence enterprise food sales, and through which channels large enterprises trade. Table 4.4 presents Pearson correlations with a two-tailed significance test for factors that influence food sales.

Table 4.4. Economic Variables Affecting Enterprise Food Sales

	Size of Enterprise (land)	Number of Workers on Enterprise	Profitable in 2000	Enterprise has Own Processing Capacity
Sell through Own Trade Networks	-.281	-.368	.231	.713
Sell to Local Processors	-.279	-.185	.191	.369
Sell to Commodity Exchange	-.230	-.206	.182	.401
Sell as State Order	-.155	-.149	.224	.216
Market Sales	-.257	-.155	.201	.427

All correlations are statistically significant at the .05 level of confidence or better.
Source: 2001 survey data.

The table shows that all of the correlations are statistically significant at the .05 level of confidence or better, which lends assurance that the findings are real and not statistical anomalies. The correlations lead to the following conclusions. First, the amount of land that an enterprise has is negatively associated with food sales through all types of channels. The strength of the correlation coefficient is not particularly strong, but it is signed negatively. What that means is that the larger the enterprise, the less likely it is to sell its raw food production off farm. While this finding seems counterintuitive, it should be noted that the largest farms are more likely to have their own processing facilities where food is processed and sold through various types of outlets, including through their own retail outlets.

Second, relatedly, the number of employees on an enterprise is negatively associated with food sales, that is, the higher the number of workers, the less likely an enterprise is to sell food through the food channels indicated. For this variable also the strength of the correlations is not high, even though the coefficents are statistically significant. This finding suggests that the larger the farm's labor pool, the more food is retained by the farm to either process itself, to use as payment in-kind, or to use for consumption on site.

Third, the profitability of the enterprise in the previous year has a positive effect on the tendency to sell food. This finding is to be expected—the more food an enterprise sells the more profitable it is likely to be.

Fourth, whether an enterprise has its own food processing capability has a positive effect on the farm's food sales. Enterprises with their own processing engage in more food sales. In particular, there is a strong relationship between a farm's processing capability and selling through its own trade networks (.71). This relationship reflects the fact that larger farms have their own retail outlets. Others have combined with processors to form a vertically integrated production and sales entity. For example, nationwide, there are reports of processing plants buying out farms, a type of vertical integration that was especially prevalent in Moscow oblast.[13] A farm's processing capability thus has a direct effect on its likelihood to sell its food production in raw form. The second strongest correlation is market sales (.42), and large farms often have their own stalls at the local collective farm market or other types of retail outlets, such as their own food stores.

Finally, the geographic location of the farm appears to have some impact on patterns of food trade. The most common channels of food trade for each of the five regions are shown in table 4.5.

Table 4.5. Channels of Trade Used for Food Sales, by Region (in percent of respondents indicating their enterprise used that trading channel)

	Novgorod	Belgorod	Krasnodar	Volgograd	Chuvashia
Sell through Own Trade Networks	37	96	19	45	25
Sell to Local Processors	97	98	81	88	68
Sell to Commodity Exchange	0	15	4	0	4
Sell as State Order	0	13	0	0	36
Market Sales	90	98	69	93	61

Source: Survey data, 2001.

In general, the table displays geographical diversity, reflecting the economic conditions and infrastructure present in each region, particularly with regard to a farm's own trading networks. In addition to diversity, there are also some commonalities: selling to local processors is a common outlet across regions, as indicated above; and market sales are likewise commonly used. In conclusion, the data strongly suggest that large farms have become much more market oriented and are more likely to use market-based channels of trade. One of those channels is explored in more detail below.

The Rise and Fall of Birzhi

An early effect of the liberalization of the food marketing system was the development (or actually, the reemergence) of commodity exchanges (*birzhi*). Commodity exchanges vary in importance by region and in general have not developed into the significant trading channel that was originally anticipated at the beginning of reform. Nonetheless, their reemergence is characteristic of change in the food marketing and trading system, and therefore warrant at least cursory attention.

The origins, development, and operation of agricultural commodity exchanges have been previously analyzed and for that reason the discussion here does not duplicate that which has been previously published.[14] *Birzhi* are privately owned and financed trading networks and were intended to compete with state-selected purchasing agents. Appearing in 1990 for the first time since 1930, *birzhi* reached their zenith in 1993. Subsequently, agricultural trade through commodity exchanges declined in significance. Although *birzhi* are more common for some food products than others, in general they have not emerged as a major channel of food trade as was originally expected.

Even during the heyday of *birzhi*, when enthusiasm was high and their numbers increasing, *birzhi* were limited in their importance. For example, the director of the first exchange in Krasnogvardeiskii raion (Belgorod oblast) was interviewed in 1992 about his exchange's activities. The director, V. Serdiukov, explained how his sugar exchange worked. Transactions with buyers were conducted on Tuesdays and Fridays in the city of Belgorod, a four hour bus trip from his raion. Trade between exchanges occurred on Wednesdays. Although a few contacts with clients existed in the north and in Siberia, his exchange concluded transactions mainly in his region, in surrounding raions and in nearby Voronezh oblast. Most of the transactions were small, and during a normal month only two to three large transactions were concluded. At the time of the interview, he was working on a transaction worth eight million rubles, which at that time was equal to about $8,000. Brokers' fees ranged from 1 to 3 percent of the value of the transaction. His own salary, as director, did "not exceed the average salary of a skilled worker." He too suffered from wage arrears due to nonpayment from clients. In order to build future business, "we try, in whatever situation that may arise, to keep our word. . . .By providing reliability, we take upon ourselves extra problems, literally tracking the path of the commodity from shipping to receipt."[15]

Not all directors were as conscientious as Serdiukov, and in general, commodity exchanges have been plagued with problems. These problems include the fact that they trade in only a limited range of agricultural products, often those that are nonperishable; there is an antiquated and rudimentary financial-credit system that stunts the development of futures contracts and leads to chronic nonpayments for purchases; there is an absence of a modern information system; there are limited storage and transportation means; and there is an absence of necessary legal protections and market infrastructure. As a result, after 1993 *birzhi* activities declined, although the strongest exchanges survived, and into 2003 one could read of new regional exchanges being opened. Nonetheless, commodity exchanges never fully supplanted state-organized trade. In fact, a key impediment to the expansion of *birzhi* trade, especially for such non-perishables as wheat (which tends to be the most common food commodity traded on the commodity market) is state price intervention and the increase in procurements by regional food funds to meet local food needs.[16] Both of these serve to divert food from the market, and one estimate claims that no more than 40 percent of grain is traded through market channels, although official data do not agree with this assessment.[17]

The decline in *birzhi* trade may be measured in two ways. First, the number of officially registered commodity exchanges has decreased, from 264 in 1992, to 180 in 1993, to 78 in 1996, to 47 at the beginning of 1999, and to only 40 in 2002.[18] Even these numbers are deceptive since only a few exchanges account for the bulk of trading operations. For example, during 1992, 16 exchanges accounted for more than 55 percent of all commodity trade. In 1994, when 168 *birzhi* existed, only 32 exchanges (19 percent) concluded deals once a week, and only 5 exchanges concluded deals at least once a day.[19] The largest and most successful exchanges are located in Moscow, and in 1998 12 of the 47 exchanges were located in Moscow. By 1998 only a handful of regions had significant trade turnover through *birzhi*, as the most active were located in Moscow, where 97.5 percent of agricultural trade turnover occurred.

Second, while food products consistently accounted for about 45 to 46 percent of national wholesale trade during the 1990s, the percentage of food trade that occurred through commodity exchanges remained low. As a nonperishable, grain is one of the most common food commodities traded by *birzhi*. However, the percentage of grain traded through *birzhi* seldom exceeded 2 percent: in 1995 *birzhi* trade involved only .2 percent of grain produced; in 1996, 1.4 percent; and in the very poor harvest year of 1998, 2 percent.[20] Under Putin, the percentage of grain traded through *birzhi* accounted for .6 percent of grain produced in 2000, .5 percent of grain produced in 2001, and 3.3 percent of grain produced in 2002.[21] Thus, even with an increase in the volume of grain sold through commodity exchanges, overall a very small amount of grain trade occurred through this channel of trade.

Although regional *birzhi* continue to exist, generally speaking regional *birzhi* have been supplanted by the rise of other forms of wholesale trade, one of which consists of regional wholesale food markets. These wholesale food markets in part represent the reintroduction of government intervention in food marketing, but at the regional level. Regional wholesale food markets arose as a consequence of the decentralization of control over food trade by the federal government. Regional wholesale food markets began to develop during 1994-1995, at which time only a handful of such markets existed.[22] One of the first regional food markets was founded in Volgograd oblast and the city of Volgograd. In 1997, regional food markets were operating in ten large cities, with another thirty cities in the process of creating food markets.[23] In 1999, some twenty regional food markets were operating, with another thirty regions in the process of introducing their own markets.

The basic function of regional food markets is to ensure that the regional population has adequate food supplies, and to stimulate an increase in the production and sale of food products within the region. Regional food markets developed in one of two ways, often spanning several years, with specialized markets (trading of one or two products) introduced first. The first form of regional food markets was based on financial, organizational, and technical assistance from regional governments. The second form of regional food markets was organized by private producers or intermediaries and trading firms which possessed transportation.[24] In the latter case, financing was arranged between organizers of the regional food market and banks regarding size of the loan, interest rates, and repayment period.[25]

Regional food markets are attractive to local politicians because experience shows that in regions where food markets were operating, there was either retail price stability or even price decreases, a growth in trade turnover, reduced food imports, and improvements in food quality and selection.[26] Moreover, regional food markets are attractive because much of the infrastructure for success already exists. During the Soviet period, food storage units, refrigerators, food cooperatives, and other objects had been constructed in all large cities and oblast centers. These were privatized during the 1990s, but often are not used for their intended purpose. However, the existence of this infrastructure provides regional and city governments with an opportunity to attract investments in order to utilize these resources for their intended purpose.

Within each regional food market, there are submarkets. Territorial (intra-oblast) wholesale markets are created to serve either certain areas of a region or selected populations. In Rostov oblast, for instance, some wholesale food markets serve industrial populations, while others serve defined zones within the oblast.[27] Each of these territorial markets is defined by area and is served by a specific number of farms. Territorial food markets also have retail outlets, selling food either through established local collective farm markets or though retail outlets of privatized companies.[28]

Food Processors and Domestic Food Trade

Despite the existence of commodity exchanges and other channels of food trade available for the sale of production, survey data confirm that local processors are the dominant outlet for food sales from large farms. Despite the increased importance of food used in barter transactions, most evidence points to the fact that during the transition period large farms maintained preexisting connections with local processors, and therefore large farms remain the primary supplier of raw food products to processors.[29] The key difference today is that the majority of contractual ties between large farm producers and processors are voluntary, not planned or regulated by the federal or regional governments.

Due to the fact that food processors continue to play an integral role in wholesale food trade and the domestic food trade system, it is worthwhile to examine how food processors have fared during the transition period, especially given that processors are, with few exceptions, neglected in analyses of economic reform in Russia.[30] This section starts with a survey of general trends, including production by food processors, employment, and financial conditions. This survey is followed by a summary of problems common to processors that must be addressed as the Russian food industry integrates into the world economy. Finally, some solutions to processors' problems are considered.

General Trends

From the start of economic reform in 1992, the number of food processing enterprises has more than tripled, due mainly to the construction of small food processing units. In 2002, the number of food processing enterprises numbered about 24,000.[31] Most food processing plants have been privatized, although municipal governments may remain an important shareholder in the enterprise. Privatization occurred rapidly, and already by September 1993, 45 percent of all processing plants in Russia had been privatized.[32]

Despite the increase in the number of processing enterprises, during 1992-2002 the number of employees in the food processing industry declined by about 4 percent, from 1.55 million in 1992 to 1.49 million in 2002.[33] This decline is much less than the contraction in the number of people employed in agricultural production during an analogous period (a decline of 22 percent, from 10.1 million in 1992 to 7.9 million in 2002). During the 1990s, labor productivity in processing plants declined, even with the contraction in the labor force, although in some exceptional cases specific processing enterprises have among the highest labor productivity in Russia.[34]

Similar to food production, food processors experienced a significant decline in output during the first half of the 1990s and then began to rebound toward the end of the decade. The decline in processed foods reflected diminished domestic demand resulting from increases in the retail price of food and an erosion in the real income of Russian families; the decline in processed food production mirrored decreases in basic food production. The result was not only lower production of processed food, but a low level of utilization of processing plants' capacity. For example, in 1997, enterprises that processed fresh meat were working at 19 percent of capacity, canned meat plants at 35 percent of capacity, bread products' plants at 37 percent of capacity, and flour plants at 48 percent of capacity. Even the production of alcohol suffered: beer plants were working at 57 percent of capacity, vodka plants at 31 percent, wine plants at 9 percent, and cognac at 17 percent. The leading alcoholic product was champagne, for which plants were working at 71 percent of capacity.[35]

However, it is interesting to note that even as the production of processed foods was declining and enterprises' capacity was underutilized, official statistics indicate that during the transition period dating from 1992, processing plants as a group have been profitable, a trend that stands in stark contrast to the levels of unprofitability experienced by large farm producers.[36] In 1998, for example, only 11 percent of large farms were profitable, and in 2001, 46 percent of large farms were profitable.[37] In contrast, in 1999 about two-thirds of food processors were profitable.[38] Processors as a group have had a net profit in every year since 1992 except 1998.

Production trends of processed foods may be divided into two stages. The first stage, 1990-1997, was characterized by a sharp decline in production.[39] Beginning in 1998, the second stage took hold; it was characterized by a rebound in the production of processed food for several categories of foodstuffs.[40] The recovery was aided in the third and fourth quarters of 1998 by sharply higher retail prices for processed imported food, which allowed domestic processed food to become more price competitive. In addition, after the ruble's collapse there was a notable improvement in the packaging of domestic processed foods which made them more attractive. In 2001, fourteen of twenty categories of processed foods experienced an increase in production compared to 1996, and for ten of those categories production increased by more than 150 percent compared to 1996.[41] This turnaround was due to several factors, including a growing preference for traditional Russian foods amidst calls for patriotism and concerns over food security; improved quality of domestic processed food; a newfound popularity of processed foods among the Russian consumer, especially for frozen foods; and competitive pricing with imports following the devaluation of the ruble in 1998.[42] The increase in production and profitability continued through 2002, with meat and milk products leading the way.[43] In 2002, the ruble value of processed was 4 times its 1997 level and almost three times the 1998 level.[44] In late October 2003, Minister of Agriculture Aleksei Gordeev noted that production of processed foods had increased 4 percent in comparison to 2002, and he noted that the processing industry as a whole is in better condition than the agricultural sector.[45]

Common Problems

Food processors, of course, are a disparate group, divided not only by the type of product they process, but also by region and size. Most food processing facilities are small. They also differ in the way the government treats them. Some processed products have received state protection in the form of import tariffs or quotas, such as sugar and meat products (import policies and trade protectionism are examined in the following chapter). Despite diversity among processors on a number of dimensions, going forward all processors share some common problems and needs which are becoming urgent as Russia integrates into the world economy and competes with foreign processors and their products.

One of the most pressing needs is the modernization of processing enterprises. Many processing enterprises were built in the 1960s or 1970s and need to be refurbished with modern equipment in order to increase automation. Mechanized labor in the food processing branch as a whole ranges from 40 to 60 percent of the labor performed, but often this level is lower, particularly in smaller processing enterprises. For example, in the meat processing branch, only 8 percent of the work is automated. In the milk branch, in which 70 percent of processing enterprises were constructed in the 1950s and 1960s, about one half of the labor to process milk, cheese, and sour cream is not mechanized. In the meat and milk branches, an estimated one-third of refrigerator units are in need of immediate repair. In the confectionary branch, 45 percent of the equipment has been in use for more than 10 years. Finally, in the sugar processing branch, an estimated 40 percent of the equipment "urgently" needs to be replaced.[46]

Related to the modernization problem is the need to bring existing processing machinery and equipment up to world standards—at the end of the 1990s only an estimated 15-19 percent of Russian processing machinery met world standards.[47] Moreover, there is a general shortage of processing machinery and equipment. One author estimates that the country produces only one-third of the needed processing equipment and machinery.[48] Finally, the processing branch faces a need to attract and retain skilled workers.

Common Solutions?

Following the financial crisis of 1998, Russian food processors rebounded quickly. They benefited from higher-priced imports, which made domestic processed food more price competitive. The rebound was indicated by two occurrences. One was the interest by Russian oil and gas companies to invest in food processing plants. The second was increased demand for processing equipment and machinery. As indicated above, most processing equipment is old and needs replacing. Following 1998, demand for processing machinery began to increase to meet growing demand for domestic foodstuffs. Russian processing plants usually preferred to purchase separate pieces rather than fully automated complete processing lines.[49] The most popular pieces of equipment are for meat and milk processing, the type of plants which most medium-sized cities have.

One solution to the continuing problems facing processors concerns investment for the modernization of processing plants. Processors have seen their fortunes improve, given that during 1994-2000 domestic investments into food processing increased from 23 to 44 percent of all investments into the agroindustrial complex.[50] Since 1998, capital investment in the food processing branch has increased significantly. The 2002 level of investment was nearly ten times the level of investment in 1998.[51] However, even in 2002, the level of investment was still insufficient. During the 1990s investments by both the federal and regional governments declined to the agroindustrial complex, while the percentage of investment coming from enterprises themselves increased.

Although foreign investment into the food processing sector has been among the most popular targets of investment, the share of foreign investments directed to food processing peaked in 2000 at 16 percent, and thereafter declined to 11 percent in 2001 and 6 percent in 2002.[52] Foreign investments have been concentrated in just a few processing industries; notable among them are beer and confectionaries. There has also been a regional concentration to foreign investment, with the overwhelming majority channeled to processors in the city of Moscow, Moscow oblast, and a few other large cities. Thus, the investment solution at present does not have the widespread national application that is needed.

Another possible answer to common problems is vertical integration between food producers and food processors. This "solution" is highly touted in the Russian scholarly literature, with elaborate schemes detailing the steps to be accomplished, and the role to be played by the state in creating conditions conducive for investors.[53] In fact, vertical integration has been endorsed by Minister of Agriculture Aleksei Gordeev as an important process to facilitate the revival and development of the agroindustrial complex.[54] Integration is important and beneficial for several reasons: (1) producers and processors often have an antagonistic relationship over wholesale prices, and integration is a way to satisfy both sides; (2) processors need reliable suppliers, and the loss of a supplier not only disrupts processing, it diminishes utilization of production capacity and entails transaction costs to find a replacement supplier; (3) processors need high-quality raw food products; (4) farms acquire secure outlets for their produce, thereby avoiding high transaction costs and the potential for added spoilage.

To date, most integration has been started by the processor. Usually, processors are interested in establishing links with only the strongest farms, despite the government's preference that weak farms combine with strong farms. Integration between producer and processor has several different variants. One form is for a processor and producer to sign long-term agreements in which the processor supplies equipment and machinery needed for production, and the producer supplies production directly to the processor. A second variant is for the processor to buy a farm outright, often restructuring it and modernizing it to fit its processing needs. A third variant is for the processor to sign long-term leases of land and fixed assets. A fourth variant is for cities to facilitate integration between processors and farms by offering financial support to processing enterprises which in turn are able to sign agreements with nearby farms.[55] The problem with the integration solution is that it has yet to become widespread. Granted, there are success stories, perhaps the most prominent being the activities of Wimm-Bill-Dann, a Moscow-based dairy and fruit processing company that during 2000 controlled 30 percent of the pasteurized milk market and 30 percent of the fruit juice market in Russia. In 2000, it had 65 dairy farms in Moscow oblast and purchased 30 percent of the fresh milk produced in the oblast.[56] The problem is that examples such as Wimm-Bill-Dann are few and far between. Vertical integration remains episodic, even exceptional.[57] Moreover, integration tends to be geographically concentrated in Moscow oblast and Leningrad oblast, where concentrated urban populations are found, consumers' purchasing power is higher, the financial condition of farms is generally better, and where most investment monies flow.

Household Channels of Food Trade

During the 1990s, household food production became more important and supplied an increasing percentage of the nation's food. Most of that food was consumed as nonmonetary income, and household sales in general pale in comparison to sales by large farms. For example, official data show that in 2001 households sold ten percent of the potatoes they produced, less than 8 percent of vegetables, 19 percent of (live weight) cattle and poultry, 21 percent of milk and milk products, and less than 8 percent of eggs.[58] Each of those numbers represents a decline in comparison to 1991.[59] Reduced sales, and increased household consumption, represent reactions to the economic environment in which rural incomes eroded compared to industrial and national indices. During the first half of the 1990s, in particular, rural incomes became demonetized (and remonetized after 1998), and the rural standard of living deteriorated. Nonetheless, despite the fact that most household food is consumed and not sold, it is still interesting to investigate through which channels of food trade households market their produce. To address this question, two different sets of data from discrete surveys are used.

1997 Survey Data

In the 1997 survey, individual and household producers were asked about how they sold their food (see note 6). The results about which channels of food trade they used are indicated in table 4.6.

Table 4.6. Channels of Food Sales for Households and Individual Producers, 1997 (in percent)

	Wheat	Milk	Meat
Sales to Processing Plants	0	22	0
Sales to Procurement Agents of Local Administration	32	0	0
Sales at City Market	0	5	27
Sales to Private Intermediary	38.5	0	73
Direct Delivery to Organizations	5	0	0
Barter	4	17	0
Use as Dividend Payment	6	0	0
Direct Sales to Population	12	56	0
Other Channels*	3	0	0

*Other channels are not defined in the Russian source.
Source: E. Serova and I. Khramova, "Struktura i funktsii agroprodovol'stvennykh rynkov v Rossii," *Voprosy ekonomiki*, no. 7 (July 2000): 49-50.

The data in the table show that the type of commodity has an influence on which channel of trade is used. The main channels of wheat trade, a nonperishable commodity, were to purchasing agents of local administrations (32

percent), and to private intermediaries (38.5 percent).[60] Meat sales had two outlets: to private intermediaries (73 percent) and the city market (27 percent). Milk
had more outlets: the majority (56 percent) of milk was sold directly to the
population, with secondary outlets to processing plants (22 percent) and as barter (17 percent).[61]

The importance of private intermediaries for wheat and meat products reflects the fact that individuals and households do not have the time, the surplus
labor, or the contacts to expend in searching out buyers, so they sell their production through intermediaries.

2001 Survey Data

A survey of 800 households in five regions of Russia during 2001 adds more
detail to what we know about household food sales (see note 12). This survey
allows us to investigate and correlate food sales to various social and economic
characteristics. In particular, the following questions are addressed below:

(1) What is the relationship between types of land usage and food sales?

(2) Are there unique social characteristics of "selling" households?

(3) What factors affect whether households sell their produce?

The first question is the relationship between land holdings and food sales.
Intuitively, we might expect that households which had expanded their
household plots the most and had the largest amount of rented land would also
have the highest levels of production and sales. In the survey, about 35 percent
of the households had expanded their household land plots since 1991, and 34
percent used a rental plot. The relationship between land usage, on the one
hand, and household production and sales on the other, however, is more
complex. As explained elsewhere, limitations on human and productive capital
lead households to choose either one type of plot or the other; very few have
both. Therefore, most households appear to have opted *either* to expand their
household plot size *or* to rent more land.[62]

These different strategies are reflected in the correlations between the
different types of land relations and production and sales. For the total sample,
an increase in plot size is strongly correlated with higher food production
($r=.524$), but has a much weaker relationship with food sales ($r=.195$). When the
small number of high-producing and high-selling private farmers are excluded
from the analysis, the different effects of the two types of land relations become
even clearer. The correlation coefficient between increased plot size and food
production is .945, but there is no statistically significant correlation between
increased plot size and food sales. Alternatively, the size of rental land is
positively correlated with food sales, $r=.125$, but there is no statistically
significant correlation between rental land and food production. These
correlations suggest that land plots are used for different purposes, with
household plots used for food consumption while rental plots are used for
commercial sales.

A second question concerns the social characteristics of selling households.
Previous research showed that private farmers, and on large farms, farm manag-

ers, sold more produce and consumed less, particularly of high-preference and high-cost food commodities.[63]

The volumes and percentages of food sales for private farmers reflect their business activity. Private farmers sell high percentages of their production, as would be expected since this is their business. This result is consistent with the fact that private farmers have the highest mean household income.[64]

On large farms, farm managers' households not only produce more, but also sell greater quantities of high-preference food commodities, as much as 2.5 times more meat than specialists and twice as much as farm workers. Farm specialists and farm workers consume comparatively more of their own meat, no doubt due to lower incomes and less disposable income to purchase from stores or the local market. Each occupational group—private farmers, managers, specialists, and workers—sells more of its high-preference, high-cost commodities (such as meat and milk), and sells lower percentages (consumes more) of its low-preference, low-cost goods (potatoes, vegetables).

For our purposes here, the question is whether individuals and households that engage in food sales have unique social characteristics. Table 4.7 presents Pearson correlations with a two-tailed significance test.

Table 4.7. Social Characteristics of Food-Selling Individuals and Households

	Size of Family	Total Family Income	Respondent's Age
Sale of Meat	.092	.484	-.080
Sale of Milk	.162	.472	-.072*
Sale of Eggs	.025*	.033*	-.028*
Sale of Potatoes	.121	.162	-.041*
Sale of Vegetables	.152	.260	-.035*

*The correlation is not statistically significant at the .05 level of confidence or lower.
Source: Survey data, 2001.

The table shows that the several correlations are statistically significant. In particular, there is a positive relationship between food sales and the size of the family. The correlations are not particularly strong, but they do suggest that larger families grow more food and tend to sell at least some of their produce. In short, the Chaianov model, which speaks to the relationship between household labor and household output, is upheld. Furthermore, the relationship between total family income and food sales is also positive and statistically significant for all food products, with the exception of eggs. Simple correlations are not able to establish the causal arrow—whether food sales cause higher income or whether higher-income families sell more because they do not need to consume the food. However, this finding suggests that the higher the family income the more likely the family is to engage in food sales. The strongest correlations are for meat and milk sales, .48 and .47, respectively, both of which are moderately strong.

The final variable in the table, respondent's age, is negatively correlated with food sales. The direction of the arrow (a negative correlation) suggests that younger individuals are more likely to engage in food sales. (All correlations except meat sales are not statistically significant at or below the accepted .05 level of confidence, so any conclusions drawn remain tentative.) This finding makes intuitive sense. Younger individuals are more likely to produce for commercial purposes, are more likely to engage in private business activity, and therefore are less dependent upon wages and transfer payments. Younger persons who are less dependent upon wages and transfer payments tend to have higher individual and household income, thus there is less need to consume household production. In contrast, older individuals are more dependent upon transfer payments, and have lower household incomes in general. Therefore, older individuals need to consume more of their household production to compensate for lower levels of income, which restrict purchasing power.

In addition to the fact that household sales are positively correlated to the size of the family and total family income, there are other explanations to help explain why households sell their food production. The most direct and strongest effect on food sales is, of course, food production. Higher production is related to higher sales, as would be expected. Factors that affect food production include access to physical capital (land, equipment, animals), the level of human capital, and access to financial capital; and these factors have an indirect effect on food sales. Using panel survey data during 1995-1997, O'Brien and his colleagues found that the degree of community involvement and integration into village life by households, and the size of household helping networks, also have a direct and fairly strong effect on household food sales.[65]

Dilemmas and Questions Surrounding Domestic Food Trade

How should changes in state intervention in food marketing be assessed? There is no generally applicable, universal answer. On the one hand, procurement policies have changed. With this transformation in policy, the importance of different channels of food trade and patterns of their use have changed considerably compared to the Soviet period. In the post-Soviet period, the federal government has withdrawn from direct control over food trade, as purchases (both planned and actual) by the federal food fund continue to decrease. Regional food funds now constitute the largest purchaser of food, which are financed and operated by local governments. As was shown at the beginning of this chapter, in the contemporary period more food flows through nonstate channels of trade, although the actual percentage varies by product. As a consequence of lower volumes of federal purchases, the center's ability to directly intervene in the food market with food supplies became weaker and more indirect, surpassed by regional influence. The amount of food purchased for state needs is now a small percent of domestic production. For example, state purchases of grain in 2002, even after the state intervention described earlier, equaled only 1.35 percent of production, and only 1.4 percent of meat and poultry.[66] Thus, in the broadest sense, during the liberalization of food marketing, there arose a food market, defined as the ability to sell food wherever and to whomever producers desired.

On the other hand, there has been vacillation between market liberalization and market regulation, the latter a reflection of enduring concerns within Russia over food supplies and agricultural production to a degree not found in most industrial nations. Having developed at least the rudiments of market structures and having adopted promarket policies, it was as if there were little trust in market processes. Attempts to regulate the food marketing system arise from a fundamental distrust of the ability of "the market" to meet demand in defined areas of social policy. As a consequence, fundamental questions about Russia's domestic food trade remain.

The first question concerns the slowly increasing intervention by the federal government in the domestic food market, eroding the progress that was achieved in the early 1990s. As the 1990s wore on, declines in domestic production, decreasing food reserves, the threat of food shortages, and Western food aid provided an environment for more state intervention.[67] The onset of Western food aid brought the reintroduction of direct federal involvement in the management of food supplies. In October 1998, the federal government created a special food reserve for the country to prevent hunger during the winter of 1998-1999.[68] In announcing the special food reserve, Prime Minister Evgenii Primakov promised "the population will have secure supplies of fruits and vegetables" during one of the country's "most difficult and complex periods in its history."[69] Primakov was implying an active role in regulating food distribution when he stated that food reserves would be used primarily for "special consumers" and "certain regions."

The federal government thus became directly involved in the management of food aid received from the United States and the European Union. In February 1999, a governmental resolution established federal control over food aid.[70] The resolution permitted Russian processing and distribution companies to bid for participation in the distribution of food aid through the regions.[71] Although many private companies existed to fill that role, in reality only monopolies with large portions of government ownership "won" during the bidding. Western governments became concerned that food aid would be used for political purposes by regional leaders to strengthen their power base. After many months of negotiation, observers from the United States and Europe were stationed throughout Russia to oversee the distribution of food aid. Despite its intended goodwill objectives, food aid was unpopular among Russian conservatives, who resented the dependency aid represented, as well as among Russian liberals, who were disturbed by the implications of food aid on reforms. For example, Eugenia Serova, an agricultural economist and former adviser to Viktor Khlystun when he was minister of agriculture, argued that food aid and, with it, federal control, threatened Russia's fledgling market system. "Eight years we have been waiting for this market system to emerge, and now we try to destroy it," she stated.[72]

Other signs are suggestive as well. It is noteworthy that the federal Food Corporation was abolished in September 1997, in part due to charges of corruption and mismanagement of funds, but it was replaced by the Federal Agency for the Regulation of the Food Market.[73] In late 1997, a federal program drafted by the Ministry of Agriculture on the creation and development of a wholesale food market was approved by an interdepartmental government commission. The program envisioned that during 1998-2000 federal wholesale food markets would be organized in large cities and industrial centers, encompassing seventy wholesale markets in twenty-nine regions. During this period, the legal base would be formed to "regulate the activities of wholesale markets."[74] By the end of 1999, wholesale markets existed in twenty regions as a result of this program.[75] These examples show that, from an institutional standpoint, the federal government has not entirely abdicated its regulatory role and has the bureaucratic apparatus in place to intervene. Going forward, the key question is to what extent wholesale food markets will be regulated by the central government. The regulation of wholesale trade and free retail trade is an odd combination.

Moreover, in April 1999 an interbranch committee for the regulation of the domestic food market was formed under order from Prime Minister Primakov.[76] Coordinating actions between the relevant federal ministries and regional governments, the committee was to analyze the food situation and draft policies to regulate domestic food market, as well as to organize the preparation of laws for such regulation. The more active, interventionist role by the federal government in the grain market, indicated by Minister of Agriculture Aleksei Gordeev in the governmental program on agrofood production to 2010, presented in July 2000, is an outflow from this committee.[77]

Later, in December 2000, Minister of Agriculture Gordeev remarked that the 2001 budget needs "to have special means in order to fulfill purchase intervention of commodities. A main role of the Ministry of Agriculture and federal agencies consists of being able to guarantee transactions in grain *birzhi*."[78] Indeed, as was discussed in the previous chapter, during the good harvest years of 2001 and 2002 the Russian government intervened in the grain market, expending more than five billion rubles in 2002. This intervention benefited grain producers, but suggests a retreat from allowing "the market" to determine transaction outcomes, replacing it with government guarantees.

The second question, and perhaps more important, is the relationship between the liberalization of food procurements and the decentralization of food marketing at the federal level on the one hand, and regional responses to those reforms on the other. Federal control over food trade has weakened, but regional intervention has increased. The main state intervention in food trade now comes from city and regional governments. Therefore, domestic restraints on food trade now originate more often at the regional level than the federal level. City and regional governments are motivated to ensure food supplies to their local population. In the spring of 1999, for example, the city administration of Kostroma adopted a program of food security for the city. As part of the program, which in general was intended to strengthen producers and processors in the oblast, export subsidies were ended for milk that was sold to other regions. Further, the head of the city committee for the agroindustrial complex suggested limits be placed on the quantity of food permitted to be sold to other regions.[79]

Ironically, one of the consequences of market reform—the use of nonstate channels of trade—reinforces motivations of regional governments to intervene in the local food market in order to ensure regional food security. The more food that is traded through nonstate channels, the greater the pressure to intervene in order to meet regional needs, and the more regional policies and regional food markets are used as a restraint on food trade.

Regional intervention is unlikely to abate any time soon. A collaborative survey conducted in 1999 by government and presidential analytical staffs during December 1998-April 1999 strongly suggested that farm managers, rural administrators, and even private farmers favor regional trade protectionism at the expense of free trade. For example, in that survey, only 59 percent of respondents were in favor of forbidding limitations on free food trade within Russia.[80] Moreover, some evidence shows that even after the food crisis of 1998 passed, regional restrictions did not diminish. In January 2000 the Center for Economic Competition (within the Russian government) conducted a survey of 1,522 agricultural specialists in regional administrations, leaders of large farm enterprises, and private farmers. According to the survey results, 45 percent answered that bans and regional limitations on food exports to other regions remained "unchanged" in 1999 compared to 1998. Another 52 percent indicated that the amount of imported raw and processed food decreased during this time period.[81]

Officially, Russia has moved beyond state orders (*goszakazy*). At the same time, it would be accurate to argue that reality is sometimes different in ways that directly affect patterns of food trade. In the summer of 1999, the president of the Grain Union complained that "[A]dministrations issue resolutions about the obligatory delivery of grain to regional and federal food funds and establish targets for deliveries from producers with fixed purchase prices."[82] The director of the Institute for the Study of the Agrarian Market supported this view when he wrote:

> Administrations and governors, using different subsidies, compensations, and sometimes even prohibitions, establish fixed prices for the processing of grain and bread products to bread factories and mills. This tendency is especially characteristic of the preharvest period.[83]

Comparing 1999 to the crisis period of 1998, the survey by the Center for Economic Competition, noted above, found that almost one-third of respondents indicated that "price *diktat*" by wholesale purchasers either worsened or remained unchanged. Furthermore, 47 percent of respondents answered that "monopolism" by procurement, processing, or trade organizations had worsened or remained unchanged.[84]

A study of the Russian grain market by a German scholar found an increasingly fragmented interregional market, characterized by a decline in domestic grain trade as regional authorities exert control over grain trade.[85] Fewer trading options, monopoly-dictated purchase prices, crumbling infrastructure, and rising regional food self-sufficiency harmed the ability of producers to receive fair market prices, as well as the development of agriculture in general.

This is not the way the internal food market was meant to develop. It is well to remember that Yeltsin's December 1993 decree "On Liberalization of the Grain Market in Russia" forbade the blocking or hindering of free trade between regions. The 1993 Constitution defines Russia as a single "unified economic space." Nonetheless, regional restraints on food trade have become significant inhibitors in interregional food marketing. Both food producing and food-deficit regions have restricted food trade with other regions. Oblast governments require producers to fill oblast reserves and to repay credit debts with food *before* exports from the oblast are permitted. Regional governments want to ensure locally produced food is available to feed their domestic population. In September 1998, Deputy Prime Minister Gennadii Kulik noted that sixteen regions forbid the export of food outside their borders.[86] A year later in September 1999, the president of the Grain Union complained in an open letter to President Yeltsin that, "practically all grain producing regions have adopted legal acts limiting or forbidding the export of grain to other territories."[87] Earlier, in March 1999, Yeltsin issued a decree directed specifically at Belgorod oblast whose administration had in December 1998 adopted a resolution that restricted the export of nonprocessed agricultural products (meat, milk, grain). The decree stated that the Belgorod resolution violated four articles of the Constitution of the Russian Federation, and instructed the Belgorod administration to stop enforcing their resolution.[88]

The governor of Tiumen oblast boasted in an interview in *Sel'skaia zhizn'* that his oblast "was one of the first in the country to actively use regional orders" to supply his regional food fund, suggesting a sensitivity to provide food for the important oil and gas sector and their workers. He indicated that contracts are signed with farms on the basis of "regional orders," and farms that signed these contracts were paid a 50 percent advance. Importantly, in the interview he repeatedly used the Soviet term "order" (*zakaz*) instead of the post-Soviet term "purchase" (*pokupka*).[89] After the harvest, the advance is repaid in-kind. Much the same was true in Saratov oblast, where, to ensure "regional food security," the oblast used "state orders" (*goszakazy*). Agricultural enterprises received fuels, seeds, mineral fertilizer, and other material-technical resources in advance of their fulfillment of their order.[90] The importance of this arrangement is threefold: it acts as a restraint on trade, it reinforces command economy-type structures and practices, and it supersedes market transactions.

Other regions envision intervention through reserve funds and price regulation. The director of a Siberian institute on the economics of agriculture suggested that the Siberian region should have a grain reserve. The reserve would be created through the purchase of 25 to 35 percent of total production, percentages that are similar to those at the national level in the late 1980s. He then commented, "In this case [with a grain reserve] there will be a real possibility, through the regulation of market prices, to balance the grain market and guarantee the necessary level of income to grain producers."[91] As another illustrative example, Tula oblast announced the establishment of a regional food fund in late 2002. According to the description in the press, large farm enterprises receive an "obligatory" advance of seed, fertilizer, and fuels in the spring, as a loan. In the fall, following the harvest, farm enterprises repay the loan with grain *at prices established by the governor.*[92]

Finally, some oblasts impose not only export controls, but import restrictions as well. For example, in Sverdlovsk oblast, the oblast legislature adopted a 50 percent import tariff on poultry meat in order to protect producers and processors there. In September 1999, then-Prime Minister Putin sent a telegram to regional heads, instructing them to "urgently stop restrictions on free trade of grain and processed grain products within the Russian Federation." He instructed regional offices of the Ministry of Internal Affairs "to ensure the unobstructed export of grain" from producing regions.[93] Given the continuation of restrictions on interregional trade, it appears that these instructions were not successful.

Conclusion

Several central themes run through domestic food trade in the post-Soviet period. First, it was shown that patterns of food trade have changed in significant ways in comparison to the Soviet period. State channels of trade are much less dominant, while private channels have emerged as common outlets for wholesale food trade. Barter has also become more important compared to the Soviet period.

Second, large farms continue to be the primary supplier of food to the wholesale food system. Household food production tends, on the other hand, to be consumed. Links between large farms and food processors have been retained, although large farms use several channels of trade and are able to change trading partners. Processors, while playing an integral role in wholesale trade, face several critical problems that must be addressed if the Russian processing industry is to be competitive with foreign companies, either in Russia or in Europe generally.

A final theme is the reduction, though not elimination, of the role of the federal government in food trade, although federal withdrawal has been offset somewhat by the increased interventionist role played by regional governments. Regarding decreased federal intervention, today the nature and degree of federal intervention is considerably different than during the Soviet period. In contemporary Russia, the federal government intervenes in food trade in the following ways: (a) through the issuance of laws and legal acts; (b) through regulation of imports; (c) through the issuance of export licenses and regulation of the quality thereof; and (d) through commodity interventions to affect domestic prices for selected food products.

Regarding the increased role of regional governments, it would be fair to conclude that they now represent the primary obstacle to a market-based food system. The reduction of federal involvement has been offset by increased intervention by regional governments; the latter intervenes in regional food markets in order to ensure adequate supplies for their population. This chapter presented evidence of significant regional restrictions on interregional food trade. In particular, there is evidence of (a) restrictions on regional food imports and exports;

and (b) regional governmental intervention through regional wholesale food markets.

However, one can hardly blame regional governments for their restraint on trade. Their restraint on trade and pricing policies serve, at least in the short term, their regional constituency. Regional politicians are mindful of the need to pursue policies that will get them reelected. Policies that facilitate regional food security are popular, even if the ramifications of such policies undercut the logic of reform and harm the national food system. Thus, tensions between the center and regions exist over domestic food trade. Collective (national) interests can only be advanced at the expense of individual (regional) interests. While reform of Russian food system, policy, and trade has been an important achievement of the overall rural economy, it is difficult to see how this basic conflict of interest between regions and the center can be easily resolved in the future.

Notes

1. "Other channels" are defined as collective farm markets, through privatized trade networks, the use of food as wage payments, through privatized food stores, and other channels.
2. See Zemfira Kalugina, "Adaptation Strategies of Agricultural Enterprises During Transformation," in *Rural Reform in Post-Soviet Russia*, ed. David J. O'Brien and Stephen K. Wegren (Washington, DC, and Baltimore: Woodrow Wilson Center Press and Johns Hopkins University Press, 2002), 367-84.
3. O. Strokova, "Adaptatsiia sel'skikh tovaroproizvoditelei k rynku," *APK: ekonomika, upravlenie*, no. 11 (November 2002): 53.
4. A. V. Petrikov, "Krupnye sel'skokhoziaistvennye predpriiatiia i izmenenie sotsial'no-ekonomicheskoi struktury agrarnogo sektora," *Ekonomika sel'skokhoziaistvennykh i pererabatyvaiushchikh predpriiatii*, no. 5 (May 2001): 7.
5. See A. I. Manellia and M. V. Goncharova, "O finansovom sostoianii kollektivnykh sel'skokhoziaistvennykh organizatsii za 1991-2001 gody," *Ekonomika sel'skokhoziaistvennykh i pererabatyvaiushchikh predpriiatii*, no. 11 (November 2002): 38-41.
6. The survey was conducted by the Center on the Agrofood Economy in Moscow and the Institute of Development, Bonn, Germany. The survey results are published in E. Serova and I. Khramova, "Struktura i funktsii agroprovodol'stvennykh rynok v Rossii," *Voprosy ekonomiki*, no. 8 (August 2000): 45-66.
7. It should be noted that food processing plants nationwide had been privatized, although in many regions and cities governments remained an important investor, if not owner. Barter trade was used to obtain inputs when cash was lacking.
8. See Stephen K. Wegren, "From Farm to Table: The Food System in Post-Communist Russia," *Communist Economies and Economic Transformation*, 8, no. 2 (1996): 149-83.
9. Carol Scott Leonard, "Rational Resistance to Land Privatization: The Response of Rural Producers to Agrarian Reforms in Pre- and Post-Soviet Russia," *Post-Soviet Geography and Economics*, 41, no. 8 (December 2000): 605-20.
10. *Sel'skoe khoziaistvo v Rossii* (Moscow: Goskomstat, 2002), 94.

11. Max Spoor and Oane Visser, "Russian Restructuring Postponed? Large Farm Enterprises 'Coping with the Market,'" *The Journal of Peasant Studies*, 31, nos. 3-4 (April-July 2004): 515-51.

12. The methodology and scope of the survey is found in Stephen K. Wegren, David J. O'Brien, and Valeri V. Patsiorkovski, "Winners and Losers in Russian Agrarian Reform," *The Journal of Peasant Studies*, 30, no. 1 (October 2002): 1-29.

13. Grigory Ioffe and Tatyana Nefedova, "Russian Agriculture and Food Processing: Vertical Cooperation and Spatial Dynamics," *Europe-Asia Studies*, 53, no. 3 (2001): 389-418.

14. See Stephen K. Wegren, "Building Market Institutions: Agricultural Commodity Exchanges in Post-Communist Russia," *Communist and Post-Communist Studies*, 27, no. 3 (1994): 195-224.

15. *Znamia truda*, 16 June 1992, 2. (Belgorod oblast.)

16. B. I. Poshkus, "Razvitie birzhevoi torgovli prodovol'stvennymi tovarami," *Ekonomika sel'skokhoziaistvennykh i pererabatyvaiushchikh predpriiatii*, no. 11 (November 2003): 40.

17. *Krest'ianskie vedomosti*, nos. 33-34 (30 September-20 October 2002), 3.

18. *Torgovlia v Rossii* (Moscow: Goskomstat, 1999), 363; *Rossiia v tsifrakh* (Moscow: Goskomstat, 2003), 263.

19. M. Alibekov and M. Lukinov, "Puti razvitiia birzhevoi torgovli sel'skokhoziaistvennymi produktami," *APK: ekonomika, upravlenie*, no. 1 (January 1995): 55.

20. Calculated from *Torgovlia v Rossii*, (1999), 105.

21. Calculated from *Torgovlia v Rossii* (Moscow: Goskomstat, 2003), 131; *Sel'skoe khoziaistvo v Rossii* (2002), 58.

22. See S. U. Nuraliev, "Sozdanie sistemy optovykh prodovol'stvennykh rynkov v Rossii i perspektivy ikh razvitiia," *Ekonomika sel'skokhoziaistvennykh i pererabatyvaiushchikh predpriiatii*, no. 7 (July 1998): 16-18.

23. K. Makin, "Optovye prodovol'stvennye rynki: sovremennoe sostoianie i perspektivy razvitiia," *Ekonomika sel'skokhoziaistvennykh i pererabatyvaiushchikh predpriiatii*, no. 10 (October 1997): 31-32.

24. A. Tarasov, "Formirovanie regional'nykh rynkov sel'skokhoziaistvennoi produktsii," *APK: ekonomika, upravlenie*, no. 4 (April 1998): 39.

25. E. Zlobin, "Formirovanie optovogo prodovol'stvennogo rynka v regione," *APK: ekonomika, upravlenie*, no. 1 (January 1996): 53.

26. A. Korolev, "Sozdanie sistemy optovykh prodovol'stvennykh rynkov," *APK: ekonomika, upravlenie*, no. 2 (February 1999): 39.

27. O. Tishchenko and L. Zakolodnaia, "Perspektivy razvitiia sistemy optovykh prodovol'stvennykh rynkov v Rostovskoi oblasti," *APK: ekonomika, upravlenie*, no. 3 (March 1999): 35.

28. G. Makin, "Mezhregional'nye sviazi i prodovol'stvennyi rynok," *APK: ekonomika, upravlenie*, no. 2 (February 1998): 9.

29. Wegren, "From Farm to Table: The Food System in Post-Communist Russia." This research, based on interviews at processing plants in the city of Kostroma, found that households seldom had direct exchanges with processors, especially for animal husbandry products such as meat. Private farmers have made some progress establishing trade ties to processors, but large farms remain the primary suppliers.

30. For exceptions see Wegren, "From Farm to Table: The Food System in Post-Communist Russia"; and Ioffe and Nefedova, "Russian Agriculture and Food Processing: Vertical Cooperation and Spatial Dynamics."

31. *Rossiiskii statisticheskii ezhegodnik* (Moscow: Goskomstat, 2003), 384.

32. M. Abdulbasirov, "Privatizatsiia predpriiatii pishchevoi i pererabatyvaiushchei promyshlennosti," *APK: ekonomika, upravlenie*, no. 3 (March 1994): 4-5.

33. *Sel'skoe khoziaistvo v Rossii* (2002), 96.

34. V. Goncharov, "Ratsional'nee ispol'zovat' proizvodstvennyi potentsial pishchevoi promyshlennosti," *Ekonomist*, no. 11 (November 2000): 91; Ioffe and Nefedova, "Russian Agriculture and Food Processing: Vertical Cooperation and Spatial Dynamics," 405.

35. A. Bondarenko, "Vozmozhnosti pishchevoi i pererabatyvaiushchei promyshlennosti," *Ekonomist*, no. 4 (April 1999): 94.

36. *Sel'skoe khoziaistvo v Rossii* (1998), 97; *Sel'skoe khoziaistvo v Rossii* (2002), 96.

37. *Sel'skaia zhizn'*, 24 September 2002, 1.

38. Goncharov, "Ratsional'nee ispol'zovat' proizvodstvennyi potentsial pishchevoi promyshlennosti," 90.

39. Bondarenko, "Vozmozhnosti pishchevoi i pererabatyvaiushchei promyshlennosti," 93.

40. Goncharov, "Ratsional'nee ispol'zovat' proizvodstvennyi potentsial pishchevoi promyshlennosti," 89.

41. A. Bondarenko, "Pishchevaia i pererabatyvaiushchaia promyshlennost': integratsiia i mirovoi rynok,"*Ekonomist*, no. 5 (May 2002): 85.

42. *Financial Times*, 5 August 1999, 2; *The Russia Journal*, 11 February 2002, 8.

43. L. M. Pod'iablonskaia and K. K. Pozdniakov, "Finansovye rezul'taty raboty pererabatyvbaiushchikh otraslei APK za 1 polugodie 2002 goda i problemy ikh platezhesposobnosti," *Ekonomika sel'skokhoziaistvennykh i pererabatyvaiushchikh predpriiatii*, no. 12 (December 2002): 23-24.

44. *Rossiia v tsifrakh* (Moscow: Goskomstat, 2003), 194.

45. *Sel'skaia zhizn'*, 9-15 October 2003, 3.

46. G. K. Vetoshkin, "Pishchevaia i pererabatyvaiushchaia promyshlennost' v sovremennykh usloviiakh," *Ekonomika sel'skokhoziaistvennykh i pererabatyvaiushchikh predpriiatii*, no. 3 (March 2000): 17-18.

47. Goncharov, "Ratsional'nee ispol'zovat' proizvodstvennyi potentsial pishchevoi promyshlennosti," 90.

48. Goncharov, "Ratsional'nee ispol'zovat' proizvodstvennyi potentsial pishchevoi promyshlennosti," 90.

49. Information from Christian Foster, Foreign Agricultural Service, U.S. Government, 29 March 2000.

50. Manellia and Goncharova, "O finansovom sostoianii kollektivnykh sel'skokhoziaistvennykh organizatsii za 1991-2001 gody," 41.

51. *Rossiia v tsifrakh*, 328.

52. *Rossiia v tsifrakh,* 332.

53. See, for example, A. S. Kirilenko, "Agropromyshlennaia integratsiia—put' k ukrepleniiu ekonomiki sel'skogo khoziaistva," *Ekonomika sel'skokhoziaistvennykh i pererabatyvaiushchikh predpriiatii*, no. 10 (October 2002): 47-48.

54. A. V. Gordeev, "Lidery Rossiiskogo agrobiznesa," *Ekonomika sel'skokhoziaistvennykh i pererabatyvaiushchikh predpriiatii*, no. 1 (January 2003): 8.

55. Ioffe and Nefedova, "Russian Agriculture and Food Processing: Vertical Cooperation and Spatial Dynamics," 408; and E. M. Bogomazova and B. D. Garbuzova, "Gorod—predpriiatiiam, predpriiatiia—gorodu," *Ekonomika sel'skokhoziaistvennykh i pererabatyvaiushchikh predpriiatii*, no. 8 (August 2001): 21-22.

56. See Grigory Ioffe and Tatyana Nefedova, "Transformation of the Russian Food System at Close Range: A Case Study of Two Oblasts," *Post-Soviet Geography and Economics*, 42, no. 5 (2001): 349.

57. Ioffe and Nefedova, "Russian Agriculture and Food Processing: Vertical Cooperation and Spatial Dynamics," 406-8.

58. *Sel'skoe khoziaistvo v Rossii* (2002), 95.

59. *Sel'skokhoziaistvennaia deiatel'nost' khoziaistv naseleniia v Rossii* (Moscow: Goskomstat, 1999), 38.

60. Clearly, the inclusion of wheat in the survey data implies that private farmers were surveyed since household land plots are too small to make grain growing realistic.

61. It is interesting to note, although I cannot explain why, milk was used for barter but not meat; and why milk was more often a barter commodity than wheat.

62. See David J. O'Brien, Stephen K. Wegren, and Valeri V. Patsiorkovski, "Rural Responses to Reform from Above: The Contemporary Period," *The Russian Review*, 63, no. 2 (April 2004): 256-75.

63. See Wegren, O'Brien, and Patsiorkovski, "Winners and Losers." High-preference and expensive food commodities are animal husbandry products (primarily meat), compared to lower-preference and lower-cost foods (such as eggs, vegetables, and potatoes).

64. Wegren, O'Brien, and Patsiorkovski, "Winners and Losers," 19-20.

65. David J. O'Brien, Valeri V. Patsiorkovski, and Larry D. Dershem, *Household Capital and the Agrarian Problem in Russia* (Aldershot, UK: Ashgate, 2000), 155-58.

66. Calculated from *Torgovlia v Rossii* (Moscow: Goskomstat, 2003), 136, and *Rossiiskii statisticheskii ezhegodnik* (Moscow: Goskomstat, 2003), 411, 420. These percentages were actually higher than in 2000 and in 2001, when the state purchased .6 and .4 percent of meat and poultry, and 1.2 and 1.25 percent of grain.

67. The paragraphs below draw from Stephen K. Wegren, "The Russian Food Problem: Domestic and Foreign Consequences," *Problems of Post-Communism*, 47, no. 1 (January-February 2000): 42-43. And see 38-41 for a review of food consumption trends.

68. *Sobranie zakonodatel'stva Rossiiskoi Federatsii*, no. 50 (14 December 1998): 11084-85.

69. Quote from Associated Press in *Dallas Morning News*, 15 October 1998, 8A.

70. *Sobranie zakonodatel'stva Rossiiskoi Federatsii*, no. 7 (15 February 1999): 1425-1445.

71. In July 2003 it was announced that the regions that had received food aid during 1998 would have to repay the value of the aid to the federal government. The money was to go into a fund for support in the social sphere and the most vulnerable strata of the population. *Sel'skaia zhizn'*, 8 July 2003, 1.

72. *Washington Post*, 29 July 1999, from website www.washingtonpost.com. (30 July 1999).

73. The main functions of the new agency were to monitor the agricultural food and raw material market, assist in the development of competition for purchases of food products, intervene in the food market for the purpose of stabilizing the agricultural market, participate in the creation of a functioning wholesale market, and fulfill state purchases for the creation of state food reserves. *Sobranie zakonodatel'stva Rossiiskoi Federatsii*, no. 40 (6 October 1997): 8070-8072.

74. Korolev, "Sozdanie sistemy optovykh prodovol'stvennykh rynkov," 40.

75. V. P. Boev, "Krupnym gorodam—nadezhnuiu prodovol'stvennuiu bazu," *Ekonomika sel'skokhoziaistvennykh i pererabatyvaiushchikh predpriiatii*, no. 6 (June 2001): 12.

76. *Sobranie zakonodatel'stva Rossiiskoi Federatsii*, no. 16 (19 April 1999): 3728-3731.

77. The program was announced in *Sel'skaia zhizn'*, 25 July 2000, 1. Elements of the program were discussed in Gordeev's presentation to the Russian government on July 27, 2000, accessed at the Ministry of Agriculture's website: www.aris.ru. (4 September 2000). A condensed summary is in A. Gordeev, "Stabil'noe i dinamichnoe razvitie APK—pervostenpennaia zadacha," *APK: ekonomika, upravlenie*, no. 11 (November 2000): 6-11; and in G. B. Bespakhotnyi, "Osnovnye napravleniia agroprodol'stvennoi politiki," *Ekonomika sel'skokhoziaistvennykh i pererabatyvaiushchikh predpriiatii*, no. 1 (January 2001): 7-9.

78. *Sel'skaia zhizn'*, 7-13 December 2000, 3.

79. *Severnaia Pravda*, 10 March 1999, 3. (Kostroma oblast.)

80. M. P. Kozlov, "O putiakh vykhoda agrarnogo sektora Rossii iz finansovogo krizisa," *Ekonomika sel'skokhoziaistvennykh i pererabatyvaiushchikh predpriiatii*, no. 2 (February 2001): 18.

81. M. P. Kozlov, "Rynochnye tendentsii v agrarnom proizvodstve Rossii," *Ekonomika sel'skokhoziaistvennykh i pererabatyvaiushchikh predpriiatii*, no. 8 (August 2001): 14.

82. *Krest'ianskie vedomosti*, no. 36 (30 August-5 September 1999), 9.

83. E. B. Tiuriina and N. S. Dem'ianov, "Sostoianie zernovogo rynka Rossii v 1999/2000 sel'skokhoziaistvennom godu," *Ekonomika sel'skokhoziaistvennykh i pererabatyvaiush-chikh predpriiatii*, no. 1 (January 2000): 67.

84. Kozlov, "Rynochnye tendentsii v agrarnom proizvodstve Rossii," 14.

85. Michael Kopsidis, "Disintegration of Russian Grain Markets in Transition: Political And Economic Dimensions," *Post-Communist Economies*, 12, no. 1 (2000): 47-60.

86. *Sel'skaia zhizn'*, 29 September 1998, 1.

87. *Krest'ianskie vedomosti*, no. 36 (30 August -5 September 1999), 9.

88. *Sobranie zakonodatel'stva Rossiiskoi Federatsii*, no. 12 (22 March 1999): 2583-84.

89. *Sel'skaia zhizn'*, 6-12 July 2000, 1.

90. *Sel'skaia zhizn'*, 31 August-6 September 2000, 2.

91. *Sel'skaia zhizn'*, 25-31 January 2000, 6.

92. *Krest'ianskie vedomosti*, nos. 35-36 (21 October-3 November 2002), 2.

93. *Krest'ianskie vedomosti*, no. 36 (30 August-5 September 1999), 2.

Chapter Five

External Food Policies and Food Trade in the Post-Soviet Period

The previous chapters explored domestic food policies and how they influence the domestic environment in which food producers operate. Those chapters showed that the core elements in post-communist Russian food policies have changed in a number of ways from those which were pursued in the Soviet Union. Procurement and marketing policies have been liberalized, moving away from compulsory deliveries at fixed prices. At the same time, obstructions by regional governments represent significant hindrances to free regional trade. Concomitant with these policy changes, new patterns of domestic food trade have emerged. Food producers have more marketing choices, and state procurements account for a much smaller percentage of raw food products than previously. Retail food prices have been decontrolled, exposing the Russian consumer to the market value of the food he purchases. New interest groups have sprung up that try to influence domestic food policies. Evidence suggests that commodity-specific interest groups play an important role during the policy-formation stage.

Food policy also has an external (international) component. In this respect, external food policies are the second half of the equation that, along with domestic demand and domestic food policies, affect in fundamental ways the financial condition of domestic producers. This chapter focuses on the international aspects of Russia's food policies and food trade, arguing that similar to domestic food policies, significant change is evident from their Soviet predecessor. The nature of that change and the patterns that emerge from it are the subject of this chapter.

The change in external food policies is important, of course, because it reflects new international realities. As Russia integrates into the global economy, its constellation of trading partners has changed, its role in the Eurasian and world economy has changed, and its international trade goals have changed. Previously, the Soviet Union pursued a more or less autarkic trade policy and concentrated its food trade with Soviet bloc nations in Eastern Europe. During the Cold War, the Soviet Union attempted to spread its economic, political, and military influence to every region of the world. Its goals were to disrupt capitalist systems and to replace regimes friendly to the United States with regimes friendly to the USSR. External food policy was a component part of that strategy. In the post-Soviet period, Russia's trade policy is more open and variegated, it has significant Western trading partners, and its goals are to integrate into the world economic system, not isolate itself.

This chapter has two primary purposes. First, the chapter is intended to address the question of how much change has occurred in the foreign trade system, in the state regulation of foreign trade, and in patterns and content of external food trade from the Soviet to the post-Soviet period. The general argument is that Russia's external food policy is considerably different from its Soviet predecessor, although that is not to say that Russia's foreign trade regime is necessarily "liberal." The second purpose is to describe the nature of state interventions and regulatory policies in food trade which directly impinge upon efforts at economic integration.

In order to examine these issues, the chapter is divided into two main sections. The first main section examines the post-Soviet foreign trade system in general, including state regulation of foreign trade and foreign trade trends during 1992-2002. The bulk of the chapter is found in a second main section that focuses on external food trade in the post-Soviet period, divided into subsections: (1) state regulation of external food trade; (2) food trade policies and general trade trends; (3) import policies for specific commodities during 1992-2003; and (4) food export policy during 1992-2003.

Post-Soviet Foreign Trade

In the post-Soviet period, foreign trade has become significantly deregulated. That is to say, the Soviet practice of centralized imports and exports through state-owned foreign trading companies has ended. Imports and exports are not planned by the Soviet-era planning committee (Gosplan, which no longer exists) or by the Ministry of Foreign Trade (which had been renamed and in 2004 was called the Ministry of Economic Development and Trade). Foreign trade has been liberalized which allows the import and export of food and other goods through nonstate channels. Private enterprises, firms, businesses, processors, and farms (large or family-peasant) are able to establish direct foreign contacts for the importation or exportation of food or other goods.

The primary role of the Russian state today is to define the parameters of external trade policies, protect national security interests through those policies, and then to implement/enforce those policies. The implementation of these basic roles is fulfilled, for example, through the issuance of import and export licenses. The state also defines tariff and customs policies and rates. The state defines health and quality standards for imports, particularly for foodstuffs, as will be examined below. In addition, the state may set import quotas or impose outright import bans for certain products, including food, as is also explained below. But within those parameters, Article 10 of the 2003 law on foreign trade permits private firms or individuals to engage in foreign trade and to maneuver within the law as they please.[1] (Interestingly, Article 11 allows regions and municipalities to engage in foreign trade only in the circumstances defined in the law.) Thus, while federal regulation of foreign trade remains, the role and nature of state intervention is very much changed from the Soviet era and is directed primarily at defining the "rules of the game," more so than interfering in the day-to-day activities of enterprises that engage in foreign trade. Having said that, under Putin the state has become more interventionist and foreign trade policies more protectionist. A brief review of how Russia got to where it is today follows.

State Regulation of Foreign Trade

Post-Soviet foreign trade is generally more open than its Soviet predecessor. A series of government resolutions, laws, and decrees have defined state policy toward foreign trade. This legislative base is summarized in table 5.1 and then discussed below.

Table 5.1. Legislation on Regulation of Foreign Trade

Name of Legislation	Date adopted
Government Resolution 854	November 1992
Government Resolutions 1102 and 1103	November 1993
On State Regulation of Foreign Trade	October 1995
On Export Control	July 1999
Commission on Defensive Measures in Foreign Trade and Customs	January 2001
On State Regulation of Foreign Trade Activities	October 2003

The 1995 law "On State Regulation of Foreign Trade," provided the legal foundation for some state protectionism.[2] For instance, Article 6 permitted the federal government to provide "economic security, defense of economic sovereignty and economic interests of the Russian Federation." Point 4 of the same article also allowed the government to define the standards and criteria for "security" from imports. Article 8 allowed regions to "coordinate and control" foreign trade activities of Russian and foreign persons. Article 12 allowed for the Russian government to introduce "temporary measures for the defense of the domestic market" of the Russian Federation, and to apply quantitative limits on imports and exports. Subsequent articles elaborated further on the rights enumerated in Article 12. Article 15 stated that quantitative limits on exports and imports may be introduced in "exceptional circumstances" with the goal of ensuring the "national security" of the Russian Federation. Article 18 stated that if a good or goods were imported in such a quantity as to create substantial damage to domestic producers, the government is entitled to adopt "defensive measures" in the form of quantitative limits or the introduction of special tariff rates, to the degree and for a period of time needed to remove the threat to domestic producers. Article 17 gave the state an export monopoly on certain goods as defined by law. Article 19 enumerated the conditions under which the state could forbid or limit imports or exports on goods, labor, or services that violate national interests. Article 20 permitted the state to define the health, veterinary, technical, and ecological standards for imports and allowed for state control over the quality of imported goods. This list of articles was chosen selectively, with the intent to show the legal rights afforded the state to regulate, and limit, foreign trade. To be fair, however, the restrictive aspects of the law were applied

only intermittently and selectively, and in general Russian importers and exporters have many more rights than under the Soviet regime.

In October 2000, a new bill, "On the Regulation of Foreign Trade," was
passed by the Duma, eventually culminating in the passage of the bill by a vote
of 372-1 in October 2003. The bill was signed into law by Putin in December
2003, and entitled "On State Regulation of Foreign Trade Activities," as mentioned above.[3] In general, the 2003 law is more open than restrictive and is not
particularly controversial. Article 5 states that trade policy is a component part
of overall economic policy. The goal of trade policy is to "create favorable conditions for Russian exporters, importers, productions and consumers of goods
and services." Article 4 defines the basic principles of state regulation of foreign
trade, some of which include: (1) defending the nation's, Russian producers',
and Russian consumers' rights and legal interests in foreign trade; (2) ensuring
equality and nondiscrimination for participants in foreign trade; (3) creating a
single custom territory for Russia; (4) creating conditions of reciprocity among
trading states; (5) fulfilling the responsibilities of Russia's international agreements; (6) ensuring the defense of the country and security of the government;
(7) creating a unified system of state regulation; and (8) applying uniform methods of state regulation across the entire area of Russia.

At the same time, the 2003 law does codify government rights to regulate
trade. According to Article 12 of the law, the state uses four main methods of
regulating external trade: (1) customs and tariffs; (2) nontariff regulations; (3)
prohibitions and limitations on the trade of services and intellectual property;
and (4) measures of an economic and administrative character. Nontariff regulations are defined by the law in Articles 21-24, 26, and 27, and include quantitative limits on imports and exports, establishment of quotas, state control over
issuance of licenses for import or export of goods, state control over list and
types of goods that may be exported or imported, and the introduction of special
defensive measures, antidumping measures, and compensatory measures.[4]

Russia also has specific legislation for the regulation of exports, although to
be fair, not all goods, information, or technology are subject to state control,
only those items with direct relevance to national security and defense. Russia's
desire to stimulate business with the outside world, and to increase global trade,
particularly with the West, represents a significant change in attitude compared
to the Soviet period.[5] In general, export trade has been deregulated and decentralized, no longer operated through state foreign trading companies. In the post-
Soviet period, aside from state prohibitions on items for export that affect national security, the primary form of state regulation in foreign export trade policy has been the use of duties on exports. The origins of export policy may be
traced to November 1992 when government resolution number 854 established a
licensing process for Russian exports and imposed duties on exports. According
to this resolution, export quotas were placed on certain goods, including fuels-
energy and raw materials.

In early November 1993 two other resolutions were adopted, government
resolutions 1102 and 1103. The first resolution eased some export restrictions
while at the same time adding grain and processed grain products to the quota

list. The second resolution placed export duties on goods being exported from Russia. About three-quarters of Russian exports were affected during 1992-1993, including fuels and raw materials, food, and semifinished industrial goods, which comprised the bulk of Russian exports.

In July 1999 a bill, "On Export Control," was signed into law by President Yeltsin.[6] A full discussion of this long law (thirty-three substantive articles) would take us far from our primary focus. But what is interesting is Article 9, which provided for an interbranch Commission on Defensive Measures in Foreign Trade and Customs-Tariff policy. A presidential decree in January 2001 brought this commission into existence, specifying twenty-two members and headed by I. I. Klebanov.[7] Among the functions given to the commission by the original January 2001 decree were the following: (a) elaboration of measures for developing export control; (b) coordination of the list of goods and technology subject to export control; (c) preparation of suggestions for drafting legal acts that would increase the effectiveness of export control; (d) examination of issues for international cooperation in the field of export control; and (e) the study and analysis of export control policies of foreign states and the preparation of policy suggestions for the president of the Russian Federation.[8]

During 2001-2002, this commission had responsibility for recommending custom tariff rates which were then considered by the Russian government. As explained to the author, the process works thusly. Producers and processors express their desires and opinions about custom tariffs to the relevant departments in the Ministry of Agriculture. The Ministry of Agriculture then forwards recommendations to relevant working groups within the Ministry of Economic Development and Trade. In turn, the working groups send recommendations to the commission, and the commission makes recommendations to the government. The government has the ultimate authority to announce custom tariffs.[9] In late 2003, the commission began to consider whether limits on the export of grain should be introduced, and in December 2003 export tariffs on grain were adopted, effective until May 2004 (see below).

General Foreign Trade Trends

The general trend for Russian foreign trade during the 1990s was an increase in trade, which is an accomplishment given the fact that the national GDP declined for much of the decade. In 1994, for example, total foreign trade totaled $101.9 billion. Foreign trade then rose during 1995-1997, before decreasing in 1998 and 1999 following the devaluation of the ruble and the government's default on loans. In 1999, following the devaluation of the ruble and financial chaos in 1998, foreign trade dropped to $103.2 billion, down from $138.2 billion in 1997. After Yeltsin left office, foreign trade resumed its growth pattern. Putin's first year in office as president in 2000 witnessed an increase in foreign trade to $136.9 billion, rising to $141.6 billion in 2001 and $151.8 billion in 2002. Aggregate foreign trade trends during 1992-2002 are shown in table 5.2.

Table 5.2. Russian Foreign Trade, 1992-2002 (in billions of U.S. dollars)

	Exports to CIS	Exports Outside CIS	Imports from CIS	Imports from Outside CIS	Total Foreign Trade
1992	NA	42.4	NA	37.0	NA
1993	NA	44.3	NA	26.8	NA
1994	14.1	49.2	10.3	28.3	101.9
1995	14.5	63.7	13.6	33.1	124.9
1996	15.9	69.3	14.6	31.9	131.7
1997	16.6	68.5	14.2	38.9	138.2
1998	13.7	57.6	11.3	32.3	114.9
1999	10.7	62.2	8.4	21.9	103.2
2000	13.8	89.3	11.5	22.3	136.9
2001	14.6	85.2	11.2	30.6	141.6
2002	15.6	90.2	10.2	35.8	151.8

NA=data not available in statistical handbooks.
Sources: *Rossiiskii statisticheskii ezhegodnik* (Moscow: Goskomstat, 1997), 581; *Rossi-iskii statisticheskii ezhegodnik* (Moscow: Goskomstat, 2001), 609; *Rossiia v tsifrakh* (Moscow: Goskomstat, 2003), 372-75.

It should also be noted that post-Soviet Russia has had a foreign trade surplus during every year since 1992, due in large part to the exportation of oil, gas, and other natural resources. In 1992, the trade surplus was just under $14 billion, rising to a surplus of about $46 billion in 2002.[10]

External Food Trade

As post-Soviet Russia moves forward with integration to the global economy, characterized by increased foreign trade with the rest of the world, Russian policy-makers are confronted with several dilemmas. In the realm external food policy, one of these dilemmas is the choice between expanding food trade in order to integrate and the need to protect domestic producers. The United States Department of Agriculture estimated that during the first ten years of reform Russia spent $70 billion on food imports, equal to three full annual budgets of the Russian government.[11] Russian foreign trade data put expenditures even higher. As will be shown below, protectionist measures and protectionism as a trade strategy have increased since the latter 1990s. The interesting question concerns Russia's ability to walk the fine line between protectionism and inter-national integration.

A related dilemma is whether to protect domestic producers or to encourage food imports with the intent to provide the population with sufficient food. Russia's domestic food production declined during much of the 1990s, and thus the Yeltsin administration found it advantageous, even necessary, to allow high levels of food imports which generally were of better quality and lower price than domestic products. The consequences of this strategy were that per capita consumption levels did not decline as much as they might have, while at the same time fueled concerns over the nation's "food security." The politics of an open trade policy and the rise of "food insecurity" are analyzed further in the following chapter.

A third dilemma facing Russian policymakers concerns the relationship between food imports and domestic food prices. The dilemma is whether the government should restrict imports in order to support higher domestic food prices, a strategy which in turn stimulates domestic agricultural production. Should the government discourage foreign imports and encourage domestic production even if it means higher food prices for the domestic population? Or should the government allow imports that lead to lower retail prices and in turn protect the poor and other targeted segments of the population such as urban industrial workers, bureaucrats and white collar workers, and the military?[12] Is it better for the nation to import cheaper foreign food in order to maintain high real incomes and to resist demands for higher salaries from urban segments of the population? It is these types of political and economic dilemmas that confront the Russian government and affect policy choices. The sections below examine the nature of state intervention and the policy choices of the government that shape and define post-Soviet external food trade policies.

State Regulation of External Food Trade

Similar to foreign trade in general, external food trade has also been significantly deregulated, as farms and processors may establish direct ties with foreign firms for either the import or export of food or other goods, assuming that the Russian farm or processor has obtained the requisite license for foreign trade operations. One of the most important methods of state regulation of food trade concerns certification. Dating from the July 1993 law "On Consumer Protection," all imported goods must receive certification that they meet Russian safety and quality standards. Certification is based on international and Russian standards, although progress has been made to standardize the quality and safety standards. Each shipment of imported food must receive certification as to its safety before it can be allowed to enter Russia. This process has been shown to vary according to political relations with a given country, and is open to bribery and corruption in the customs service.

To say that Russia's external food trade policies have been deregulated is not to say that food trade has become entirely open. The poor performance of Russian agriculture in the 1990s created political pressures for more restrictive trade policies, about which more will be said in a separate section. As a result of conflicting trends, it is difficult to generalize about Russian external food trade. On the one hand, as domestic food production plummeted during the early 1990s, the amount spent on food imports increased (see table 5.4). One might even argue that on a macropolitical level, Yeltsin's strategy was to let imports feed the cities as his "agrarian policy" attempted to destroy the last vestiges of the Stalinist system and communist influence. Under Putin, political rhetoric has been more protectionist, but the amount spent on food imports actually increased during 2000-2002.

On the other hand, the decline in domestic production during the 1990s created distinctive political pressures for trade restrictions, and a number of policies and laws were passed in an attempt to protect domestic producers and to limit food imports. A number of policy levers were used. For example, import duties were changed and raised numerous times during the 1990s. In 1995, on the advice of the International Monetary Fund, import tariffs were established on most food goods ranging from 5 to 30 percent. From the mid-1990s onward, food products were also subject to the VAT, assessed at 10 percent (lower than the 20 percent on most other imported goods). The Russian government in February 1996 imposed a ban on imported poultry from the United States, but this ban was quickly removed in March 1996 after the two sides reached an agreement on inspection and sanitary conditions. Following the ban on imported U.S. chicken, Prime Minister Chernomyrdin stated that other "tough measures" would be needed to protect the Russian market from imported foods.[13] Shortly thereafter, import quotas were introduced for the first time in July 1996 on meat, milk, and poultry products, but withdrawn in December 1996 under U.S. pressure. Concerning legislation, by early 2001 there was a legislative base of federal laws that regulated the quality of domestic and imported food. A summary of these laws is presented in table 5.3.

Table 5.3. Legislation on Regulation of External Food Trade

Name of Legislation	Date adopted
Certification by Veterinary Services	March 1993
On Consumer Protection	July 1993
On Genetic Engineering	July 1996
On State Regulation of the Agroindustrial Complex	July 1997
On Protection of Economic Interests of Russian Federation	April 1998
On State Control for Quality and Rational Use of Grain	December 1998
On Quality and Security of Processed Food Products	January 2000

One early law concerned certification by veterinary services to ensure the safety of animal husbandry products, adopted in March 1993. By 2000, there were several ministries and committees that had responsibility for ensuring that food imports met sanitary and health criteria: the Ministry of Health, the Ministry of Trade, the State Tax Service (to ensure state monopoly on alcohol production), the State Bread Inspectorate, the State Customs Committee, the State Committee on Standards, and the Veterinary Service of Russia.[14] In general, responsibility for the quality and safety of food products, both raw and processed, was divided among six ministries and departments in 2000.[15] Another law concerned the certification of products and services, and was adopted in June 1993 and then amended in December 1995 and July 1998. In July 1996 a law on genetic engineering was adopted, with amendments added in July 2000.[16]

Other laws either in full or in part regulated food trade. One such law was "On State Regulation of the Agroindustrial Complex," adopted by the Duma and Federation Council in 1996 and signed by Yeltsin in July 1997.[17] Article 17 of this law provided for trade protection either in the form of quantitative limits or tariffs. Another federal law, "On Food Security of the Russian Federation," was adopted in late 1997 by the Duma and signed by Yeltsin. This law authorized the government to create and implement a special program at the federal level that would provide food security.[18] In mid-April 1998, a bill was signed into law on the protection of Russia's economic interests against imported goods, providing preferential protection for poultry, vegetable oils, and meat producers.[19] In December 1998, a law, "On State Control for the Quality and Rational Use of Grain and Its Processed Products," was signed by President Yeltsin.[20] This law expanded responsibilities and the authority of the state grain inspectorate for the quality of domestically produced grain and especially imported grain.[21]

The restrictive legislative acts discussed above demonstrate growing Russian protectionism in the latter 1990s. Not all attempts to restrict food trade were successful, however. One bill that did not become law was entitled "On State Regulation of Imports of Agricultural Products, Raw Materials, and Food." The first reading of the bill was adopted by the Duma in May 1999.[22] After undergoing amendments and changes in the Duma Committee on Agrarian Problems during 2000 and 2001, the bill was rejected by the Duma in April 2002.[23]

Nonetheless, it is fair to say that since 2000 President Putin and Minister of Agriculture Gordeev have followed a more protectionist course, at least for animal husbandry products. This course was originally set by former Minister of Agriculture Viktor Semenov, who in 1998, distanced himself from his predecessor, Viktor Khlystun, by adopting an explicit policy of defending the economic interests of domestic producers. Semenov announced that he favored raising import tariffs on those products that compete directly with domestic products, and lowering tariffs on goods which were not produced domestically.[24]

In his speeches and actions, Putin himself supports less open food import policies. One of the very first bills signed into law by Putin upon becoming acting president was entitled "On the Quality and Security of Processed Food Products," signed in January 2000.[25] This law signified a centralization of control over imported food. Article 10 allows for the registration of imported processed foods. Article 21 permits banning imported processed foods that are deemed as not meeting health standards established by the Russian government. The organizations in charge of verifying health and sanitary standards have the authority to refuse acceptance of a specific cargo, and to issue broader prohibitions of foodstuffs from specific nations. Although these conditions sound reasonable, the application of the term "unhealthy" food has been used as a political weapon in the "chicken wars" with the United States. Thus, the law gives wide latitude to restrict trade for political reasons as well as legitimate health reasons cited in the law.

In addition, food trade has been regulated not only by law, but also through tariff policy. Almost immediately after Putin became acting president (January-March 2000), tariffs on many types of poultry meat and fish were changed.[26] During this time, Putin remarked that tariffs on imports should be used not only to protect domestic producers, but also to stimulate production of high-quality products.[27] Subsequently, Putin repeated on numerous occasions the theme that the country needs to reduce imports and become more food self-reliant. The use of custom and tariff policies to protect domestic producers was included as a plank in the government's ten-year agricultural program to 2010 that was presented in June 2000.[28] From the earliest days of the Putin administration, Minister of Agriculture Gordeev has advocated the use of custom and tariff policies to protect domestic producers.[29]

The Putin administration was prepared to go even further than the use of tariffs. In February 2000 the Russian government imposed an import quota of 3.5 million tons on sugar and levied import tariffs ranging from 10 to 45 percent, depending on the time of year. In March 2000, import quotas on fish and sea products were renewed for 2000, having been originally introduced in 1999 when Putin was prime minister.[30]

The next year, import tariffs were expanded. In May 2001, Gordeev expressed support for the use of import quotas on foodstuffs, stating that "we need to increase the protectionist role of the state with regard to our food producers and protect them from unfair competition."[31] In July 2001 import quotas were announced for several food commodities, including meat. These import quotas established a bifurcated system of import tariffs, with higher tariffs applied to imports above the quota. This bifurcated tariff system is called a "tariff-rate quota" system.

Thus, in terms of policy, legislation, and rhetoric, Russia clearly has become more protectionist under Putin. Ironically, growing protectionism has occurred as Russia has accelerated its attempts to integrate into the world economy. However, as is shown below, while protectionist rhetoric and policies have increased under Putin, the amount spent on food imports and volumes of selected commodities has increased, even as domestic agricultural production has rebounded. The growth in both production within Russia and the amount spent on food imports is due to the economic recovery in Russia and the growth in real incomes of its citizens. By using protectionist rhetoric, even as the amount spent on imports increases the Russian government "wins" in the following ways: (a) it wins by seeming to protect domestic producers, which is politically popular; (b) it wins by ensuring adequate food supplies and satisfying consumer desires; and (c) it wins by reaping a financial benefit from import duties, particularly the higher tariffs from above-quota imports.

Import Policies Toward Selected Food Commodities, 1992-2003

International food trade policy under Yeltsin was relatively open compared to its Soviet predecessor, and import tariff rates were comparatively low, on average about one-half the world average. For example, in the European Union some tariffs on specific food imports reached 200 percent in the mid-1990s.[32] Worldwide, agricultural tariffs averaged 40 percent in the late 1990s.[33] In contrast, under Yeltsin, aggregate Russian import tariffs were only about one-half of world levels, ranging from about 5 percent to 35 percent (sugar had seasonally higher tariffs). Following the liberation of food trade in the early 1990s and through the mid-1990s, meat and meat products had an import tariff of 15 percent, milk and milk products a tariff of 15 percent, potatoes a tariff of 25 percent, cabbage a tariff of 10 percent, grain a tariff of 1 percent, and white sugar a tariff of 20 percent.[34]

The combination of declining domestic production, relatively low import tariffs, and cheaper foreign imports meant that during the 1990s Russia spent much more on food imports than was allocated to the agricultural sector in the federal budget. The sum of imports as a percentage of total food supplies reached its peak in 1997—an estimated 40 percent of the nation's food according to some sources. In that year, Russia spent over $13 billion on food imports. Thereafter, the amounts spent on food imports declined to a low of $7.4 billion in 2000, before increasing again to $9.2 billion in 2001 and $10.3 billion in 2002. In contrast, in 2001, which witnessed a large increase in funds allocated to agriculture, the equivalent of less than $1 billion from the federal budget was assigned to support domestic producers.[35] Expenditures on food imports are shown in table 5.4.

Table 5.4. Russian Food Imports, 1992-2002 (in billion U.S. dollars)

	Amount Spent on Total Imports	Amount Spent on Food Imports	Food Imports as % of Total Imports
1992	37.0	9.6	26
1993	26.8	5.9	22
1994	38.7	10.7	28
1995	46.7	13.2	28
1996	46.0	11.6	25
1997	53.1	13.3	25
1998	43.6	10.8	25
1999	30.3	8.1	27
2000	33.8	7.4	22
2001	41.8	9.2	22
2002	46.0	10.3	22

Sources: *Rossiia v tsifrakh* (Moscow: Goskomstat, 1997), 164, 580-81; *Rossiia v tsifrakh* (Moscow: Goskomstat, 2001), 366-67; *Rossiiskii statisticheskii ezhegodnik* (Moscow: Goskomstat, 2001), 609-10; *Rossiia v tsifrakh* (Moscow: Goskomstat, 2003), 372-75; and author's calculations.

Immediately following the collapse of the USSR, the amount spent on food imports was depressed during 1992 and 1993 due to declining demand for food and falling standards of living for the vast majority of the Russian population. However, as a percentage of total imports, food imports increased significantly in 1994 and 1995, totaling 28 percent of all imports. During a three-year period, 1996-1998, food imports accounted for 25 percent of total imports in each year.[36] Following the financial crisis of 1998, food imports rose again in 1999 to 27 percent of all imports. Food imports as a percentage of all imports fell significantly in 2000, and did not exceed 22 percent during 2000-2002. Even as dollar amounts spent on imports increased during 2000-2002, the percentage of total imports comprised of food imports did not increase, explained by the fact that domestic food production was growing during these years by more than an average of 5 percent per annum.

From where did Russia import its food? Table 5.5 disaggregates food imports into two broad regions: trade with the nations of the Commonwealth of Independent States (CIS), and the rest of the non-CIS world. In the latter category, the primary food exporters to Russia are the United States, the European Union, and China.

The data in the table illustrate three main trends that warrant mention. First, although Russian foreign policy has emphasized trade relations with CIS nations, food imports from CIS nations account for only 20 percent of the total amount spent on food imports during 1992-2002. This pattern is not what one would expect, given geographical proximity, the existence of established trading partners, a shared language (Russian), and infrastructural links. Second, and conversely, Russia is much more dependent on non-CIS nations, having imported close to $88 billion worth of food during 1992-2002. Third, Russia is very much a food importing nation, with a net food trade balance of more than minus $92 billion during 1992-2002.

Table 5.5. Regional Food Imports, 1992-2002

	Food Imports from CIS, Billion Dollars	Food Imports from CIS as % of All Imports	Food Imports from Outside CIS, Billion Dollars	Food Imports from Outside CIS as % of All Imports	Net Food Trade Balance (exports minus imports), Billion Dollars
1992	NA	NA	9.6	26.0	-8.0
1993	NA	NA	5.9	22.2	-4,3
1994	2.1	20.1	8.6	30.4	-9.3
1995	3.5	25.4	9.7	29.4	-11.8
1996	3.8	26.1	7.8	24.5	-9.9
1997	3.2	22.6	10.1	26.0	-11.7
1998	2.2	19.2	8.6	26.8	-9.3
1999	1.8	21.0	6.3	28.8	-7.1
2000	2.1	17.8	5.3	23.9	-5.8
2001	2.0	17.4	7.2	23.6	-7.3
2002	1.8	17.3	8.5	24.0	-7.6
Totals	22.5	--	87.6	--	-92.1

NA=data not available in statistical handbooks.
Sources: table 5.4; table 5.9; *Rossiia v tsifrakh* (Moscow: Goskomstat, 1997), 164, 580-81; *Rossiia v tsifrakh* (Moscow: Goskomstat, 2001), 366-67; *Rossiiskii statisticheskii ezhegodnik* (Moscow: Goskomstat, 2001), 609-10; *Rossiia v tsifrakh* (Moscow: Goskomstat, 2003), 372-75; and author's calculations.

Having shown that Russia is a food importing nation, and that most imports come from the "Far Abroad," it is also necessary to note that the composition of

Russian food imports began to change during the 1990s. Russia imported much less grain in the 1990s than it had during the 1980s, and grain imports were a fraction of the levels during the latter Soviet period. For example, during 1981-1985 the Soviet Union imported an average of more than 40 million tons of grain a year; during 1986-1990, the Soviet imported an average of more than 35 million tons annually. In the post-Soviet period, smaller animal and livestock herds decreased the need for grain imports and increased the need for meat imports. As a result, meat imports became the most important food import, measured in dollar value. Because meat imports are "high-value" imports—they are more costly—this explains in part why the dollar value of imports has remained high even as physical volumes of imports may decline. The subsections below survey state policies toward the importation of selected food commodities.

Grain Imports
During the Soviet era, most food imports consisted of what economists call "bulk products," which include grains, oilseeds, cotton, and other plant fibers. Conversely, the Soviet Union imported lower volumes of "high-value products" which include processed meat and dairy products.[37] During the post-Soviet period those patterns have been reversed. Imports of bulk products have decreased significantly, from 28.8 million tons of grain in 1992 to 1.6 in 2002. In 2002, Russian grain imports consisted primarily of barley used for the production of beer. Russia also imported small amounts of wheat from Kazakhstan and corn from several European nations, as well as the United States.[38] Grain import trends during 1992-2002 are shown in table 5.6.[39]

Along with changes in patterns of food imports, import policy also underwent revision, and this was nowhere more apparent than with the importation of grain. The first hints of change in import policy became evident in late 1992, when officials mentioned that grain imports needed to be reduced. By late 1993 explicit statements by high-ranking government officials indicated that a change in Russian grain import policy would be introduced in 1994. In mid-November 1993, during a visit to Stavropol krai, Deputy Prime Minister Aleksandr Zaveriukha announced that in 1994 the Russian government would not import foreign grains.[40] He explained that the purpose of the policy was to strengthen state and collective farms, agroindustrial enterprises, and peasant farmers, as well as to stabilize the domestic grain market and to stimulate higher domestic grain production.[41] Since that original announcement, the basic intention to stop or reduce grain imports was repeated in the press, although a slight softening was detected in early May 1994 when Zaveriukha admitted that although the Russian government did not intend to import grain—specifically wheat—it could not stop former state enterprises, now private joint stock corporations, from concluding contracts for foreign grain. This remained the policy for the remainder of the decade: virtually nonexistent imports by the federal government, and low levels of imports by commercial organizations. Thus, throughout the 1990s, grain imports remained low, both in terms of actual volumes and as a percentage of total supply. What were the factors that contributed to a policy of greatly reduced grain imports?

**Table 5.6. Russian Grain and Cereal Imports, 1992-2002
(in million tons)**

	Imports	Domestic Production	Imports as % of Total Supply
1992	28.8	107	21
1993	11.1	99	10
1994	2.0	81	2
1995	2.7	63	4
1996	3.2	69	4
1997	3.5	89	4
1998	1.7	48	3
1999	6.8	55	11
2000	4.7	65	7
2001	1.8	85	2
2002	1.6	87	2

1992 data do not include imports from CIS countries.
Sources: *Sel'skoe khoziaistvo Rossii* (Goskomstat, 1995), 125; *Rossiiskii statisticheskii ezhegodnik* (Moscow: Goskomstat, 1997), 584, 588; *Sel'skoe khoziaistvo Rossii* (Goskomstat, 2002), 57; *Rossiia v tsifrakh* (Moscow: Goskomstat, 2003), 210, 379; and author's calculations.

First, it may be argued that the low level of imports was largely a market-driven response, that is, in reaction to reduced need and declining demand. During the 1990s, a significant decline in animal herds reduced demand for feed grains and thus the need for grain imports.[42] Cattle stocks declined from 58.8 million head in 1990 to 27.1 million head in 2002 (from all categories of farms). The number of pigs declined from 40 million to 16 million during the same time period.[43] Large farms experienced the greatest losses.

A second factor was financial, at least early in the reform period. In the past, Soviet grain imports from the United States were paid on a cash basis. In 1990, however, due to dwindling hard-currency reserves, the Soviet government requested credits for grain exports from the United States. This request meant that henceforth imports from the United States would be financed through credits and agricultural assistance from the U.S. government. Following President George H. W. Bush's waiving of emigration requirements stipulated in the Jackson-Vanik amendment, in December 1990 the U.S. administration approved the first export credit guarantees in the amount of $1 billion.[44] In June 1991, President Bush approved another $1.5 billion in agricultural guarantees to the Soviet Union. In November 1991, the Bush administration expanded the scope of agricultural assistance to include food aid, technical assistance, and training programs.[45] Overall, from December 1990 to November 1992 the U.S. government extended $6.5 billion worth of agricultural assistance in various forms to Russia and other newly independent states, including $250 million in emergency food aid in 1992.

By late 1992, however, Russia failed to meet scheduled payments. By November 1992, Russia defaulted on its repayments, thereby precluding new loans from the Commodity Credit Corporation (CCC).[46] As a result, in November 1992, the United States Department of Agriculture suspended Russia's access to $386 million in credit guarantees that were still available until Russia repaid all delinquent payments and/or the debt was rescheduled.[47] Already by the end of 1992, Russian indebtedness for grain was nearly $200 million to the United States alone, and a similar situation was said to exist with Canadian exporters.[48] By mid-1993, Russia was almost $850 million in arrears to the United States for its agricultural exports.

Due to Russia's default on previous loans, a new approach to assistance was necessary. Immediately after the Vancouver summit with President Yeltsin in April 1993, President Bill Clinton announced a new program of assistance entitled "Food for Progress" that would not require new appropriations from Congress. Of the $1.6 billion pledged, $924 million took the form of agricultural assistance, including $700 million in agricultural loans and $194 million in food grants. Under the terms of this program, the agricultural loans were granted on highly concessionary terms. Russia was given food credits for fifteen years, with repayments to begin after seven years at below-market interest rates. This program stood in contrast to the CCC agricultural credit guarantees that comprised the bulk of the Bush administration's assistance, which were three-year loans at market rates of interest.[49] With this and other agricultural aid, Russian grain imports in 1993 were financed using credits from the United States, France, and the European Community. Nonetheless, despite new U.S. assistance, a significant constraint on further grain imports was the financial ability of the Russian government to repay, as well as its ability to make delinquent payments.

Third, it is also necessary to consider food reserves. Owing to sharply higher purchase prices, grain sales to the federal food fund exceeded planned targets in 1993. As of early 1994 there were more than ten million tons of grain still in the federal fund.[50] In mid-1994 the head of the grain inspectorate of the Russian government indicated that grain reserves in federal and regional funds, on state and collective farms, and held by commercial operations were "sufficient to provide the country with bread for six months."[51] Later in the decade, in the wake of a poor harvest, grain reserves fell to dangerously low levels—an estimated one million tons. Instead of increasing imports for payment, Russia accepted humanitarian food aid, as discussed below.

A final consideration is structural and concerns seaports and port access. When the former Soviet Union existed, most of its grain imports arrived through non-Russian ports. For example, in 1988, 41 percent of grain and milled imports arrived through Ukrainian ports, with 38 percent arriving in Odessa alone, and another 22 percent came through various Baltic ports. Russian ports received 36 percent of imports grains, with St. Petersburg the single largest Russian recipient (15 percent).[52] With the dissolution of the USSR, Russia "lost" nearly two-thirds of its access to port cities that had been used for grain imports. Those access points were not easily replaced or compensated for by other existing ports, a fact that surely affected grain import policy and even affected grain exports a few years later.

One exception to the federal government's aversion to foreign grain was Western food aid following the disastrous harvest of 1998, and subsequent U.S.-Russian agreements in 1999-2000. Following the disastrous 1998 harvest, during which Russia harvested only 47.9 million tons of grain after threshing, foreign governments and international donors offered food assistance to Russia.[53] In November 1998, the United States set up a $1 billion food aid package: $600 million as humanitarian assistance, and a $400 million line of credit at 2 percent interest for 20 years to purchase additional food.[54] Also in November 1998, the European Union provided a $480 million package of food aid, including 1 million tons of wheat, 500,000 tons of rye, 150,000 tons of beef, 100,000 tons of pork, and 50 tons of dry milk, for free.[55] Although food aid agreements were reached in November 1998, a lengthy delay ensued due to negotiations about how the food would be distributed. In the end, Western monitors (mostly from the EU donor countries) were stationed throughout Russia to oversee distribution. Food aid began to arrive in Russia in March 1999 and continued through October 1999, being distributed in sixty regions of Russia.[56] Despite Western attempts to ensure that food aid was distributed properly, Russia's Audit Chamber found shortcomings in the distribution of food aid. In particular, one state organization that had been contracted out to sell food aid in the regions was found to have violated the procedures that had been established. *Rosmiasomoltorg* sold to some regions more than their allocated quota of poultry, meat, and pork; and to other regions meat was sold that had no quota at all. In sum, the Audit Chamber found that more than one-half of the produce that *Rosmiasomoltorg* sold was in non-conformity with established distribution plans.[57]

Even before the original food aid package was fulfilled, Russia and the United States began discussions on a new food aid package. In September 1999, Russia formally requested another humanitarian aid package from the United States, consisting of 5 million tons of grain, 1 million tons of food wheat, 1.5 million tons of fodder grain, 1.5 million tons of feed corn, and 1 million tons of soy beans and meal.[58] A new administration under Vladimir Putin, and expectations for a better harvest in 2000, led the Russians to lower their request, and the two sides agreed on a package of 500,000 tons of grains.[59] Under the agreement reached in February 2000, the United States supplied 300,000 tons of wheat, 200,000 tons of food products, and 20,000 tons of crop seeds to Russia during 2000. This aid package, termed "Food in the Name of Progress" stipulated that the United States would pay for transportation from the United States to Russian ports.[60]

Thus, a variety of factors played a role in Russia's declining grain imports. When grain imports were needed for humanitarian reasons at the end of the decade, improved political relations led to partial free assistance and partial agricultural credits. During the Putin administration, better harvest results combined with a goal to improve the nation's food independence lessened the need for grain imports even more.

Meat Imports

As noted above, one of the key changes in Russian import trends during the 1990s was an increase in the importation of meat (exclusive of poultry meat, which is discussed below). From 1993 through 1997, total meat imports increased more than 300 percent. Meat imports rose from 4 percent of total supply in 1993 to 19 percent in 1997. Following the collapse of the ruble in August 1998, meat imports declined significantly in the third and fourth quarters of 1998, and overall fell to 15 percent of total supply for the year. However, in 1999, meat imports (not including poultry) surpassed their precrisis levels, increasing 135 percent over 1998 levels and comprising 22 percent of total supply. Meat imports reached a low in 2000, and then began to increase rapidly. It should be noted that despite more protectionist policies and rhetoric, meat imports increased significantly during 2001-2002, with 2002 levels almost three times the level of 2000. Meat import trends during 1992-2002 are shown in table 5.7.

The dramatic increase in meat imports during the 1990s led the Russian government to use non-market policies in order to limit imports. Import quotas on meat were first introduced in July 1996, but removed in December 1996.

Table 5.7. Russian Meat Imports, Fresh and Frozen, 1992-2002 (in thousand tons)

	Imports	Domestic Production	Imports as % of Total Supply
1992*	288	6,832	4
1993	260	6,236	4
1994	515	5,735	8
1995	702	4,937	12.5
1996	779	4,646	14
1997	967	4,224	19
1998	733	4,013	15
1999	990	3,565	22
2000	517	3,665	12
2001	873	3,567	20
2002	1,151	3,684	24

Table does not include poultry.
*1992 data do not include imports from CIS countries.
Sources: *Sel'skoe khoziaistvo Rossii* (Moscow: Goskomstat, 1995), 82, 120, 122, 125; *Rossiiskii statisticheskii ezhegodnik* (Moscow: Goskomstat, 1997), 584, 587; *Rossiiskii statisticheskii ezhegodnik* (Moscow: Goskomstat, 2001), 416, 611, 614; *Rossiia v tsifrakh* (Moscow: Goskomstat, 1997), 168-69; *Rossiia v tsifrakh* (Moscow: Goskomstat, 2003), 214, 378-79; and author's calculations.

Under Putin and Gordeev, the federal government became much more interventionist in agricultural production and the food market, in contrast to the relative neglect of the second Yeltsin term. Among the first moves in a more restrictive environment under Putin was one to prohibit imports of substandard meat that potentially posed a health danger. Toward this end, in April 2000 the Veterinary Service of Russia prohibited the importation of meat and animal feed from China, South Korea, Vietnam, and Japan.[61]

Less than a year later, in February 2001, the Russian government imposed a ban on meat imports from the United Kingdom in reaction to the mad cow disease scare. This ban was expanded in March 2001 to countries stricken with foot-and-mouth disease, and later expanded again to include all meat and meat products from European Union nations, Eastern Europe, and the Baltic states.[62] Prior to the March 2001 decision, imports of meat and milk products were prohibited from Argentina, Mongolia, and China.[63] As the epidemic in Europe receded, the ban was lifted in late April and early May 2001 for countries that had not experienced foot-and-mouth disease, while retaining the ban on meat and dairy products from the Netherlands and the United Kingdom for several months.

Thereafter, a generally restrictive policy toward meat imports was adopted. In July 2001, the Ministry of Agriculture proposed a quota on imported beef, pork, and poultry, thereby establishing a dual system of import tariffs: lower tariffs on imports below the quota levels, and higher custom duties on any imports above the quota. This meat quota was maintained during 2002. Even with higher tariffs, meat imports increased during 2002. In December 2002, the Russian Ministry of Agriculture proposed to reduce food imports by 1.5 million tons in 2003. The head of the Ministry Department for Animal Husbandry, Vasilii Shapochkin, complained at the time that the state's economic policies did not take into account the interests of domestic producers, citing lower levels of trade protectionism than in developed countries, and noting that while poultry imports from the United States declined by 16 percent, higher imports from Brazil and France compensated for the decrease.[64] A few days later, Minister of Agriculture Gordeev stated that the Ministry was preparing to introduce quotas and tariffs for selected food products, noting that "annually, Russia spends abroad about $8 billion for the development of others' production instead of supporting our food producers and developing our domestic economy."[65]

In late 2002, the Commission on Defensive Measures in Foreign Trade and Customs-Tariff recommended import quotas of 420,000 tons of beef and 450,000 tons of pork.[66] In January 2003, the Russian government announced that import quotas would be introduced on frozen meat, effective April 1, 2003. When the tariffs were announced, however, the quotas were even lower than had been recommended: 315,000 tons of beef, for which the import tariff would be 15 percent of the declared value at customs, but not less than .15 euro per kilogram; and an import quota of 337,500 tons of pork, for which the import tariff would be 15 percent of the declared value at customs, but not less than .25 euro per kilogram.[67] Imports of beef or pork above these import quotas faced considerably higher import tariffs—for beef, 60 percent of the declared value at customs, but not less than .6 euro per kilogram; and for pork, 80 percent of the declared value at customs, but not less than 1.06 euro per kilogram.[68] After the import quotas were announced, 141 U.S. congressmen and 51 senators signed a letter to President George W. Bush requesting that he obtain from the Russian side an agreement to abolish subquota limits on American meat and poultry exports.[69]

In July 2003, a Russian government resolution introduced import quotas on fresh and refrigerated beef, effective August 1, 2003, to the end of the year. The quota was set at 11,500 tons, with a tariff of 15 percent or .2 euro per kilogram for beef below the quota and a tariff of 60 percent or .8 euro per kilogram for beef above the quota.[70] In September 2003, Gordeev announced that the quotas were working, as domestic meat production increased by 6 percent. At the same time, Gordeev stated that "Western partners, after receiving access to our market, do not always act conscientiously" and that "the Russian side should not be ashamed about the introduction of necessary measures to defend the interests of domestic producers."[71] In October 2003, Minister of Economic Development and Trade German Gref noted that quotas on imported beef from the United States would be retained for five years, with the size of the quota established yearly, with the goal to reduce the U.S. presence on the Russian meat market.[72]

In November 2003, it was reported that for 2004 Russia would adopt a meat quota of 420,000 tons of frozen beef and 27.5 tons of fresh beef. Frozen beef would have an import tariff of 15 percent of the declared value at customs, but not less than .15 euro per kilogram. Imports above the quota faced import tariffs of 60 percent of the declared value at customs, but not less than .6 euro per kilogram. Fresh beef would have an import tariff of 15 percent of the declared value at customs, but not less than .2 euro per kilogram; and imports above the quota would have a tariff of 60 percent, but not less than .8 euro per kilogram.[73]

Poultry Imports

Poultry meat has been among the most important, and most politically sensitive, food imports during the post-Soviet period. Imports of poultry meat are important because they have comprised such a large percentage of total supply, and poultry meat has been politically sensitive because the United States is the single largest exporter of poultry meat to Russia. This latter fact has made U.S. poultry meat a controversial issue as the political relationship between Washington and Moscow waxes and wanes. Trends in the importation of poultry meat during 1992-2002 are indicated in table 5.8.

During 1992-1995, poultry meat imports grew significantly while domestic production fell. As domestic poultry production declined 40 percent during this period, imports as a percentage of total supply increased dramatically, accounting for almost one-half of Russia's poultry meat supply in 1995.[74] By 1996, Russia had become the world's largest importer of poultry meat, and poultry meat comprised about 45 percent of Russia's total meat imports. In 1996, U.S. meat exports to Russia totaled about $1 billion, 80 percent of which was from the sale of poultry meat, the so-called "Bush legs" which in themselves were controversial.[75] The increase in imported poultry meat dipped in 1996 due in part to a political dispute with the United States. In February 1996, a controversy arose over the quality of American poultry meat. The Russian Ministry of Agriculture announced that its veterinary service would deny import certification to many U.S. poultry processing plants, in effect placing a temporary ban of American poultry exports. The issue was settled in March 1996 following negotiations that led to Russia accepting the U.S. poultry inspection system. The issuance of import licenses was resumed and chicken imports that were en route when the dispute arose were admitted into the country by Russian customs. For the remainder of the Yeltsin period, levels of imported poultry meat varied significantly. In 1997, poultry meat imports surged, but then declined about 25 percent in 1998, with most of the decrease occurring in the fourth quarter. In 1999, poultry imports dropped again, reaching only 28 percent of the 1998 level and 21 percent of the 1997 level. The decrease was a result of the devaluation of the ruble. As a result, domestic poultry meat was better able to compete with imports on price.

Table 5.8. Russian Poultry Imports, Fresh and Frozen, 1992-2002 (in thousand tons)

	Imports	Domestic Production	Imports as % of Total Supply
1992	56	1,428	4
1993	178	1,277	12
1994	501	1,142	30
1995	824	859	49
1996	754	690	52
1997	1,149	630	65
1998	843	690	55
1999	242	748	24
2000	694	766	47.5
2001	1,391	884	61
2002	1,382	962	59

Data for 1992 and 1993 are partial and do not include CIS countries.
Sources: *Rossiiskii statisticheskii ezhegodnik* (Moscow: Goskomstat, 1994), 436; *Rossiiskii statisticheskii ezhegodnik* (Moscow: Goskomstat, 1997), 584, 587; *Rossiia v tsifrakh* (Moscow: Goskomstat, 1997), 168-69; *Sel'skoe khoziaistvo Rossii* (Goskomstat, 1998), 75; *Rossiiskii statisticheskii ezhegodnik* (Moscow: Goskomstat, 2001), 611, 614; *Rossiia v tsifrakh* (Moscow: Goskomstat, 2003), 378-79; and author's calculations.

Under Putin, poultry imports have increased to their highest levels in the post-Soviet period, even as tariffs have increased and import quotas have been introduced. In 2000, poultry imports nearly tripled compared to 1999, due in part to the fact that effective April 1, 2000 tariffs on imported poultry meat were lowered slightly.[76] In 2001, imports doubled over their 2000 level and reached a high of 1.3 million tons, 1 million of which came from the United States. While poultry imports declined slightly in 2002, they still were about twice the 2000 level. Even though domestic production of poultry meat increased 26 percent during 2000-2002, imports still comprised almost 60 percent of total supplies in 2002.

The increase in imported poultry meat was due to rapidly growing consumer demand for this relatively cheap source of meat, a demand that domestic production could not meet.[77] Thus, the growth in poultry imports occurred despite import quotas and renewed tensions in poultry trade between the United States and Russia. In July 2001, poultry imports were included in the Ministry of Agriculture's quotas on imports, with higher custom duties on any imports above the quota.

During early 2002, Russia and the United States engaged in a minor trade "war" over poultry meat imports into Russia. In February 2002, the Russian government increased its import tariff on American poultry to 30 percent, up from 25 percent.[78] There were also Russian concerns over the U.S. use of chlorine-based chemicals as disinfectors.[79] Mayor Yurii Luzhkov ordered Moscow's municipal food department not to buy "Bush legs" from the United States because U.S. "biological additives...are dangerous and may cause a negative impact at the genetic level for generations to come."[80]

On March 10, 2002 Russia banned the import of U.S. poultry over alleged sanitation and health violations. The foreign minister, Igor Ivanov, stated at the time that the ban was temporary and was not in retaliation for U.S. tariffs applied to Russian steel exports. Despite the fact that Russia insisted the ban was due to "repeated" U.S. violations of Russian veterinary requirements, many analysts at the time believed that the banning of U.S. chickens was in fact a form of retaliation.[81] The United States responded in kind by withdrawing funding for Russian students to study agriculture in the United States.[82]

After negotiations, the Russian government stated it would partially lift the ban on April 15, 2002—with the exception of poultry imports from Pennsylvania, Virginia, North Carolina, and Maine, for which the ban extended an additional six months. The partial lifting of the ban came after inspections of poultry-producing facilities. Negotiations led to an agreement whereby all veterinary certificates to U.S. poultry exporters would be annulled and new ones obtained in conformity with new standards as stipulated between the two sides.[83] On April 15, Russia extended the ban for an extra two days in order to study the evidence that proved U.S. poultry meat was safe. Minister of Agriculture Gordeev stated that "without analyzing how the United States meets our demands, it is impossible to lift the restrictions on U.S. poultry imports."[84] On April 17, the ban was partially lifted, but the new certificates were temporary, and the Russian side indicated that a series of issues would have to be dealt with during the next two to three months.

Even after the ban was partially lifted, the "chicken war" had a residual effect on U.S.-Russian relations. In May 2002, Gordeev stated that the Russian government intended to introduce quota imports for all categories of meat in 2003. A few days after that announcement, the U.S. Senate passed a nonbinding resolution calling for permanent normal relations with Russia, but stopped short of lifting the Jackson-Vanik restrictions (dating from 1974, which linked Most Favored Nation status to Jewish emigration from the USSR), in large part because of lingering problems in U.S.-Russian poultry trade. In particular, when referring to the tensions over U.S. chicken exports, Senator Joseph Biden, chairman of the Senate Foreign Relations Committee, was quoted as saying, "I can either be Russia's best friend or worst enemy. They keep fooling around like this, they're going to have me as their enemy."[85]

Poultry trade slowly resumed in the period prior to the meeting in Moscow between Presidents Bush and Putin in May 2002. However, several issues remained outstanding, and the disagreement did not fully end in April or May 2002. As poultry trade remained below previous levels, new negotiations were opened between the two sides on June 26 over import certifications, testing requirements and procedures, hygienic requirements, and inspection guidelines.[86] Negotiations continued for nearly two months, with agreement finally being reached on new health certificates in late August 2002.[87] Although poultry trade resumed thereafter, the effects of the nearly six-month ban were significant and U.S. poultry exports to Russia declined 40 percent during 2002 in comparison to 2001.[88]

As Gordeev promised, strict quotas were enacted in January 2003 for the importation of poultry meat, using a bifurcated tariff system as explained above.[89] The import quotas reduced poultry imports to 744,000 tons in 2003, and 1.05 million tons in 2004 and 2005. Quota amounts were assigned by country. According to the government resolution, the United States would remain the primary exporter to Russia, allowed to export 553,500 tons in 2003.

It was not the end of the tension in trade relations, however, as in February 2003, the Ministry of Agriculture revoked, without explanation, all import licenses for meat and poultry. Minister of Agriculture Gordeev was quoted as saying that "Western companies want to gain ground on the Russian market, and we should take steps to curb these aspirations."[90] Importers had to reapply for permits, a process that took several weeks to complete. In early April 2003 an agreement was reached that allowed industries in both countries to use different sanitary methods as long as they were scientifically based and achieved the same results. Further, U.S. producers had to certify that antibiotics were not used in the processing or to enhance growth in the birds.[91] In May 2003, Gordeev visited the United States and signed a memorandum on agricultural cooperation, and poultry imports resumed in July 2003. However, U.S. exports remained limited by the import quotas and higher tariffs on above-quota imports. In September 2003, a new trade agreement was reached that increased U.S. poultry exports to Russia by guaranteeing 74 percent of the low tariff quota to American poultry.[92] This agreement allowed the United States to export about 740,000 tons of poultry meat at the lower tariff level, compared to the 553,500 tons under the original terms. Higher volumes of imports were possible if importers were willing to pay a higher duty.

Food Exports, 1992-2003

One does not normally think of Russia as a food-exporting nation. In fact, as was shown previously, Russia is a food-importing country and the net balance of food trade heavily favors imports. However, official data show that Russia has been an exporter of food, although to be sure the dollar value of exports has been low and export trade does not comprise a significant percentage of total export trade. Food exports were limited during much of the 1990s by domestic production declines and production shortfalls that required imports, as seen above. For that reason, little attention was devoted to the development of a coherent food export policy. Food export trends during 1992-2002 are shown in table 5.9.

The table shows that during 1992-2002 Russia exported a total of $18 billion worth of foodstuffs. If Russia's food exports are broken down regionally, just under one-third of food exports went to CIS countries, with the other two-thirds to non-CIS nations. In the post-Soviet period, food trade among CIS nations has been constrained by a number of barriers. Grain is the primary commodity traded among CIS nations. On the one hand, grain trade has been limited by government actions, including the use of quotas, taxes, customs regulations and certifications, and direct limitations on trade. Russia and Ukraine in particular have increased tariffs on the importation of grain. On the other hand, other factors that do not involve state policies or actions also constrain trade, including undeveloped infrastructure, lower purchase prices, and a growing criminal element and/or corruption that increases the cost of transportation.[93]

Table 5.9 Russian Food Exports, 1992-2002

	Food Exports to CIS, billion dollars	Food Exports to CIS as % of All Exports	Food Exports Outside CIS, billion dollars	Food exports Outside CIS as % of All Exports	Total Food Exports, billion dollars
1992	NA	NA	1.6	3.9	1.6
1993	NA	NA	1.6	3.8	1.6
1994	0.5	3.7	0.9	1.8	1.4
1995	0.4	2.8	1.0	1.5	1.4
1996	0.5	3.4	1.2	1.7	1.7
1997	0.6	3.6	1.0	1.5	1.6
1998	0.6	4.3	0.9	1.5	1.5
1999	0.5	4.3	0.5	0.8	1.0
2000	0.7	5.3	0.9	1.0	1.6
2001	0.9	6.2	1.0	1.2	1.9
2002	1.1	7.1	1.6	1.8	2.7
Total	5.8	--	12.2	--	18.0

NA=data not available in statistical handbooks.
Sources: *Rossiiskii statisticheskii ezhegodnik* (Moscow: Goskomstat, 1997), 580-81; *Rossiiskii statisticheskii ezhegodnik* (Moscow: Goskomstat, 2001), 609-10; *Rossiia v tsifrakh* (Moscow: Goskomstat, 2003), 372-75.

The value of food exports increased after Putin became president—a result of increased domestic production—and in particular grain exports have increased owing to several good harvests. Trends in the export of grain are discussed in more detail next.

In 2001, Russia exported 3.2 million tons of grain, a significant increase over the level of 2000 (715,000 tons).[94] Experts commented that the potential for Russian grain exports was even higher, but export levels were constrained by insufficient port capacity.[95] Almost one-half of Russia's grain exports leave from the port of Novorossiisk on the Black Sea, while most grain used for export comes from Krasnodar krai and Rostov oblast to the west, and ports in Rostov were in need of repair and not able to handle a large export capacity.[96] This situation led to Russian exporters using some Ukrainian ports in an effort to export grain to Western Europe, the Middle East, and Northern Africa.[97] Since then efforts have been concentrated on improving port facilities and making it possible to export more grain.

In 2002, Russia exported about 10 million tons of grain, including 9.2 million tons of wheat.[98] In October 2002 alone, a record 1.78 million tons of grain were exported, including 1.4 million tons of wheat.[99] In the spring of 2002 it was announced that Russia was exporting grain to 23 countries in the world. Moreover, in response to increased exports, it was necessary to work out an export policy, and in mid-2002 a government program for the exportation of grain began to be developed.

In 2003, the grain market was somewhat mismanaged. Early forecasts estimated a gross harvest of about 75 to 77 million tons, with a domestic need of about 70 million tons, leaving 5 to 7 million tons for export. Based on this forecast, exporters were encouraged to sign contracts for the export of grain. However, in reality, the domestic grain harvest came in at about 20 million tons less in comparison to 2002. By midyear, some press reports began to question whether Russia would have enough grain for domestic needs. However, any potential shortfall was denied, both by the Ministry of Agriculture and the Grain Union. For example, in June 2003, the chairman of Russia's Grain Union, Arkady Zlochevksii, responded that fears about a grain deficit were unfounded, although he did support distribution of coupons to some 8.7 million of the very poorest Russians to ensure their access to bread as domestic prices rose.[100] Also in June 2003, Gordeev stated that the state would not impose limits on grain exports.[101] Some strains on domestic supplies were suggested, however, by restrictions in the Kuban placed on the export of grain from the region in midyear, by Gordeev's suggestion of limits on price markups for bread, and by increased imports of grain from Kazakhstan as the year progressed.[102] In November 2003, some sources were suggesting it might be necessary to introduce export tariffs on wheat, although by November grain contracts had already been fulfilled for the 2002-2003 agricultural year (June 2002-July 2003). In early December, it was announced that the government Commission on Defensive Measures in Foreign Trade and Customs-Tariff policy had begun to consider export tariffs on grain, a move that was supported by Russia's Grain Union.[103] As 2003 came to a close, Prime Minister Kasianov signed a government resolution to impose an export tariff of .025 euro per kilogram on rye and wheat effective from January 1, 2004 to May 1, 2004 in an effort to support domestic supplies.[104] While domestic shortfalls did not occur—the state utilized its state grain reserve—domestic grain purchase prices increased substantially, reaching world market levels and in regions surpassing it.[105] In addition, retail bread prices also increased. During 2003 grain exports declined in comparison to 2002. Russia finished 2003 with an export of approximately 5 million tons of grain, 4 million of which were exported after July 1, 2003.

Conclusion

This chapter demonstrated significant change in the nature of the food trade system, as well as in patterns of trade and content of international food trade in the post-Soviet period. Imports and exports are no longer centrally managed, patterns of external food trade have changed so that most food trade is conducted with non-CIS nations, and high-value animal husbandry products have replaced grain as Russia's primary import. In recent years Russia has become a rather significant exporter of grain.

The chapter also demonstrated an evolution of external food trade policy. Russia's early strategy was to feed the population with cheaper imports during much of the 1990s when domestic production was declining. In short, when incomes and standards of living were falling (in real terms), a choice was made to prioritize protection of the consumer over protection of domestic producers. When Putin became president, a shift in priorities became evident, one that emphasized protection of domestic producers even at the cost of higher-priced food. A calculation was made that, with increases in real incomes and higher standards of living, consumers could afford higher prices from domestic producers.

Thus, contemporary issues surrounding food trade have greater political and economic complexity. On the one hand, farm producers, processors, and interest groups representing producers and processors want higher food prices and protection. On the other hand, consumers want low-priced food. In the middle is the Russian government, which is responsible for protecting domestic producers, encouraging domestic production, and protecting the poorest sectors of society. In this respect, the 25 to 35 percent of the Russian population living at or below the poverty line is the most vulnerable to significant increases in food prices. The critical question for the future is how Russia will balance these competing political, economic, and social requirements, and how the policy choices that emerge impinge upon efforts to integrate with the global economy.

Notes

1. "Ob osnovakh gosudarstvennogo regulirovaniia vneshetorgovoi deiatel'nosti," *Sobranie zakonodatel'stva Rossiiskoi Federatsii*, no. 50 (15 December 2003): 12044.
2. "O gosudarstvennom regulirovanii vneshetorgovoi deiatel'nosti," *Sobranie zakonodatel'stva Rossiiskoi Federatsii*, no. 42 (16 October 1995): 7406-24.
3. "Ob osnovakh gosudarstvennogo regulirovaniia vneshetorgovoi deiatel'nosti," 12038-12065.

4. The special defensive, antidumping, and compensatory measures are covered in great detail in a separate law that was also signed by President Putin in December 2003. This law is called "On Special Defensive, Anti-Dumping, and Compensatory Measures for Imported Goods," *Sobranie zakonodatel'stva Rossiiskoi Federatsii*, no. 50 (15 December 2003): 12065-12105.

5. Russia's opening to the world was also evidenced by the fact that at the beginning of 1993 there were more than 3,250 registered joint ventures employing more than 195,000 persons. "Sovmestnye predpriiatiia," *Vestnik statistiki*, no. 4 (April 1993): 15-18; and *Rossiiskaia Federatsiia v 1992 godu* (Moscow: Goskomstat, 1993), 61.

6. "Ob eksportnom kontrole," *Sobranie zakonodatel'stva Rossiiskoi Federatsii*, no. 30 (26 July 1999): 6795-6810.

7. "O Komissii po eksportnomy kontroliu Rossiiskoi Federatsii," *Sobranie zako nodatel'stva Rossiiskoi Federatsii*, no. 6 (5 February 2001): 1620-24. The decree was amended by a subsequent decree signed in June 2002, which among other things, expanded the membership to twenty-four and named A. L. Kudrin head of the commission. *Sobranie zakonodatel'stva Rossiiskoi Federatsii*, no. 25 (24 June 2002): 6351-53. In July 2003 the composition of the commission was changed again by changing the head to B. S. Aleshin and reducing the commission to twenty-two members. *Sobranie zako-nodatel'stva Rossiiskoi Federatsii*, no. 30 (28 July 2003): 7455-56. In December 2003 the commission was expanded to twenty-three and a new head, Iu. K. Demchenko, was named. *Sobranie zakonodatel'stva Rossiiskoi Federatsii*, no. 50 (15 December 2003): 12183-84.

8. "O Komissii po eksportnomy kontroliu Rossiiskoi Federatsii," 1621.

9. Interview by author of Sergei Kisilev, Moscow State University, 17 May 2004.

10. See *Rossiiskii statisticheskii ezhegodnik* (Moscow: Goskomstat, 1994), 342; *Rossiiskii statisticheskii ezhegodnik* (Moscow: Goskomstat, 2001), 604; and *Rossiia v tsifrakh* (Moscow: Goskomkstat, 2003), 363.

11. *Krest'ianskie vedomosti*, nos. 3-4 (15-28 January 2001), 5.

12. Paul Streeten, *What Price Food? Agricultural Price Policies in Developing Countries* (Ithaca: Cornell University Press, 1987), chap. 16.

13. *Kommersant*, 19 April 1996, 2.

14. In addition, there is a Veterinary Inspectorate within the Ministry of Agriculture. See A. Korolev and V. Yudin, "Kontrol' za kachestvom prodovol'stviia," *Ekonomist*, no. 2 (February 2000): 82.

15. See Korolev and Iudin, "Kontrol' za kachestvom prodovol'stviia," 82.

16. See V. Plotnikov, "O kachestve importnogo prodovol'stviia," *Ekonomist*, no. 8 (August 2001): 87.

17. "O gosudarstvenom regulirovanii agropromyshlenogo proizvodstva," *Sobranie zako nodatel'stva Rossiiskoi Federatsii*, no. 29 (21 July 1997): 5689-5698. For an analysis of the ineffectiveness of this law, see A. Gordeev, "Ekonomicheskie mekhanizmy reguli-rovaniia agropromyshlennogo proizvodstva," *Ekonomist*, no. 6 (June 1998): 90-93.

18. "O prodovol'stvennoi bezopasnosti Rossiiskoi Federatsii," photocopy of final version of law.

19. "O merakh po zashchite ekonomicheskikh interesov Rossiiskoi Federatsii pri osushchestvlenii vneshnei torgovli tovarami," *Sobranie zakonodatel'stva Rossiiskoi Federatsii*, no. 16 (20 April 1998): 3395-3412.

20. "O gosudarstvennom kontrole za kachestvom i ratsional'nym ispol'zovaniem zerna i produktov ego pererabotki," *Sobranie zakonodatel'stva Rossiiskoi Federatsii*, no. 49 (7 December 1998): 10746-10751.

21. By 2000 there were 1,600 employees in the State Grain Inspectorate. Each inspector had an annual budget of not less than 2 million rubles, but inspection of domestic grain trade was insufficient due to an inadequate number of inspectors. *Krest'ianskie vedomosti*, no. 7 (14-20 February 2000), 2. On the responsibilities of the inspectorate in general, see the interview with the chief of the grain inspectorate, Oksana Labutina, in *Krest'ianskie vedomosti*, nos. 17-18 (1-15 May 2001), 6; and with the deputy head in *Krest'ianskie vedomosti*, nos. 25-26 (1-15 July 2001), 4.

22. *Sobranie zakonodatel'stva Rossiiskoi Federatsii*, no. 22 (31 May 1999): 4982-83.

23. *Sobranie zakonodatel'stva Rossiiskoi Federatsii*, no. 18 (6 May 2002): 4610.

24. *Krest'ianskaia rossiia*, no. 27 (13-19 July 1998), 2; and V. Semenov, "Novyi kurs agrarnoi politiki," *Ekonomist*, no. 1 (January 1999): 14.

25. "O kachestve i bezopasnosti pishchevykh produktov," *Sobranie zakonodatel'stva Rossiiskoi Federatsii*, no. 2 (10 January 2000): 613-632.

26. *Krest'ianskie vedomosti*, no. 1 (1-9 January 2000), 2.

27. *Krest'ianskie vedomosti*, no. 3 (17-23 January 2000), 2.

28. A. Gordeev, "Stabil'noe i dinamichnoe razvitie APK—pervostepennaia zadacha," *APK: ekonomika, upravlenie*, no. 11 (November 2000): 10.

29. A Gordeev, "Stabil'noe i dinamichnoe razvitie APK,"10.

30. *Krest'ianskie vedomosti*, no. 11 (13-19 March 2000), 2.

31. *Krest'ianskie vedomosti*, nos. 19-20 (16-31 May 2001), 2.

32. S. Pilaev, "Ob obespechenii prodovol'stvennoi dostatichnosti naseleniia Rossii," *Ekonomist*, no. 7 (July 1998): 25.

33. "World Trade: Fifty Years On," *The Economist*, 16 May 1998, 22.

34. G. I. Shmelev, V. I. Nazarenko, and E. N. Blinova, "Prodovol'stvennaia bezopasnost' Rossii: puti dostizheniia,"*Problemy prognozirovaniia*, no. 1 (January-February 1999): 33.

35. *Krest'ianskaia rossiia*, no. 13 (2-8 April 2001), 1.

36. It is interesting to note that the financial crisis of 1998 had little effect even though the amount spent on imports declined.

37. These definitions are taken from Economic Research Service, *Former USSR Situation and Outlook Series*, WRS-95-1 (Washington, DC: USDA,1995), 18.

38. *Krest'ianskie vedomosti*, no. 47 (November 2003), 3.

39. During the early reform period, 1992-1993, imports of high-value products also declined—a reflection of lower consumer demand due to price liberalization—but then, unlike grain imports, began to increase again to pre-reform levels.

40. *Rossiiskaia gazeta*, 11 November 1993, 2.

41. *Sel'skaia zhizn'*, 11 November 1993, 2.

42. However, it should be noted that opponents to imports argued that the importation of meat had a grain equivalent. Looked at in this way, grain continued to be imported but in a different form.

43. *Sel'skoe khoziaistvo Rossii* (Moscow: Goskomkstat, 2002), 67.

44. Remy Jurenas, "U.S. Agricultural Assistance to the Former Soviet Union: Policy Issues," *CRS Issue Brief*, Report no. IB90139 (Washington, DC: Congressional Research Service, Library of Congress, 1993), 3.

45. Remy Jurenas, "U.S. Agricultural Exports," in Joint Economic Committee, *The Former Soviet Union in Transition*, vol. 2, Joint Committee Print, 103rd Congress, 1st session (Washington, DC: Government Printing Office, 1993), 542.

46. The CCC is a federal corporation. Its credit guarantee programs use commercial banks. Thus, money came from banks, but the CCC (the U. S. government) guaranteed repayment in the case of default. I thank Allan Mustard for this clarification.

47. Jurenas, "U.S. Agricultural Assistance to the Former Soviet Union," 5.

48. *Finansovye izvestiia*, 24-29 December 1992, 4.
49. Curt Tarnoff, "U.S. and International Assistance to the Former Soviet Union," *CRS Issue Brief*, Report number IB91050 (Washington, DC: Congressional Research Service, Library of Congress,1993), 6.
50. *Sel'skaia zhizn'*, 13 January 1994, 2.
51. "Kachestvo zerna, produktov ego pererabotki i ikh ispol'zovanie—pod strogii kontrol'," *Vash partner*, no. 20 (May 1994): 23.
52. The World Bank, *Food and Agricultural Policy Reforms in the Former USSR: An Agenda for the Transition* (Washington, DC: The World Bank, 1992), 108.
53. This description of food aid draws from Stephen K. Wegren, "The Russian Food Problem: Domestic and Foreign Consequences," *Problems of Post-Communism*, 47, no. 1 (January-February 2000): 46.
54. *New York Times*, 4 November 1998, A5; *Financial Times*, 10 November 1998, 2. In early 2000, it was announced that Russia would purchase an additional 300,000 tons of corn from the United States as part of the food aid package, paying $32 million for the corn.
55. *Krest'ianskie vedomosti*, no. 3 (18-24 January 1999), 2; and see *New York Times*, 10 November 1998, A6; *Financial Times*, 10 November 1998, 2, for coverage in English.
56. Food aid was sold at local market prices, with some of the revenue going to local budgets and some to the federal pension fund. By August 1999, more than 1.7 billion rubles had been directed into the pension fund from the sale of humanitarian food aid. Originally, it was hoped that 18 billion rubles would have been directed to the pension fund. *Krest'ianskie vedomosti*, no. 34 (16-22 August 1999), 2.
57. Information from Christian Foster, Foreign Agricultural Service, 24 July 2000.
58. *Krest'ianskie vedomosti*, no. 44 (25-31 October 1999), 2.
59. *Krest'ianskaia rossiia*, no. 14 (10-16 April 2000), 2; and *Krest'ianskaia rossiia*, no. 16 (24-30 April 2000), 2.
60. See Government Resolutions 1177, 1178, and 1188 in *Sobranie zakonodatel'stva Rossiiskoi Federatsii*, no. 11 (13 March 2000): 2534-2540; 2570-2574.
61. *Krest''ianskie vedomosti*, no. 15 (10-16 April 2000), 3.
62. *Krest'ianskie vedomosti*, nos. 13-14 (1-15 April 2001), 2.
63. *Krest'ianskaia rossiia*, no. 14 (9-15 April 2001), 2.
64. *Krest'ianskie vedomosti*, nos. 37-38 (4 November-15 December 2002), 4
65. *Krest'ianskie vedomosti*, nos. 39-40 (15-31 December 2002), 2.
66. *Krest'ianskie vedomosti*, nos. 1-2 (1-31 January 2003), 2.
67. *Krest'ianskie vedomosti*, no. 16 (14-20 April 2003), 3.
68. *Krest'ianskie vedomosti*, nos. 1-2 (1-31 January 2003), 2.
69. *Krest'ianskie vedomosti*, nos. 10-11 (24-30 March 2003), 2.
70. *Krest'ianskie vedomosti*, no. 32 (August 2003), 2.
71. *Krest'ianskie vedomosti*, no. 37 (September 2003), 2.
72. *Krest'ianskie vedomosti*, nos. 40-41 (October 2003), 2.
73. *Krest'ianskie vedomosti*, no. 48 (November 2003), 2.
74. *Sel'skoe khoziaistvo v Rossii* (Moscow: Goskomstat, 1998), 75.
75. After the fall of the Soviet Union, Russians believed that the so-called "Bush legs" (referring to imported chicken legs) were exported to Russia because they were an inferior part that was unwanted by American consumers. The Russian mass media fed the perception that America was dumping an unwanted chicken part onto Russian consumers, and the term "Bush legs" became a term of derision.

76. Effective April 1, 2000, poultry meat was subject to a 30 percent tariff or .2 euro per kilogram, whereas the previous tariff had been 30 percent, or .3 euro per kilogram. *Krest'ianskie vedomosti*, no. 1 (1-9 January 2000), 2.

77. *Krest'ianskie vedomosti*, nos. 23-24 (16-30 June 2001), 14.

78. *The Russia Journal*, 11 February 2002, 4.

79. *Sel'skaia zhizn'*, 27 February 2002, 1-2.

80. *RFE/RL Newsline*, 6, no. 93, part 1, 20 May 2002. Moscow was not the only Russian city to stop importing U.S. poultry.

81. On Russian reasons for the ban, see *Sel'skaia zhizn'*, 2 April 2002, 2.

82. *The Russia Journal*, 18 March 2002, 5.

83. *RFE/RL Newsline*, 6, no. 71, part 1, 16 April 2002.

84. *The Russia Journal*, 15 April 2002, 19.

85. *RFE/RL Newsline*, 6, no. 96, part 1, 23 May 2002.

86. *State News Service*, 5 July 2002, accessed through web.lexis-nexis.com (10 February 2004); *Krest'ianskie vedomosti*, nos. 29-30 (16-31 July 2002), 3; *Johnson's Russia list*, no. 6344, 8 July 2002; and *Financial News*, 25 July 2002, accessed through web.lexis-nexis.com (10 February 2004).

87. *World Financial Post*, 24 August 2002, FP8, accessed through web.lexis-nexis.com (10 February 2004).

88. The value of U.S. poultry exports during 2002 fell to $400 million, compared to $700 million in 2001.

89. Resolution no. 48, "O merakh po zashchite Rossiiskogo ptitsevodstva," 23 January 2003, available at agronews.ru/ (30 January 2003); and *Krest'ianskie vedomosti*, nos. 1-2 (1-31 January 2003), 2.

90. Article from NewYorkTimes.com, (1 February 2003).

91. *Business*, 5 April 2003, 37, accessed through web.lexis-nexis.com (10 February 2004).

92. *New York Times*, 30 September 2003, C2, accessed through web.lexis-nexis.com (10 February 2004).

93. See K. Borodin, "Ustranit' bar'ery agrarnogo rynka SNG," *APK: ekonomika, upravlenie*, no. 3 (March 2002): 42-48.

94. *Krest'ianskaia rossiia*, nos. 7-8 (25 February-3 March 2002), 2; *Krest'ianskie vedomosti*, nos. 11-12 (16-31 March 2001), 2. The 2000 level was 42 percent higher than the 1999 export level.

95. *Krest'ianskie vedomosti*, nos. 11-12 (16-31 March 2002), 2; *Krest'ianskaia rossiia*, no. 25 (24-30 June 2002), 2.

96. *Krest'ianskie vedomosti*, no. 29 (July 2003), 2.

97. *The Russia Journal*, 4 November 2002, 13.

98. *Sel'skaia zhizn'*, 3 December 2002, 1; and *Krest'ianskie vedomosti*, nos. 5-6 (16-28 February 2003), 2.

99. *Krest'ianskie vedomosti*, nos. 37-38 (4 November-15 December 2002), 2.

100. *Krest'ianskie vedomosti*, no. 24 (June 2003), 2.

101. *Krest'ianskie vedomosti*, no. 25 (June 2003), 3.

102. On this latter point, see *Krest'ianskie vedomosti*, no. 38 (September 2003), 3.

103. *Krest'ianskie vedomosti*, no. 50 (December 2003), 2.

104. *Krest'ianskie vedomosti*, nos. 51-52 (December 2003), 2.

105. Information from Allan Mustard, minister-counselor, Foreign Agricultural Service, U.S. Embassy in Moscow, 28 May 2004.

Chapter Six

Conclusion: Russia's Food Policies and Globalization

To this point, previous chapters have focused on the nature of domestic food polices and the nature of external food policies. Specifically, the analysis has examined Russia's domestic food policies and patterns of food trade, and external food policies and patterns of trade. This concluding chapter ties the previous chapters together by addressing the third broad question on which this book is based: How do Russia's domestic and external food policies affect its efforts at international integration? To put it somewhat differently, how prepared is Russia for global economic integration, at least as far as food trade is concerned? How much integration actually occurred in the 1990s and what are Russia's prospects for the future?

The core argument of this concluding chapter is that post-Soviet Russia has become more interdependent with other nations in its food trade—as in the economy as a whole. Increased interdependence is seen, for example, by expanded foreign trade, as chapter 5 demonstrated (see table 5.2). However, Russia has not attained integration, shown by the fact that Russian food exports accounted for 1.3 percent of world agricultural exports in 2002, and only 1.9 percent of world food imports. These numbers contrast with the European Union (EU), which accounted for 40 percent of world food exports and 41 percent of world food imports in 2002.[1]

For Russia to become a more important world participant in food trade, national policies in the United States, and among EU nations, will need to change, such as export subsidies provided by Western states to their agricultural sectors. Some of these policies are crucial topics being negotiated at the Doha round of trade talks under the auspices of the World Trade Organization (WTO). In this respect Russia is in a similar situation as many other developed nations. But within Russia as well there are factors at play that affect the process of and prospects for integration, and it is those factors that concern us in this concluding chapter. The nature and direction of Russia's food policies, the unintended by-products of food policies such as concerns over the nation's food security, and the perceived effects and consequences of globalization are likely to hinder actual integration for quite some time. Thus, this chapter sees a Russia in the foreseeable future that stands apart from full integration, a Russia that does not fully participate in the globalization process, even while foreign trade expands and interdependence increases. The question to be discussed is: what factors hinder Russia's food trade in its attempt to integrate globally?

The discussion surrounding this question is divided into sections. The first section below briefly discusses globalization and integration. The second section examines structural factors to trade protectionism that affect food trade, that is, factors that are common transnationally. The third then examines factors that are operational in Russia, including concerns over national "food security." The fourth section examines the policy issues surrounding Russia's entry into the World Trade Organization. The fifth section analyzes different factors in agriculture that affect Russia's ability to compete successfully during global integration. The conclusion summarizes Russia's prospects for global integration.

Globalization: A Macro View

Globalization is the new world system that emerged after the Cold War and, it might be argued, replaced the bipolar world of the Cold War era. What is globalization? There are numerous understandings and nuances, with little common consensus. A neutral definition is presented by Rosa Dierks, who states that globalization is a process by which technological, political, economic, and cultural dimensions interconnect individuals, governments, and business firms across borders.[2] In short, global telecommunications and computer technologies facilitate the transfer of ideas, capital, goods, services, information, and knowledge across borders with unprecedented speed. In addition, attendant to those processes is increased movement of peoples. Globalization, therefore, is a process that increases integration among nations along a number of dimensions.

At the core of globalization is increased global trade, based on the goal of free trade among states. What is controversial is the issue of whether trade is value free or not, and therefore whether globalization carries with it values and norms that may displace indigenous cultures, norms, and behaviors. This issue is particularly important because it shapes how governments assess the benefits of international trade and globalization. Relatively closed societies want the benefits of trade—more goods—but do not want the value transference that accompanies trade. A perfect example is the trade relationship between the United States and China. Liberal politicians in the United States during the 1990s justified trade with China (which resulted in a trade deficit with China) and granted most favored nation status precisely on the grounds that trade would help engender political values and respect for human rights in China that the United States desired.

Thomas Friedman, one of the best-known writers about globalization, argues that globalization is value laden and clashes with local traditions, culture, geography, and community.[3] Samuel Huntington and Samuel Berger likewise see globalization as value laden and argue that at least four distinct types of cultural transmission occur during globalization.[4] The first is the so-called Davos culture which is carried by business elites and which entails the homogenization of the business culture across borders. The second is the Faculty Club culture which is carried by foundations, NGOs, academic networks, and some governmental and multinational networks. This cultural transmission entails the Westernization of social and public policy agendas in developing nations, in short, post-materialist agendas that are popular among Western intellectual elites. The third type of cultural transmission is directed at consumer masses and is termed McWorld culture. This entails the Westernization of consumer tastes and values, and in particular American food, music, and dress. Finally, the fourth type of cultural transmission is aimed at both elites and masses and is called "Evangelical Protestantism," flowing from the ideas of Max Weber and his Protestant work ethic. This idea imbues the receiving country with attitudes toward work and the value placed on work that is found in the United States and other developed nations.

On the other hand, the view of globalization as value laden is contradicted by James Rosenau, who argues that globalization is value neutral.[5] According to Rosenau, globalization, which he terms "boundary expanding," occurs simultaneously with "localization," which is "boundary heightening." In short, processes of integration and "fragmentation" occur simultaneously. Thus, he argues that a nation may become more open and more protectionist at the same time, which means that indigenous values coexist at the same time new values are being incorporated into society.

In this vein, Ronald Inglehart and Wayne Baker argue that while globalization transmits values across borders, preexisting cultural norms and values influence the outcomes of the modernization processes. As a result, even nations that undergo modernization are able to retain a certain degree of their cultural identity. The authors show, for example, cultural uniqueness even among countries with similar per capita GDP.[6]

Views of globalization are not simply dichotomized between value laden and value neutral. Michael Pettis supports Rosenau in essence by arguing that globalization is primarily a monetary phenomenon and driven by expansions in global capital. His emphasis is on monetary flows and opportunity-versus-risk calculations, although it may be argued that monetary flows (as with free trade) carry with them implicit and inherent values.[7]

Supporters of globalization argue that the processes of open trade are "good" for both sender and recipient, and therefore that open trade is more beneficial than not. Advocates point to higher standards of living, reduced poverty, higher incomes, and increased life expectancies in developing nations as beneficial byproducts of globalization and open trade.[8]

At the same time, there is a significant line of analysis within the globalization literature that argues globalization and free trade lead to increased inequity, both within a country and transnationally, increased poverty, environmental destruction; and a host of other negative aspects.[9] These critics argue that "successes" in globalization may be the exception, not the rule.[10] In short, critics of globalization and free trade point to processes that perpetuate a global system of haves and have nots.[11]

Globalization and Food Policy

As the collapse of the Doha round of WTO negotiations in late 2003 shows, agriculture and food trade are among the most controversial aspects of free trade and global integration. In September 2003, the talks at the Doha round collapsed, in large part because of disagreement over export subsidies provided by developed states and domestic support to their farm producers.[12] An attempt to restart the talks occurred in February 2004, but early efforts stalled because of lack of movement on these issues.[13]

Therefore, it is relevant and necessary to discuss the intersection between integration and globalization on the one hand, and Russia's attempt to integrate on the other, with particular focus on food trade. Advocates of globalization argue that an integrated Russia is preferable to an isolated Russia, and therefore the world should prefer an integrated Russia. In this sense, there are strong political, military, and security reasons for this position, based upon the lessons drawn from the treatment of Germany in the interwar years. There are also strong economic reasons why it is beneficial for Russia to integrate. Russia is a vast, but relatively untapped, consumer market that provides enormous opportunity for foreign investors and firms. Russia has abundant natural resources that are attractive to foreign investors.

Moreover, advocates of globalization argue that Russia has something to gain from pursuing comparative advantage that is inherent to integration. Integration with the world, or at least parts of it, is likely to lead to higher standards of living and more consumerism for much of the Russian population. Foreign trade can bring in much-needed technology and modernization. "Free" domestic and foreign trade requires producers to become more efficient in order to compete effectively.

Based on the assumption that global integration is desirable along several dimensions, the primary purpose of this chapter is to assess whether Russia is prepared for integration, and if not, why not. The chapter examines Russia's "readiness" by examining the obstacles and challenges to integration in the realm of its food policies and trade. Domestic food policies at both the federal and regional levels directly influence the operation and the openness of internal markets. External food policies influence international relations with other states and also directly affect the larger economic environment in which domestic producers operate. Thus, Russia's food policies are directly relevant to processes of global integration.

Structural Factors of Trade Protectionism

Flowing from the discussion above, it is clear that issues about Russia's integration and in particular its food trade are set in a broader context of globalization and its effects. That is to say, what is at stake, at least as far as public policy debates go, is not simply the question "should we import food or not" or "should we integrate or not." Rather, the issues surrounding globalization are inherently tied to the larger costs of integration in terms of its impact on national culture, norms, and values, *as well as* the economic impact and competitiveness of domestic producers.

Chapter 5 depicted Russian external food policies as increasingly protectionist under President Putin. Why has this happened, particularly since Russian agricultural production has rebounded since 2000? There are two types of explanations. The first explanation is policy related and has two dimensions. The first dimension is that it is perfectly understandable, even rational, for Russia to become more protectionist as part of the strategy to revive domestic agricultural production. During the latter 1990s in particular, Russia's meat and poultry producers complained that they were being undercut on price by foreign imports, with the consequence that both domestic production and animal stocks decreased. As long as consumers preferred imports, and imports had relatively unfettered access to the Russian market, there was little economic incentive for domestic producers to reverse the trends of decline. Seen in this light, rising protectionism is a response to the needs and appeals of domestic producers. The second dimension is that Putin, who indicated as early as 2001 Russia's desire to join the WTO, and subsequently repeated that desire on numerous occasions, decided to put Russia's food producers and processors on a firmer financial footing prior to entry into the WTO because he understood that they were not ready to compete after the disastrous trends of the 1990s. In this way, increased protectionism would buy time for domestic producers before they would be exposed to increased foreign competition.

The second explanation why Russia has become more protectionist concerns structural reasons. A policy of protectionism is not only common among developing economies in order to protect domestic producers, but perhaps is the dominant model to economic development. This is true for both agricultural and nonagricultural trade and is one of the reasons that "free trade" is so controversial. One of the arguments of developing nations is that their producers are not able to compete due to export subsidies given by developed nations, and therefore reductions in their import barriers are resisted. One author argued the point concisely:

> Competition is meaningful only if competitors are able to survive. This is especially true for agriculture, where labor productivity varies by a factor of a thousand to one between a grain farmer on the plains of the Middle West and a spade-wielding peasant in the heart of the Sahel. . . .How can there be a level playing field in the same market between a majority of 1.3 billion farm workers who harvest the land with their hands or with harnessed animals, and a tiny minority of 28 million mechanized farmers formidably equipped for export? How can there be "fair" competition when the most productive farmers of rich countries receive emergency subsidies and multiple guarantees against falling prices on top of their direct and indirect export bonuses?[14]

Even among developed economies protectionism is sometimes employed, Japan being a prime example. Japan, for a long time after World War II, was permitted to have high import barriers, and attempts are still being made to reduce the obstacles that block access to the Japanese market, with limited success. Thus, significant progress in international free trade, while a long-standing U.S. foreign and economic policy goal, is relatively recent. And even then, the current reality is that regional free trading blocs have developed instead of truly free global trade. Regional free trading agreements are evidenced, for example, by NAFTA, the European Union, and the South East Asian Nations pact (ASEAN).

Turning to agricultural trade, one set of authors has argued that agricultural protectionism "is a common phenomenon in countries whose agricultural competitiveness is declining," citing the cases of France, Germany, Japan, and Italy in the late nineteenth-early twentieth centuries.[15] From these case studies, several hypotheses have been postulated that have relevance to the rise of agricultural protectionism in Russia today.[16] These hypotheses include:

H1. Agricultural competitiveness is a key criterion for a government to decide to erect import barriers.

H2. Agricultural protectionism is more amenable to urban interests as the share of agriculture in national income and employment declines, thereby making protectionism less burdensome for nonagricultural producers to support domestic agricultural producers.

H3. There is often a political link between government and rural interests in which the government needs rural support.

H4. Agricultural protection is more palatable when real incomes per capita and real wage rates are rising.

H5. Import controls are less efficient in a comparative sense than some other measures such as production subsidies or income supports. However, they do not require government payouts and may even add to the treasury through duties on imports.

Assessing the Russian situation today shows the relevance of those hypotheses. As such, the hypotheses above provide a partial understanding as to why Russia has become more protectionist. Below each of the structural hypotheses indicated above are applied to Russia.

(1) While Russian agricultural production has reversed its decline and the rural economy grew during 1999-2002, the competitiveness of Russian agriculture still lags.[17] Russian grain yields are lower, labor productivity is lower, animal husbandry productivity is lower, farms are less mechanized, and production costs remain higher compared to agriculture in most Western states, including the United States and European Union (EU). Shortfalls in deliveries of fuels, spare parts, and agricultural machinery underlie lower productivity. A year prior to becoming minister of agriculture, Gordeev argued that "the main reason for the growth in food imports. . . .is the low competitiveness of domestic agriculture." Gordeev noted that the biological potential of agricultural land was on average 2.5 times lower than in Western Europe and the United States.[18] In short, while Russian agricultural production began to rebound in the latter 1990s and early 2000s, the sector as a whole is not competitive with foreign farms or processors.

(2) The percentage of the Russian labor force employed in agricultural production has declined, though is still high in comparison with developed countries. During 1992-2002, the percentage of the labor force employed in agriculture declined from 14 percent to about 11.5 percent.[19] In addition, agricultural output as a percentage of GDP has declined, from about 14 percent in 1991 to approximately 7 percent in 2002.

(3) During much of the 1990s, when the Yeltsin administration pursued a relatively open trade policy, rural producers suffered and as a result it was no

surprise that conservative communist political candidates, and the Communist Party as a whole, fared quite well in the countryside at election time. Voter support for Yeltsin in rural areas lagged significantly behind urban areas in the June 1991 presidential election, the April 1993 referendum, and the presidential election of 1996. Rural support for Communist candidates was also high in the Duma elections of 1993, 1995, and 1999. In 1996, when some modest steps toward import protection were introduced, they received the explicit endorsement of the peasant association AKKOR, the interest group representing private peasant farmers.[20] The Agrarian Party and Communist Party also supported protectionism for rural producers, specifically large farms.

In contrast to the Yeltsin period, increased protectionist rhetoric and policies under Putin have coincided with increased rural support for reformist political candidates and parties. Based on survey data from rural households, there was already evidence in 2001 of weakness in rural support for Communist candidates and growing support for the government-backed party Unity (*Edinstvo*) among rural voters.[21] While this type evidence and its relevance to food policies was circumstantial and not direct, the suggested link was borne out by recent election results. In the December 2003 Duma election, the Communist Party received about one-half of the support that it received in 1999, and much of the erosion in support was attributable to the defection of the rural voter. In contrast, support for United Russia (the successor to Unity) increased so much that it received more than 37 percent of the party-list vote and as a result had by far the largest single bloc of representation in the Duma; in addition United Russia was granted the chairmanships of all twenty-nine legislative committees. In the March 2004 presidential election, Putin swept to an easy victory, capturing 71 percent of the vote nationwide, which means that he was dominant in both urban and rural areas, as well as across all income, occupational, and educational levels.

(4) When Yeltsin was president, real incomes and wages were declining for most of the population during the 1990s, while under Putin Russians have experienced real increases in incomes and wages. Nationally, real increases in monetary incomes compared to the previous year reached 12 percent in 2000, 8 percent in 2001, and 9 percent in 2002, while real increases in wages were somewhat higher.[22]

(5) Import quotas have not protected Russian producers entirely. This reality is seen, for example, by increased import levels of poultry meat in 2001 and 2002. However, import quotas have made domestic production more price competitive with foreign imports. Moreover, unlike direct production subsidies, the two-tiered import quota system discussed in the previous chapter adds to government revenues and does not require government payouts. This latter point is important because agrarian policy under Putin and Gordeev has attempted to reduce agricultural subsidies by channeling government support to the most productive and profitable producers.

Challenges to Integration: Russian Factors

Beyond structural factors that help illustrate the obstacles to Russia's integration in food trade, there are reasons operational within Russia that affect its readiness for integration. These reasons have a direct bearing on Russia's global integration and why its government has tended toward more protectionist measures. These factors are discussed in the following subsections.

The Rise of Food Security

The concern over Russia's "food security" as a political and economic issue has influenced the course of food policy and naturally lends itself to food trade protectionism. What is food security as defined in Russia? One author has defined the concept broadly, consisting of several separate elements: (1) satisfaction of physiological needs of the population; (2) a level of physical and economic accessibility to food products by different groups of the population; (3) price stability on the Russian food market; (4) independence from foreign imported foods so as to provide food to Russian citizens; (5) development of domestic branches of the agroindustrial complex and providing means to them to expand production; and (6) strategic supplies and reserves of food held by the state.[23]

Perhaps more useful for our purposes here are three broad dimensions of food security that are commonly mentioned by Russian policymakers and analysts. The first dimension, of course, is the volume of foreign imported food, the openness of Russia's foreign trade policies, and the dependence of Russia on foreign food, in particular meat and meat products, which have political sensitivity. Supporters of national food security argue that reliance on foreign imports is dangerous. An example from a leading agricultural newspaper illustrates the sentiment. The title of the article is "Imported? It Means it is Bad." The author argues that "more than 80 percent" of meat and meat products in Moscow are imported and that this situation has exceptionally negative consequences because "the quality of imported food is of significantly lower quality than the food products of Russian producers."[24]

Advocates of Russian food security favor higher trade barriers in the form of tariffs or even import quotas in order to protect domestic producers. In 1997 and 1998, for example, a central issue in the food security campaign was the fact that Russia was spending many times more on imports than on support for domestic producers—in 1997 Russia spent over $1 billion a month on food imports, comprising 28.5 percent of the amount spent on all imports.[25] It was pointed out that this was a level of spending almost double that of 1990, and that some three-quarters of food imports came from non-CIS nations, thereby requiring expenditures of hard currency.[26] The policy remedy suggested by advocates of food security is that the state become interventionist and regulatory with regard to foreign food trade.[27] In addition, the vice president of the Russian Academy of Sciences for Agriculture suggested that the state should consider measures for limiting foreign companies' participation in domestic food wholesale markets.[28]

A second dimension of food security is linked to decreasing state support for the agricultural sector as a whole and the reduction in domestic food production. These two occurrences were a direct result of lower levels of state financial support and the "price scissors" that the government refused to address in the 1990s. When talking about the low level of state financial support to Russian agriculture, Chairman of the Committee on Agrarian Policy in the Federation Council, V. Zvolinskii, stated in 1995 that "such relations of the state to agriculture are unknown in any other developed country in the world."[29] Nikolai Kharitonov, a former leader in the Agrarian Party of Russia and chairman of the Agrarian Deputy group in the Duma during 1996-1999, went even further in his criticism. He blamed the "profoundly mistaken agrarian policy that was based on the program...prepared by several international organizations under the leadership of the World Bank." Moreover, he criticized the political leadership of President Yeltsin, noting that a 1996 international agreement to invest in agriculture and fight against hunger as a top priority "was ignored by the government of the Russian Federation in its budget of 1997 and 1998. Further, the president...has not signed such a law for the Russian Federation, although its own agricultural complex is suffering an economic catastrophe."[30] The policy remedy favored by advocates of food security was for more state support for Russian agriculture.

Conversely, Eugenia Serova, who served as an assistant to Minister of Agriculture Khlystun in the early 1990s, argued that support for the domestic agriculture at the expense of macroeconomic stabilization only aggravates the food problem and could lead to reduced food output. Moreover, she argued that the growth in food imports signified improved quality of food consumed by Russians.[31]

Finally, a third dimension of food security is lower consumption levels, insufficient caloric intake, and malnutrition. Kharitonov noted that during the 1990s Russia's ranking of per capita consumption fell from sixth place in the world to forty-second place.[32] Analysts noted that in the 1990s per capita consumption of foodstuffs declined for most every food commodity in comparison to 1990. Moreover, daily per capita caloric intake fell from 3,420 in 1990 to 2,190 in 1997, while the recommended norm by the FAO was 3,000 calories.[33] It was further alleged that both domestic and foreign foodstuffs were suffering from lower quality, with the result being higher disease and sickness.[34]

From the beginning, concern over Russia's "food security" has been an elite-driven campaign that arose in the mid-1990s. As early as 1995 the concept of food security began to appear in specialized academic and policy publications. In early 1996, Deputy Prime Minister Zaveriukha, in charge of agriculture, took up the cause and warned of the danger from the "invasion" of imported foods. He noted that the import of food from abroad was not new to Russia, but what was new were the volumes of food being imported, particularly meat products into large cities. Further, he stated that "our agriculture is not able to compete on the food market with more advanced countries and therefore it is necessary to maintain the course" of restricting the purchase of food imports.[35] By 1995, the statistic of 70 percent of meat supplies being imported into Moscow and St. Petersburg had already entered the political dialogue and became conventional wisdom, to be repeated often in the years ahead.[36]

Once food security entered into the public domain as a public policy issue, in subsequent years a literal mountain of articles appeared on the theme in the popular and specialized academic press, reaching a peak in 1998 and 1999 when Russia was accepting food aid from the US and EU. The food security cause was consistently furthered by policymakers in the Ministry of Agriculture. One of the strongest proponents for more protection of domestic producers was former Minister of Agriculture Viktor Semenov (March 1998-May 1999), who advocated a system of higher tariffs and quotas on imported food products that-compete with Russian products, and lower tariffs on products that Russia did not grow.[37] Semenov's views echoed those of agrarian conservatives. More recently, Putin has supported the concept of food security by speaking often on the need to reduce imported food.

It would be one thing if concerns over food security were restricted to the Ministry of Agriculture. In that case, the influence of food security advocates would be limited. However, there is significant bureaucratic support for protection of domestic producers among those who participate in food production and food trade. In short, support for food security extends far beyond the Ministry of Agriculture and specialized institutes.

Over time, concerns over food security spread to agricultural academic institutes and the printed mass media. Supporters of the nation's food security are drawn from managers of large farms and private farmers, from regional leaders of food producing regions, from food processors, and from various agricultural interest groups such as the Meat Union, the Grain Union, the Sugar Union, and the Poultry Union. In addition, political parties and movements such as the APR and, more recently, RAD, support agricultural protectionism. Thus, food security has wide appeal and support from a broad spectrum of what may be considered political and economic elites.

Of course, Russia is not the only nation to express fears over food security. For example, in 1985 the United States adopted a law on national food security. But in Russia's case, the fear of losing food security took on something of a political and media campaign that has endured even after domestic agricultural production rebounded and the government began to protect domestic producers. After imports became somewhat more restricted by the introduction of a dual tariffs system that treated below-and above-quota imports differently, advocates of food security shifted the bulk of their attention to strengthening domestic agriculture by improving mechanization and capitalization of large farms, by protecting large producers from price *diktat* of natural monopolies, by increasing capital investments into agriculture, and by increasing domestic production and limiting food exports.

The fact that food security remains an important public policy issue even after five years of agricultural recovery is not to suggest that concerns over food security are a cynical manipulation of popular sentiment. Indeed, there is clear evidence that food security is directly linked to economic security and national security in general. Three examples illustrate the point.

First, even prior to becoming minister of agriculture, Gordeev was explicit about his feelings regarding food security, beginning one article published in

1998 with the sentences: "Food security of the Russian Federation is a component part of its economic security. [Food security] is seen as the ability of the
state to guarantee the satisfaction of food requirements to the population of the
country at a level that provides it a normal existence."[38]

Second, in late 1998, the Security Council approved a draft state doctrine on
food security in Russia. In particular, part of the document stated that "the draft
doctrine provides the requirements for providing food security of the country. . .
.[F]ood security is considered as one of the main components of economic security to the Russian Federation."[39]

Third, in the government's "Priority Tasks," released in mid-2000 after
Putin became president, the section on the agroindustrial complex states as one
of the national goals to "obtain food security for the country."[40] In 2004, a draft
law on the development of agriculture explicitly links foods security to food
self-sufficiency. Thus, it would be fair to conclude that "food security" is part of
the everyday political dialogue among policymakers and has become a corner-
stone of the nation's overall food policy strategy.

Today, policy advice for the amelioration of the "food security problem,"
coming from a variety of sources, all point to more state regulation, more protectionism, and less dependence on Western nations for food supplies. External
food trade—both imports and exports—are seen as dangerous and not in the
national interest. Clearly, Putin has no desire to construct "fortress Russia" or to
return to the relative autarky of the Soviet period. Nonetheless, it is important to
note that elite circles, those who attempt to influence food policy, share a consensus that Russian agriculture cannot compete and should be protected until it
can.[41] This shared consensus, coming from the Ministry of Agriculture, agricultural institutes and academies, and the media (both specialized and mass), means
that a policy of greater integration will have to override significant elite opposition.

Russia and Entry into the World Trade Organization

The negotiation process for Russia's entry into the WTO actually began in 1995,
although early on the process was primarily of an informational nature. Serious
discussions about Russia's entry did not begin until 1997, although little progress was made.[42] After Putin became president, accession became a priority,
and Putin repeatedly stated that Russia's future is linked to integration into the
world economy, and specifically to entry into the World Trade Organization.
For example, as early as 2001 Putin predicted that by the end of the year Russia
would be a member of the WTO. In his annual speech before the federal As-
sembly in April 2002 he stated that globalization was already upon Russia, and
that there was "no choice" but to join world markets.[43] Predictions of Russia
completing the accession negotiations appeared in 2002 and 2003, each time
ending in disappointment. As of mid-2004, it was expected that Russia would
enter the WTO in 2005, and this prospect was considered more realistic. On the
other hand, some Russian observers state that "Russia is in no hurry" and will
take as long as necessary in order to protect its interests and make sure that accession does not unduly harm its economy. For instance, Sergei Kiselev, a pro-

fessor of agricultural economics at Moscow State University and adviser to the Russian government on the WTO, would not be surprised to see negotiations extend into 2007.[44] In this respect, it is interesting to note that Russia's integration into the world economy has very little importance with the Russian population. A survey conducted in February 2004 and published in a special insert to *The Economist* in May 2004 found that less than 5 percent of respondents felt that economic integration should be a priority and only 10 percent felt it was likely to be achieved.[45]

Despite ongoing reservations, in May 2004, during a EU-Russia summit in Moscow, agreement was reached on outstanding issues, and by the end of the summit the EU formally declared its support for Russian entry.[46] EU support was an important step both politically and economically. Politically, accession would increase the stature of Russia, consolidate its standing among major nations, and facilitate political integration. As one Russian academic noted, "Entry into the WTO is one more circle of interests between us and the world community, corresponding to the course of integration of Russia into the world community."[47] Russia remains the only major power in the world that is not a member of the EU. Other former Soviet republics—nations that are considerably smaller than Russia—are already members, such as Latvia (2001), Georgia (2000), and Moldova (2001). Moreover, several very poor nations—Botswana (1995), Zimbabwe (1995), and Mongolia (1997)—joined several years ago. EU support will help pave the way for other countries to support Russia's accession. After the EU promised its support, all that remained for Russia was to complete bilateral negotiations with several major countries, including the United States and China.

Economically, the EU accounts for about 50 percent of Russian foreign trade. Agreement on WTO issues lessens somewhat the losses that EU expansion in May 2004 represented, when eight former communist nations joined the EU, in effect placing Russia outside the EU trading zone and thereby raising tariffs and trade barriers for Russian products. For example, according to one economic model, the "loss" of markets by EU expansion is estimated to cost Russian agriculture a minimum of $20 million in the short term and perhaps $200 million over the longer term. [48]

Some observers argue that Western nations have more to gain by Russia's accession into the WTO than Russia has to gain.[49] Nonetheless, entry into the WTO is important because "joining the WTO would provide Russia with a chance to diversify its economy away from oil exports. . .and producers would have to modernize to beat the competition or face extinction."[50] However, as other observers have commented, "Putin has talked like a true reformer, but his actions have been more ambiguous."[51] Thus, the question is not whether Russia is experiencing globalization and participating in increased interdependence. Instead, the question is how Russia reacts to those processes. In this respect it appears that Putin may be pursuing something of a "dual policy" with regard to entry into the WTO and trade protectionism, which, if true, would not be the first time Russia conducted a dual policy in its foreign or economic relations.[52] Putin has talked about the need to integrate and about how Russia's economic future is tied to integration into the global economy at the same time he has pursued more protectionism, particularly concerning imports of meat and poultry.

The issues surrounding Russia's entry into the WTO are complex and numerous.[53] A full discussion of the accession process, requirements, and status of negotiations not only would take us far afield from our primary focus, but is worthy of a separate article, or even book.[54] Therefore, we will proceed with a short overview of some of the most salient issues before turning our attention to agriculture. An ordering of the difficulty of issues to be resolved may be divided into two groups. In the first group, the issues are the most contentious and will be the most difficult: (1) energy, specifically domestic prices for natural gas; (2) banking; and (3) telecommunications. The problem with energy is that Russian domestic prices are considerably lower than in the EU. For example, industrial users in the EU pay as much as four times more for natural gas than do Russian industrial users, a situation which is said to give Russian producers an unfair price advantage for their products. The other issue surrounding energy was whether Gazprom would retain its export monopoly. In the fall of 2003 Russia warned the EU that it would "not abandon the export monopoly of Gazprom as a condition for entry into the WTO."[55]

At the May 2004 EU-Russia summit, Russia agreed to increase domestic gas prices from its 2004 level of $28 per 1,000 cubic meters to between $37 and $42 per 1,000 cubic meters by 2006 and between $49 and $57 per 1,000 cubic meters by 2010. Gazprom will retain its export monopoly. The EU will gain limited access to Russian pipelines, but not transit rights. Export duties on gas will be capped at 30 percent.[56] Russia also promised, without working out specifics, to liberalize the financial services and telecommunication sectors. However, Russia remained adamant about its ban on foreign banks operating in Russia.

The second group of issues is somewhat less problematic, but questions still remain that require resolution. This group includes aircraft, automobiles, furniture, and agriculture. Russian observers note that, in principle, economic interests in Russia support entry into the WTO, which is not to suggest that different sectors of the economy do not have concerns about the consequences and effects.[57] As concerns agriculture, entry is expected to increase access to other countries' markets, while at the same time reducing barriers to food imports and increasing competition for domestic producers and processors. Academic observers in particular express several concerns over the effects of entry into the WTO on Russian agriculture, and in this respect enthusiasm is more muted than among governmental policymakers. Apprehension over the effects of WTO accession also support concerns over national food security. Some of the concerns expressed over WTO accession are discussed below.

• Russian export of food. One Russian academic has argued that Russia faces inherent natural disadvantages stemming from its climate, geographical location, land quality, etc. Combined with natural disadvantages are the conditions of Russian agriculture. Specifically, the author points to a decrease in livestock herds, low consumption levels of domestic production, and particularly low wages in the agricultural economy. For example, in 2002-2003, average incomes of agricultural workers were one-third the national average, eight times less than average incomes in the energy sector, and eleven times lower than lower than average incomes in the financial sector.[58] The author argues that with low wages it is "impossible to expect a growth in labor productivity, skilled workers, or attracting young workers to agricultural work."[59] As a result of this combination of factors, the author argues that as domestic consumption increases, Russia will have little surplus food to export and therefore agriculture will not benefit very much from entry into the WTO.[60]

A related worry expressed by the director of the Union of the Wholesale Food Market concerns regional restrictions on the export of food, as was discussed in chapter 4. The question posed by the director was how Russia could export food, even if national policy allowed it, when regional leaders often forbid food to be sold beyond regional borders. Further, he wondered how a real wholesale food market could develop to the benefit of Russian producers when the Russian government "remains only a passive observer" in the face of market interventions in the Russian food market by Ukraine and Belarus.[61]

• Agricultural protection. The Russian side argues that European nations are more protectionist than is Russia, which puts Russian agricultural producers, processors, and exporters at a disadvantage.[62] For example, the average 2001 level of tariffs on imported agricultural goods into Russia was 14.7 percent, compared to a world average of 62 percent.[63] In 2003, the average level of tariff protection for Russia's agricultural goods averaged 11 percent, in comparison to 12 percent in the United States and 20-30 percent in the EU.[64] At the EU-Russia summit in May 2004, the two sides agreed that Russia would not exceed tariff levels of 11 percent for fish products and 13 percent for agricultural goods in general. Thus, Russia has some latitude to increase tariff protection for agriculture, and indicated that it might do so to help the hard-hit sector as a "defensive measure."[65]

• Levels of domestic support for agriculture. The Russian side argues that European nations provide higher levels of subsidies than does Russia, which puts Russian agricultural producers, processors, and exporters at a disadvantage.[66] The key issue is the base period to be used to calculate domestic support.[67] The question is not trivial, for levels of subsidization were considerably higher during 1990-1991 than later in the decade. The United States has for several years insisted that Russia cut its level of subsidization to agriculture, although this position was consistently rejected as hypocritical, given the higher levels of subsidization received by American farmers.[68] The subsidization issue was partially resolved at the May 2004 EU-Russia summit when the two sides agreed on domestic government support for Russian agriculture up to $13 billion a year, which actually is more than the Russian government allocates in direct agricultural support.[69] At the May 2004 EU-Russia summit, Russia also asked for the use of export subsidies, which historically have not been used, claiming it needs to level the playing field with EU nations.[70]

Clearly, Russia is on the path to accession to the WTO, whether it be in 2005 or later, and in that respect concerns expressed by academics over the effects of WTO conditions on Russia's agricultural sector will not prevent Russia's entry. However, it is worthwhile to examine the question of whether WTO accession is good for Russian agriculture, at least in the short term. Specifically, we turn our attention to factors that will influence how well Russian agriculture may be able compete once the requirements for entry are completed.

Integration and Russian Agriculture:
Is Russia Able to Compete?

In addition to the rise of food insecurity and the policy issues surrounding WTO accession, there is another issue that acts as a restraint to Russia's global integration, and that is whether Russia is able to compete, and to compete successfully. The ability of Russia to compete, which is to say the competitiveness of Russian food products, has been a subject of discussion among Russian academics. Their general line of analysis is that in the short term at least, the Russian government needs to protect the agricultural sector and provide more support, thereby warning of the consequences to agriculture if certain advantages that are provided to agriculture are ended as a result of WTO negotiations.[71]

The discussion below focuses on this question by examining four factors, each suggesting that Russia may not be able to compete successfully: (1) the ability of Russia's domestic producers to compete with international competitors; (2) trends in agricultural science and technology; (3) trends in rural social development and capital investment; and (4) rural demographic and personnel trends.

Can Russia's Producers Compete Internationally?

Chapter 1 examined Russia's three main food producers: large farms, households, and private farms. In terms of those food producers, one of the main beneficiaries from Putin's domestic agricultural and protectionist policies has been large farms. Though clearly a "loser" during much of the 1990s, large farms' production has rebounded since 1998, although by 2003 still not reaching 1990 levels of production. But the economic recovery of large farms is fragile, shown by the drop-off in economic growth in the agricultural sector in 2003. Large farms are important because, as chapter 1 showed, they sell most of their production, and among Russia's three food-producing sectors are more likely to produce for export. The question is whether large farms, as a domestic winner under Putin, would "win" when exposed to open competition that will come with entry into the WTO and greater economic integration. The prospects in the short to medium term are not especially optimistic: Russia's large farms face low efficiency, relatively low levels of mechanization, a deteriorated capital stock, lack of investment capital, and severe infrastructural obstacles.

With regard to the second producing sector, households, chapter 1 also showed that households became the dominant sector during the 1990s, and this trend has continued into the new century. As such, households may be considered a domestic winner. But chapter 1 also demonstrated significant stratification among households, not only in terms of income but also food production. While most food production from households is consumed, higher-income households grow significantly more food and sell higher volumes as a result. From that basis, two comments are necessary.

First, the bulk of rural households will remain relatively unaffected by globalization, that is, they will emerge as neither winners nor losers in the process of integration, but rather somewhere in-between. This is because such households are and will remain largely insulated from integrative food policies and the trade effects of globalization. Instead, they will remain content growing and consuming most of their food. Thus, the vast majority of rural households producing food have little to worry about in terms of competing with foreign competitors as a result of Russia's entry into the WTO and greater global integration. What this means is that global integration is unlikely to exacerbate rural poverty in Russia, which is already quite high, but it also means that integration is not likely to be a source for the amelioration of poverty.[72] The vast majority of rural households have much more to worry about in terms of maintaining sustainable rural communities, improving social services, and trying to prevent the extinction of their village through outmigration.

Second, the "elite" stratum of households—the income category labeled "very rich" (see table 1.5)—does have to worry about foreign competition. These households derive more of their income from business activities, that is, the sale of their food production. But let us consider the ability of these households to compete with American or EU competitors. The land and productive assets of "elite" household producers in rural Russia are shown in table 6.1, as well as their mean level of food sales.

Table 6.1. Mean Levels of Production Capital and Food Sales of "Very Rich" Households

Size of Household Plot (ha)	.26
Size of Rental Plot (ha)	2.1
Tractors	.45
Poultry	127.5
Pigs	5.1
Cows and Calves	5.8
Meat sold (kg)	1,842
Milk Sold (liters)	8,457
Eggs Sold (number)	325
Potatoes Sold (kg)	667
Vegetables Sold (kg)	270

"Very rich" is defined as a household with 3,149 rubles per month per capita in 2001.
Source: 2001 survey data.

The table shows that even the "richest" rural households are woefully under-capitalized and have low levels of production capital. Their commercial activity, while relatively better than non-elite households by Russian standards, does not approach the level of world standards for even middle-income nations. It is not at all clear that these types of households would be able to compete with large mechanized and modern farms in the EU, let alone the United States. Nor are there realistic prospects for improvement given the low level of investment into the household sector. Household producers often have difficulty obtaining credit or loans from commercial banks and are ineligible for loans from the state agricultural bank.[73]

In addition, the level of assistance from large farms to households has decreased during the period of reform. A 2002 survey of 6,300 agricultural workers on agricultural enterprises in 18 regions found that 90 percent of respondents reported no improvement in help from large farms during the last year.[74] The author's 2001 survey of 800 rural households, cited above in table 6.1, found that 83 percent of households received either "no support" or "very little" support from a nearby agricultural enterprise. Only 4 percent of households received "a lot" of assistance.

Turning to the third source of food production in Russia, it may be argued that private farmers were domestic "winners" during the 1990s in terms of increasing incomes, improved household welfare, and engaging in private business activities.[75] However, doubt about the ability to compete with foreign competitors pertains to Russia's private farmers as well. Russian private farmers have more land capital than households (an average of 67 hectares per farm in 2003), but otherwise have low levels of mechanization. In 1993, for example, there was an average of 79 tractors, 20 grain combines, and 42 trucks per 100 private farms in Russia.[76] In 1999, the private farming sector averaged 76 tractors, 28 grain combines, and 36 trucks per 100 private farms.[77] In other words, the level of large machinery possessed by private farmers was not much better, and in some cases worse, at the end of the decade than at the beginning. Nor is the situation likely to improve in the near term. In 2003, only 1,000 private farmers were able to take advantage of the state's special program to obtain advantageous credits to lease farm machinery and equipment.[78] Only 1,000 private farmers in 2003 were able to obtain crop insurance.[79] Moreover, private farms—which average three to four members—tend to rely on their own labor and use very little hired labor. In 1999, for example, the average annual number of workdays performed by hired labor on a private farm was 10.3.[80] Thus, the lack of mechanization on private farms is not compensated with hired labor.

Private farmers also suffer from myriad other problems endemic throughout Russian agriculture such as poor infrastructure, shortages of storage and refrigeration, inadequate transportation, insufficient access to credit, a weak information system, and monopoly pricing practices by input suppliers and processors. As a result of these rural realities, it is not clear that private farmers are well armed to compete with Western agrofirms that do not face this same array of problems.

Agricultural Science and Technology

A second factor that raises questions about Russia's ability to compete is spending on agricultural science and technology. In the United States, there is a special relationship between the government and public universities, especially land grant universities, which usually have departments of agricultural economics and other subjects relevant to agriculture and rural development. These universities are important centers of research and offer extension programs that disseminate information to farmers, which in turn helps them stay current with the latest technology and production techniques. In short, there is a firm base of scientific support and technological assistance that is designed to help American farmers.

In the United States and other developed nations, agricultural research has led to genetically modified (GM) foods that are more resistant to insects and disease. Although highly controversial, especially in Europe where a premium is placed on organic and "pure" food, GM food products are bred for increased yields with less fertilizer, and some GM foods have higher nutritional value.[81] GM foods can also be "engineered" to "turn off" attributes that consumers find unappealing, such as squishy tomatoes.[82] Putting aside long-term health concerns, high yields translate into lower export costs which help capture export markets abroad. Moreover, in the West, agribusiness farms use sophisticated technology, for example satellite imaging to tell what parts of a field need watering and how much.

In contrast, in Russia spending on agricultural science and technology was reduced significantly during the 1990s, affected by the reduction in capital investments into the agricultural sector and state support for agriculture in general. While it would be an exaggeration to say that agricultural science collapsed, it is fair to conclude that the technology gap between Russia and the West increased during the 1990s. In addition, contributions of science to Russian agricultural production had a less significant impact on the agroindustrial complex as a whole, as scientific achievements were restricted to a small minority of leading farms that remained profitable during the 1990s.[83]

Having said that, there are signs that the Putin administration is intent on improving the situation in science. In March 2003, a joint meeting of the Security Council and the Council on Science and Higher Technology, the latter existing within the presidential analytical and administrative apparatus, convened to discuss the importance of agricultural science, and science and technology in general. At this meeting, it was acknowledged that "scientific achievements and new technologies determine the dynamic of economic growth, the level of state competitiveness in the world community. . . . This is why the development of domestic science and technology is considered among the highest priorities of our government."[84] The meeting produced a program, "Basic Policies of the Russian Federation for the Development of Science and Technology to 2010," that was subsequently approved by President Putin. As regards agriculture, the program envisioned three initiatives in the short to medium term:

(1)"Restructure" the system of financing the agricultural scientific-technological complex, most of all by increasing budgetary means allotted to it.

(2) Increase state regulation of science and technology by introducing a system of "state orders" for scientific-technological work and by specifying a list of innovative projects that the state could use. During the first quarter of 2003 a list of scientific projects was considered and approved, and two billion rubles were allocated in the 2003 budget for the funding of those projects. According to Gordeev, the goal of state regulation is to create "demand" for scientific work that benefits the state and to put Russian science in the greatest advantageous position as the country integrates into the world economy.

(3) Conduct an inventory of state scientific organizations, including educational facilities, institutes doing basic research, and experimental laboratories. During the inventory the financial status of the organizations will be reviewed. Over the longer term, as scientific-technological organizations are restructured, federal centers of science and higher technology are planned to be created.[85]

Despite these initiatives, it is too early to say whether Russia's goals will be met or whether the impact will achieve the competitiveness that is desired. There is a lot of ground to be made up if Russian agricultural science is to regain a competitive status with foreign technology.

Rural Social Development

The third factor affecting Russia's ability to compete is rural social development, attendant with capital investments. In order to make agricultural products price competitive, Russia needs a modern rural infrastructural network of roads, storage and refrigeration capacity, communications, and transportation. To achieve these aspects of modernization, money is needed. However, capital investment into the rural economy from federal sources fell from about 16 percent of budgetary allotments in 1990 to 1.3 percent in 2001.[86] In late 2002 the Russian government adopted a program for the social development of the countryside, a special-purpose program that was to run to 2010. For development of the social sphere in the countryside the program estimated that 187.5 billion rubles would be needed. Even assuming this sum was sufficient, which some Russian academics do, the federal government was obligated to provide only 11 percent of the funding—a total of 5.87 billion rubles. In comparison, for the 300th anniversary of St. Petersburg, the government expended 40 billion rubles.[87]

The shortfall in federal investment has not been compensated by either regional or foreign investment. The program on social development calls for regions to provide 43 percent of the funding, but this is a highly unrealistic target and unlikely to be fulfilled. Regional governments are strapped for money and expend little on rural social development. One Russian analyst summed up the situation thusly by using Ul'ianovsk oblast as an example, where, "as everywhere, kopecks are spent on the social needs of the countryside, but then for a personal automobile for the governor the oblast spends 15 million rubles."[88] Foreign investment, to the extent it is invested in the food sector at all, tends to flow to food processing industries. The burden for capital investment thus falls on large farms, which themselves are burdened with debt and for much of the 1990s experienced cash flow problems that led to significant wage arrears to farm employees. The result of these financial trends has been the virtual stoppage of construction of rural infrastructure, housing, and buildings.

Agricultural Personnel and Rural Demographics

A fourth factor concerns agricultural personnel and rural demographics in general. Low wages in the agricultural sector, a high incidence of poverty and unemployment, significantly lower standards of living among rural residents, and a general lack of amenities in rural areas have caused problems in trying to staff and retain agricultural personnel on large farms. For example, during the years of reform, the percentage of leaders on large farm enterprises with a higher education decreased from 86 to 73 percent, and the percentage of chief specialists on large farms with a higher education decreased from 63 to 55 percent. Decreases in education levels were also experienced among workers who performed mechanized labor and those who were in employed in animal husbandry.[89]

In addition, several regional examples further illustrate the nature of the problem. In Krasnodar krai, for example, increasingly "unqualified, untrained" individuals enter into farm leadership. In the krai, "only one-fourth of farm leaders are sufficiently capable of introducing new economic principles to their collectives." At the same time, there is a high turnover rate among preexisting leaders, with turnover rates as much as 16 percent who leave due to demoralization.[90]

In Kaluga oblast, analysis shows that those with higher levels of agricultural education are more likely to leave than those with only a secondary education. For example, among individuals with a higher education, 48 percent of agronomists, 37 percent of livestock experts, and 43 percent of accountants expressed an interest in working in an agricultural enterprise. It appears that the oblast is losing its "best and brightest" to other sectors of the economy. As a result, in 2001 only 56 percent of chief agronomists, 42 percent of chief veterinarians, 25 percent of chief accountants, and 67 percent of chief economists had a higher education throughout the oblast.[91] Nor was the outlook for the future much better. A survey of students in their last year of study at an agricultural academy in Kaluga indicated that only 11 percent could say with certainty that they intended to remain in the countryside and work on an agricultural enterprise. Those who indicated either a desire to leave or were uncertain about their future work cited low wages, nonprestigious work, poor working conditions, and a low level of culture as the main reasons.[92]

In Altai krai, the story is much the same. During 1997-2001, farm leadership turnover increased 1.5 times, and in 1999 alone 1 in 7 farm managers was replaced. In addition, similar to other regions, the quality of farm personnel is declining. In Altai krai in comparison to 1991, in 2001 the percentage of farm managers with a higher education declined 9 percent and 15 percent for chief specialists.[93] As a result of lower personnel quality and the out-migration of the most educated, the majority of farms are not able to adjust to new economic conditions. These personnel factors, affecting the way in which large farms are managed and operated, have a direct impact on the ability of Russia's large farms to compete with international competitors on price and quality, and affect export potential.

There is not only a personnel problem affecting farm management, but there is also a broader rural demographic problem. Russia's demographic problem consists of a shrinking population as a result of low fertility, continued high mortality, and an aging population. From 1989 to 2002, Russia's population decreased from 147 million to 143.9 million. The average estimate for Russia's population envisages a decline to 138 million in 2015.[94] The effects of this decline will drop Russia from the sixth largest country in the world to about the fifteenth by mid-century. The population decline will have implications for the country's labor force, military, pension, and health care systems, as well as other aspects of Russian society and economy. In addition to the quantitative drop, disease rates and deaths from all types of infectious, circulatory, and other illnesses have increased significantly since 1992. There is also concern about a qualitative decline in the health of the population and several emerging health threats such as tuberculosis and HIV/AIDS. Many health experts consider Russia to be a ticking time bomb with respect to AIDS since Russia is ill-equipped to cope with the few thousand cases officially reported; some believe there may be as many as a million unreported cases.[95]

The general demographic problem affects the rural labor force and the composition of the rural population.[96] During 1992-1995 the rural population increased due in large part to in-migration from the Near Abroad. Starting in 1996, however, the rural population resumed its decades-long decrease, which continued through 2002 despite nearly a decade of net in-migration. In particular, the 2002 census revealed that 13,000 villages are completely empty, and some 35,000 villages have fewer than 10 inhabitants.[97]

During the 1990s several trends emerged that represented reversals of Soviet-era patterns and demonstrated significant deterioration in the human capital stock in rural Russia. Several of the most important rural demographic trends are discussed below.

(1) The rural population's natural increase coefficient changed from positive to negative. In 1990, the rural natural increase coefficient was +2.2, but deteriorated to -6.1 in 1994.[98] To state the natural increase coefficient differently, in 1992 the number of rural deaths began to outnumber rural births for the first time in decades (even as rural areas experienced net in-migration and an increase in the total rural population). The population's natural increase improved to -5.4 in 1998 before falling to -7 in 1999 and -7.3 in 2001.[99]

(2) Life expectancies decreased, from 62 in 1990 to 57.9 in 2001 for rural males, and from 73.9 in 1990 to 71.8 in 2001 for rural females.[100] At the same time that average life expectancies were decreasing, the rural population was aging. In 1989, there were 27.1 million rural males and females past the retirement age (60 for males, 55 for females), comprising 18.5 percent of the total population. In 2002, in a smaller rural population, there were 29.8 million rural males and females past the retirement age, comprising 20.7 percent of the total rural population.

(3) Rural deaths from virtually every kind of disease (circulatory, respiratory, infectious, and digestive) increased, as did rural suicides, rural homicides, and rural alcohol poisonings. With regard to rural deaths by various diseases, in 2001 there was some improvement in comparison to 1994, but compared to the pre-reform period the numbers remained very high.

(4) Migration patterns turned negative. Starting in 1991, rural areas experienced a net migration inflow for the first time in many decades, a result of ethnic Russians returning home as the USSR crumbled. Positive net migration flows occurred during 1991-2000, reflecting the general decline of the economy and suggesting that individuals pursued survival strategies by taking up residence in the countryside.[101] However, as the economy recovered and began to grow under Putin, net in-migration virtually stopped—a net of only 4,800 persons moved into the countryside in 2000, and in 2001 out-migration once again was evident as a net of 86,700 persons moved out of the countryside.[102]

Thus, there is an inverse relationship between rural migration inflows and the strength of the economy, suggesting that what is good for the country is not necessarily good for rural demographics. As economic growth is expected to continue and remain strong under Putin's policies, the rural demographic situation may become exacerbated, thereby raising questions about the long-term adequacy of labor sources for agricultural work on large farms and private farms. In this context it is worth noting that among the highest economic priorities of Putin's second term are improving standards of living and reducing the occurrence of poverty, as expressed by Prime Minister Fradkov in early March 2004, and repeated by President Putin following his reelection in mid-March.

Nor are demographic problems restricted to northern, poor agricultural areas. Statistics show a decline in the number of agricultural workers in the regions comprising the Volga economic region—one of the most productive regions where growing conditions are more favorable, incomes are higher, and farms more profitable. Even here rural births are declining, rural deaths are increasing, the percentage of working-age people is contracting, and the number of pensioners is growing.[103] Thus, the broad demographic problems affecting Russia's countryside are widespread and geographically diverse.

Conclusion

This chapter examined some of the factors that affect Russia's integration during globalization. Protectionism is the opposite of integration, and Russia appears to be becoming more, not less, protectionist. Part of Russia's increasing protectionism may be attributed to structural factors common among developing nations. In addition, the rise of elite concerns over the nation's food security is an important factor, and those concerns have remained salient even after Russian agriculture began to rebound. Food security has entered the national vocabulary and remains politically important, making it difficult for politicians and policy makers to ignore, just as "national security" and the "war on terrorism" cannot be ignored in the United States. Concerns over Russian food security are bolstered by the fact that bureaucratic interests support restrictive trade policies that shelter their constituents from foreign competition.

Not only are there strong elite pressures for protectionism, but there are valid concerns about whether Russia is or would be able to compete successfully if it were to integrate more fully and become more open. This chapter showed that the three food producers in Russia would face severe challenges trying to compete with more mechanized and modernized Western farms that are not as constrained by infrastructural shortcomings as are Russian producers. The Russian agricultural science and technology sector is far behind the West. Russia also faces serious problems in retaining the most highly educated and skilled personnel in the countryside. Finally, there are broader demographic processes underway, in Russia as a whole as well as in the countryside, which raise questions about the size and composition of the labor force in the coming decades.

President Putin was correct when he stated that globalization has arrived and Russia has no choice except to join. The issue is how to react to globalization, that is, what is the nature of "joining"? There are numerous variables and questions, each of which leads to different options and policy choices, so reactions are not predetermined or foreordained. One of the most important variables is politics and political attitudes. Political attitudes are as important to global integration as economic trade, and thus political attitudes have a direct effect on the degree and nature of integration.

Politically, it would be fair to conclude that the era of relative liberalism that existed under Yeltsin is over. Liberalism carried with it pro-Western, pro-integrationist messages. Despite the relative liberalism under Yeltsin, previous chapters demonstrated that even during this time protectionist and anti-integration policy measures were engendered, but never implemented fully or consistently. Today, a more nationalist, pragmatic, and conservative regime is in place under Putin, one that emphasizes order and stability. Thus, numerous questions arise regarding the future of liberalism in Russia and its global integration. How successfully will Putin be able to pursue his dual policy of talking about the need for integration while introducing protectionist policies? How vigorously will Prime Minister Fradkov pursue economic integration, or will he continue the trend of protectionism? What effect will the defeat of liberals in the December 2003 Duma election have on foreign economic policies? What impact will the rise of nationalist parties in the Duma have on legislation and external trade policies? How much influence will "liberal" cabinet members have on domestic and foreign economic policies? How much influence will the so-called *siloviki* have on Fradkov and on economic policy?[104] Will Fradkov become a pawn of the *siloviki*, as some suggest?[105] Is there a real danger of Russia "slipping away" into semi-isolationism and semi-anti-Westernism, or will global integration remain a policy goal? Thus, the questions are many, and the answers remain to be seen. Russia's food policies reflect and are influenced by these larger economic questions and policies. If Russia's prospects are judged by the trajectory of trends in its food policies, the outlook for Russia's future integration is fraught with numerous obstacles.

Notes

1. World Trade Organization, *International Trade Statistics 2003* (Geneva: WTO, 2003), 109.

2. Rosa Gomez Dierks, *Introduction to Globalization: Political and Economic Perspectives for the New Century* (Chicago: Burnham Publishers, 2001), 6.

3. Thomas L. Friedman, *The Lexus and the Olive Tree* (New York: Farrar, Straus and Giroux, 1999), 35.

4. See Peter L. Berger, "Four Faces of Global Culture," in *Taking Sides: Clashing Views on Controversial Global Issues*, eds., James E. Harf and Mark Owen Lombardi (Guilford, CT: McGraw-Hill/Dushkin, 2001), 235-42.

5. James N. Rosenau, "The Complexities and Contradictions of Globalization," in *Global Issues 2003/04*, 19th ed., ed. Robert M. Jackson (Guilford, CT: McGraw-Hill/Dushkin, 2003), 60-65.

6. Ronald Inglehart and Wayne E. Baker, "Modernization's Challenge to Traditional Values: Who's Afraid of Ronald McDonald?" in *Global Issues 2003/04*, 212-16.

7. Michael Pettis, "Will Globalization Go Bankrupt?" in *Global Issues 2003/04*, 74-78.

8. See for example, Anne O. Krueger, "Supporting Globalization," in *Taking Sides: Clashing Views on Controversial Issues in World Politics*, 11th ed., ed. John Rourke (Guilford, CT: McGraw-Hill/Dushkin, 2004), 138-42.

9. See for example, Scott Marshall, "Imperialist Globalization" in *Taking Sides: Clashing Views on Controversial Issues in World Politics*, 10th ed., ed. John T. Rourke (Guilford, CT: McGraw-Hill/Dushkin, 2002), 12-19; James K. Galbraith, "The Crisis of Globalization" in *Global Issues 2000/01*, 16th ed., ed. Robert M. Jackson (Guilford, CT: McGraw-Hill/Dushkin, 2000), 97-100.

10. Galbraith, "The Crisis of Globalization," in *Global Issues 2000/01*, 97-98.

11. Friedman, *The Lexus and the Olive Tree*, 267-84.

12. See *Financial Times*, 11 September 2003, 7; 15 September 2003, 1; and 13 January 2004, 6.

13. *Financial Times*, 14-15 February 2004, 2.

14. Jose Bove, "Globalization's Misguided Assumptions," in *Taking Sides: Clashing Views on Controversial Issues in World Politics*, 11th ed., 144.

15. Yujiro Hayami, "The Roots of Agricultural Protectionism," in *The Political Economy of Agricultural Protection*, ed. Kym Anderson and Yujiro Hayami (Sydney: Allen and Unwin and the Australia-Japan Research Centre, Austrialian National University, 1986), 31-32.

16. These hypotheses are derived from Hayami, "The Roots of Agricultural Protectionism," 33-38.

17. On the growth of agricultural production, see "O sostoianii sel'skogo khoziaistva Rossiiskoi Federatsii v 1998-2002 gg. (ekonomicheskii obzor)," *APK: ekonomika, upravlenie*, no. 11 (November 2003): 10. Preliminary reports on gross agricultural production in 2003 (January-September) indicated a slight decline of –1.3 percent. See V. Bezrukov, B. Safronov, and B. Mel'nikov, "Sotsial'no-ekonomicheskoe razvitie Rossiiskoi Federatsii v 2003 godu i prognoz na 2004 god," *Ekonomist*, no. 1 (January 2004): 11-12.

18. A. Gordeev, "Obespechenie prodovol'stvennoi bezopasnosti Rossii—zadacha strategicheskaia," *APK: ekonomika, upravlenie*, no. 8 (August 1998): 10.

19. *Rossiia v tsifrakh* (Moscow: Goskomstat, 2003), 78.

20. *Finansovye izvestiia*, 31 March-6 April 1994, 1.

21. See Stephen K. Wegren, David J. O'Brien, and Valeri Patsiorkovski, "Russian Agrarian Reform: The Gender Dimension," *Problems of Post-Communism*, 49,

no. 6 (November–December 2002): 54-55; and Stephen K. Wegren, "Rural Support for the Communist Party and Implications for the Party System," *Party Politics*, 10, no. 5 (2004): 565-82.

22. *Rossiia v tsifrakh*, 97.

23. I. N. Buzdalov, "Strategiia prodovol'stvennoi obespechennosti Rossii v perekhodnykh usloviiakh," *Agrarnaia Rossiia*, no. 5 (September-October 2003): 4.

24. *Krest'ianskaia rossiia*, no. 35 (3-9 September 2001), 3.

25. *Sel'skaia zhizn'*, 3 November 1998, 1.

26. A. Altukhov and D. Vermel', "Prodovol'stvennoe samoobespechenie strany: sostoianie i perspektivy," *APK: ekonomika, upravlenie*, no. 11 (November 1997): 21.

27. See, for example, the policy suggestions made by I. G. Ushachev, "Strategicheskie napravleniia obespecheniia prodovol'stvennoi bezopasnosti Rossii," *Ekonomika sel'skokhoziaistvennykh i pererabatyvaiushchikh predriiatii*, no. 5 (May 2002): 9.

28. I. G. Ushachev, "Sovershenstvovat' gosudarstvennuiu agrarnuiu politiku," *APK: ekonomika, upravlenie*, no. 11 (November 2003): 6.

29. V. Zvolinskii, "Obespechenie prodovol'stvennoi bezopasnosti Rossii," *APK: ekonomika, upravlenie*, no. 1 (January 1996): 25.

30. N. Kharitonov and N. Radugin, "Agrarnaia reforma i prodovolstvennaia bezopasnost' Rossii," *APK: ekonomika, upravlenie*, no. 8 (August 1998): 15, 16.

31. Her views and views of others are summarized in V. V. Miloserdov, "Politika obespecheniia prodovol'stvennoi nezavisimosti Rossii," *Ekonomika sel'skokhoziaistvennykh i pererabatyvaiushchikh predriiatii*, no. 3 (March 2000): 14.

32. Kharitonov and Radugin, "Agrarnaia reforma i prodovolstvennaia bezopasnost' Rossii,"15.

33. Iu. Ugriumova, "Prodovol'stvennaia bezopasnost' Rossii i neobkhodimost' sel'skokhoziaistvennoi kooperatsii v eyo obespechenii," *Agrarnaia Rossiia*, no. 2 (March-April 2003): 11.

34. V. Zvolinskii, "Prodovol'stvenoe obespechenie—faktor sotsial'no-politicheskoi stabilizatsii obshchestva," *Ekonomist*, no. 9 (September 1995): 91.

35. *Sel'skaia zhizn'*, 4 April 1996, 1.

36. See V. Zvolinskii, "Prodovol'stvenoe obespechenie," 92. At the time the article was published, Zvolinskii was chairman of the Committee on Agrarian Policy in the Federation Council.

37. V. Semenov, "Novyi kurs agrarnoi politiki," *Ekonomist*, no. 1 (January 1999): 14; and *Sel'skaya zhizn'*, 25 July 2000, 1.

38. A. V. Gordeev, A. I. Altukhov, and D. F. Vermel', "Prodovolstvennaia bezopasnost' Rossii: sostoianie i mery obespecheniia," *Ekonomika sel'skokhoziaistvennykh i pererabatyvaiushchikh predriiatii*, no. 10 (October 1998): 10.

39. Press Service of the Security Council of the Russian Federation. Draft doctrine and quote taken from: www.scrf.gov.ru/scripts/querycgi.exe/default?q=624&d=0 (27 March 2002).

40. Taken from: www.kommersant.ru/Docs/high-priority-task.htm (29 June 2000).

41. See, for example, the open letter to President Putin entitled "The Country is Losing its Food Independence," *Sel'skaia zhizn'*, 13-19 February 2003, 3.

42. For a historical review of the negotiation process and its different stages, see S. V. Kiselev and R. A. Romashkin, "Sel'skokhoziaistvennaia politika i vstuplenie Rossii v VTO," *Ekonomika sel'skokhoziaistvennykh i pererabatyvaiushchikh predriiatii*, no. 10 (October 2003): 10-15.

43. His speech in Russian was accessed at analytics.ed.ru (7 March 2004).

44. Interview by author with Sergei Kiselev, Moscow State University, 17 May 2004.

45. *The Economist*, 22-28 May 2004, 13.

46. *The Moscow Times*, 24 May 2004, 1, 2.

47. L. V. Popova, "Politicheskii aspekt vstupleniia v VTO," *Agrarnaia Rossiia*, no. 1 (January 2003): 38.

48. Interview with author with Sergei Kiselev, Moscow State University, 17 May 2004.

49. Maxim Medvedkov, "Russia's Accession to the WTO: The View From Russia," in Katinka Barusch, et al., *Russia and the WTO* (London: Centre for European Reform, 2002), 44.

50. *The Moscow Times*, 20 May 2004, 2. See also "Recommendations to CIS States on WTO Accession" (www.aris.ru/WIN_E/TACIS_2001/01.html, accessed March 5, 2003), which focuses on agriculture and discusses the different categories for negotiation (or green, yellow, and red boxes), and describes where negotiations stand on each of the issues.

51. James R. Millar, "Putin and the Economy," in *Putin's Russia: Past Imperfect, Future Uncertain*, ed. Dale R. Herspring (Lanham, MD: Rowman and Littlefield, 2003), 119.

52. A dual policy in foreign policy was a well-known Bolshevik strategy that dates from the 1920s. See Edward Hallett Carr, *The Bolshevik Revolution: 1917-1923*, vol. 3 (New York: The Macmillan Co. 1953), chap. 22.

53. The following websites have useful information about the WTO and/or issues surrounding Russian entry: www.wto.ru; www.rian.ru; www.economy.gov.ru; and www.rsppr.biz.

54. For an excellent background primer on the range of issues surrounding accession, including the views of the Russian side, see Katinka Barusch, et al., *Russia and the WTO*.

55. *The Financial Times*, 17 October 2003, 8.

56. *The Moscow Times*, 24 May 2004, 1, 2.

57. See the special report by the East-West Institute entitled "Attitudes Toward the WTO in Russia's Regions," in *Russian Regional Report*, 7, no. 22 (10 July 2002): 1-4.

58. A. F. Serkov, "Vstuplenie v VTO: riski i posledstviia dlia sel'skogo khoziaistva," *Agrarnaia Rossiia*, no. 1 (January 2003): 37.

59. A. F. Serkov, "Vstuplenie Rossii v VTO: problemy agrarnogo sektora," in *VTO i sel'skoe khoziaistvo Rosssii*, ed. S. V. Kiselev (Moscow: Moscow State University, 2003), 59.

60. Serkov, "Vstuplenie Rossii v VTO: problemy agrarnogo sektora," 57-60.

61. S. U. Nuraliev, "Vstuplenie Rossii v VTO: problemy i perspektivy razvitiia optobykh prodovol'stvennykh rynkov," *Ekonomika sel'skokhoziaistvennykh i pererabatyvaiushchikh predpriiatii*, no. 4 (April 2002): 7.

62. Iu. S. Khromov, "O nekotorykh posledstviiakh vstupleniia v VTO dlia agrarnogo sektora ekonomiki Rossii," in Kiselev, ed., *VTO i sel'skoe khoziaistvo Rossii*, 60-64.

63. E. G. Mikailov, "Nekotorye problemy razvitiia sel'skogo khoziaistva Rossii v kontekste prisoedineniia k VTO," in Kiselev, ed., *VTO i sel'skoe khoziaistvo Rossii*, 118-22.

64. Interview by author with Sergei Kiselev, Moscow State University, 17 May 2004.

65. Mikailov, "Nekotorye problemy razvitiia sel'skogo khoziaistva Rossii v kontekste prisoedineniia k VTO," 118, 121.

66. For a comparison of Russian domestic support for agriculture with that in the United States and Europe, see Kiselev and R. A. Romashkin, "Sel'skokhoziaistvennaia politika i vstuplenie Rossii v VTO," 10-15.

67. I. Starikov, "Agrarnye aspekty vstupleniia Rossii v VTO," *APK: ekonomika, upravlenie*, no. 7 (July 2002): 11-12.

68. See, for example, *The Russia Journal*, 14 December 2002, 3.

69. See S. V. Kiselev, "O prisoedinenii Rossii k VTO v oblasti sel'skogo khoziaistva," in Kiselev, ed., *VTO i sel'skoe khoziaistvo Rosssii*, 44-46.

70. For an explanation of Russia's position and justification for this request, see S. A. Dankvert, "Sel'skokhoziaistvennyi aspekt peregovorov po prisoedineniiu rossii k VTO," in Kiselev, *VTO i sel'skoe khoziaistvo Rosssii*, 21.

71. See, for example, S. Dankvert, "Razvitie zhivotnovodstva i usloviiakh vstupleniia Rossii v VTO," *APK. ekonomika, upravlenie*, no. 2 (February 2004): 17-24.

72. For an in-depth analysis of rural poverty in Russia, see David J. O'Brien, Valeri V. Patsiorkovski, and Stephen K. Wegren, "Rural Poverty and Adaptation," *The Journal of Peasant Studies*, 31, nos. 3-4 (April-July 2004): 457-88.

73. A. V. Petrikov, "Prioritety v gosudarstvennoi podderzhke LPKh," *Ekonomika sel'skokhoziaistvennykh i pererabatyvaiushchikh predpriiatii*, no. 8 (August 2002): 10.

74. G. I. Shmelev, "Vashniyi vnutrennii rezerv povysheniia prodovol'stvennoi obespechennosti Rossii," *Agrarnaia Rossiia*, no. 5 (September-October 2003): 7.

75. See Stephen K. Wegren, David J. O'Brien, and Valeri V. Patsiorkovksi, "Winners and Losers in Russian Agrarian Reform," *The Journal of Peasant Studies*, 30, no. 1 (October 2002): 1-29.

76. *Itogi khoziaistvennoi deiatel'nosti krest'ianskikh (fermerskikh) khoziaistv Rossiiskoi Federatsii v 1993 godu* (Moscow: Goskomstat, 1994), 5.

77. "O deiatel'nosti krest'ianskikh (fermerskikh) khoziaistv Rossiiskoi Federatsii," *Statisticheskii biulleten'*, no. 10 (October 2000): 8.

78. *Fermerskoe samoupravlenie*, no. 3 (March 2004): 4, 13-14.

79. *Fermerskoe samoupravlenie*, no. 3 (March 2004): 4.

80. V. I. Kudriashov and S. V. Polunin, "Trudoresursnyi potentsial krest'ianskikh khoziaistv," in *Agroprodovol'stvennaia politika i vstuplenie Rossii v VTO*, ed. A. V. Petikov (Moscow: Vserossiiskii institut agrarnykh problem i informatiki, 2003), 312.

81. C. Ford Runge, et al., *Ending Hunger in Our Lifetime: Food Security and Globalization* (Baltimore: Johns Hopkins University Press, 2003), 91-96.

82. See J. Madeline Nash, "Grains of Hope," in *Global Issues 2001/02* 17th ed., ed. Robert M. Jackson (Guilford, CT: McGraw-Hill/Dushkin, 2001), 46-53.

83. For a discussion see E. Ogloblin and I. Sandu, "Nauchno-tekhnicheskii progress v sel'skom khoziaistve," *APK: ekonomika, upravlenie*, no. 2 (February 2001): 8-13.

84. A. Gordeev, "Priumnozhat'vklad nauki v agropromyshlennoe proizvodstvo," *APK: ekonomika, upravlenie*, no. 4 (April 2003): 3.

85. Gordeev, "Priumnozhat'vklad nauki v agropromyshlennoe proizvodstvo," 4-5.

86. Buzdalov, "Strategiia prodovol'stvennoi obespechennosti Rossii v perekhodnykh usloviiakh," 5.

87. Buzdalov, "Strategiia prodovol'stvennoi obespechennosti Rossii v perekhodnykh usloviiakh," 5.

88. Buzdalov, "Strategiia prodovol'stvennoi obespechennosti Rossii v perekhodnykh usloviiakh," 5.

89. E. Semenova and T. Borzunova, "Ekonomiko-pravovoe razvitie rynka zemli v Rossiiskoi Federatsii," *Ekonomist*, no. 4 (April 2004): 90.

90. N. Shokov, "Kadrovyi potentsial APK Krasnodarskogo kraia," *APK: ekonomika, upravlenie*, no. 12 (December 2001): 25.

91. A. Gorbatov and A. Migel', "Zakrepliaemost' spetsialistov na sele," *APK: ekonomika, upravlenie*, no. 11 (November 2002): 22-23.

92. Gorbatov and Migel', "Zakrepliaemost' spetsialistov na sele," 24.

93. E. Sheludchenko, "Glavnyi factor uspekha—liudi," *APK: ekonomika, upravlenie*, no. 1 (January 2002): 29.

94. *Ob osnovnykh tendentsiiakh razvitiia demograficheskoi situatsii v Rossii do 2015 goda* (Moscow: Gosmkomstat, 1998), 3.

95. See Timothy Heleniak, "Russia's Demographic Challenges," in *Russia's Policy Challenges: Security, Stability, and Development,* ed. Stephen K. Wegren (Armonk, NY: M. E. Sharpe, 2003), 200-21.

96. For a general review of rural social and demographic problems see L. Bondarenko, "Sotsial'no-demograficheskaia situatsiia na sele," *APK: ekonomika, upravlenie,* no. 12 (December 2002): 13-19.

97. *The Moscow Times,* 30 April 2003, 1; and *New York Times,* 5 February 2004, A4.

98. Natural increase is a standardized measure, calculated by subtracting the number of births from the number of deaths per 1000 persons.

99. *Demograficheskii ezhegodnik Rossii* (Moscow: Goskomstat, 2002), 57.

100. *Demograficheskii ezhegodnik Rossii,* 105.

101. See Stephen K. Wegren and A. Cooper Drury, "Patterns of Internal Migration During the Russian Transition," *Journal of Communist Studies and Transition Politics,* 17, no. 4 (December 2001): 15-42.

102. *Demograficheskii ezhegodnik Rossii,* 21.

103. A. Cherniaev, A. Kruglikov, and V. Trofimova, "Ekonomicheskie i sotsial'nye problemy sela i puti ikh resheniia," *APK: ekonomika, upravlenie,* no. 12 (December 2002): 7-8.

104. *Siloviki* is a term referring to persons with ties to, or work experience in, Russia's intelligence agencies. Lilia Shevtsova also refers to it as Russia's ruling class and analyzes its influence on Putin and national politics. See Lilia Shevtsova, *Putin's Russia* (Washington, DC: Carnegie Endowment for International Peace, 2003).

105. Leading TV-Tsentr political analyst Aleksei Pushkov told viewers in March 2004 that through Fradkov, the so-called *siloviki* will have greater influence in government, and said Fradkov's appointment is the strongest blow yet to the liberals in government, especially acting Finance Minister Aleksei Kudrin and acting Economic Development and Trade Minister German Gref. *RFE/RL Newsline,* 8, no. 44, part 1 (8 March 2004), accessed at www.rferl.org (8 March 2004).

Index

About the Author

Stephen K. Wegren is an Associate Professor in the political science department at Southern Methodist University in Dallas, TX. He is the author of more than six dozen articles and book chapters on various aspects of reform in post-communist states. He is the author or editor of the following: *Land Reform in the Former Soviet Union and Eastern Europe* (1998); *Agriculture and the State in Soviet and Post-Soviet Russia* (1998), which won the Hewett award for best book in political economy from AAASS; *Rural Reform in Post-Soviet Russia* (2002); *The Land Question in Ukraine and Russia* (2002); *Russian Policy Challenges: Security, Stability, and Development* (2003); and *Building Market Institutions in Post-Communist Agriculture: Land, Credit, and Assistance* (2004). Two books are forthcoming in mid-2005. The first is entitled *The Moral Economy Reconsidered: Russia's Search for Agrarian Capitalism*; and the second is entitled *Rural Adaptation in Russia*.